W9-AJI-231

Salute to a Bug

Bug, insect, oh giant beast,

If you were taller,

And I were smaller,

I'd run from you

at a hundred miles an hour

at least.

Volusia County Public Library
ORANGE CITY
PUBLIC LIBRARY
148 Albertus Way
Orange City, FL 32763
DISCARD

Introduction

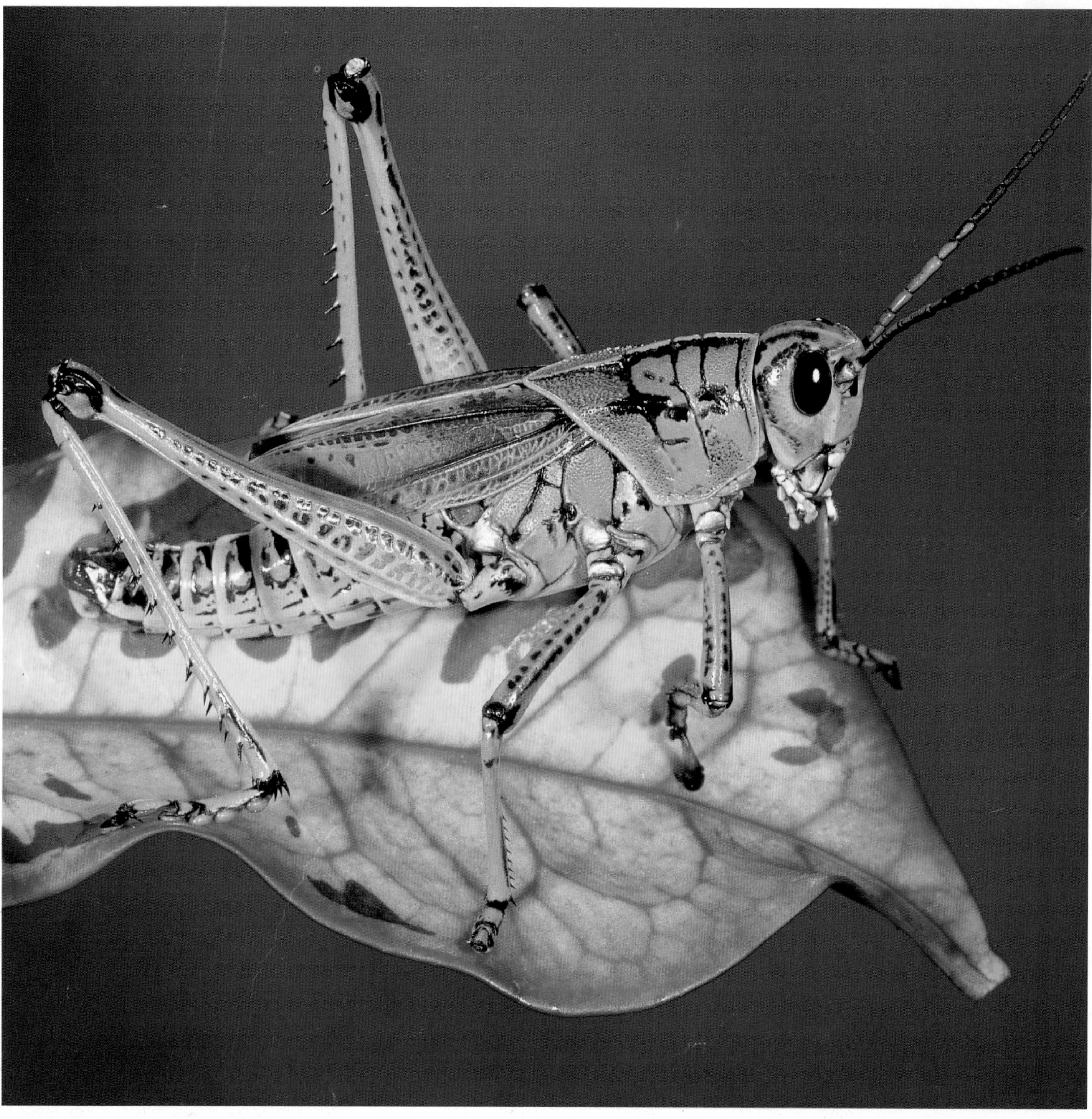

PC

Top: **a lubber grasshopper on an equally colorful croton leaf. These hoppers are familiar to Florida gardeners.** **See page 37 for** **their fascinating story. The bright colors of this grasshopper warn birds that it is inedible.**

There are a lot of insects out there. They are by far the most diverse creatures on earth. Nobody could name them all—not the brilliant professors at the University of Florida, not the famous entomologists at the Smithsonian Museum. Certainly not the author of this book. This book is to the world of Florida insects as a nature trail is to a great national park. A nature trail identifies some conspicuous species and explains some important processes, but there is much, much more out there in the wilderness. There is so much to explore in Florida that no guided nature trail and no guide book to insects can do more than introduce their subjects.

Insects have always been part of mankind's environment, and the number of dangerous or disease-bearing species is very small. Country children, who grow up romping through an outdoor world teeming with thousands of kinds of insects are at least as healthy as city children whose environment contains far fewer. Native peoples of the Amazon Basin, which has one of the world's richest concentrations of insects, can get by with minimal protective clothing. In Florida, as elsewhere, a little knowledge and common sense rapidly separate real insect problems from unnecessary worries.

The color photographs in this book record moments in the lives of living insects. After their portraits were taken, they resumed their careers. Their descendants are probably still out there.

Silverfish

ORDER THYSANURA

A colony of silverfish, living under a pile of old dot-matrix computer printouts in the corner of an office, symbolizes the fact that extraordinarily old and primitive organisms, unlike much human technology of a decade ago, are not necessarily obsolete. The body plan of silverfish is older than that of beetles, dragonflies, and cockroaches. It dates from before the time that wings evolved in insects. The development of wings was an evolutionary breakthrough in transportation seen in all successful groups of advanced insects.

BK

Silverfish have several other antique features, including external fertilization. When a friendly pair of male and female silverfish encounter each other, they perform a little dance, running and touching antennae. The male quickly spins a series of fine threads that are attached to the ground at one end and angled up to attach to some raised object. Under this set of threads he deposits a packet of sperm. The female follows him with her three long, antenna-like tails raised in the air. When the tails contact the threads above the sperm packet, the female begins to search for the sperm with her genital opening.

Silverfish are better known for their tendency to eat documents than for their charming courtship ceremonies. They are among the few insects able to digest cellulose without the help of bacteria living in the gut. Some species of silverfish can survive without water. A covering of scales helps hold moisture in the body and helps the silverfish slip from the grasp of enemies, such as ants and spiders. Although silverfish can't travel very far on their own, in the last few centuries humans have been carting them around when moving stored food products, books, and papers.

There are about six species of free-living and domestic silverfish found in Florida. Several additional species live as scavengers in ant nests. Some silverfish are more silver-colored than others. The color often depends on the lighting.

Springtails

ORDER COLLEMBOLA

Springtails are among the most common animals found in Florida soil, but they are so small (usually less than 1/8th of an inch) that they are seldom noticed. If a handful of moist leaf litter is placed on a dark piece of paper, springtails can usually be seen, sometimes by the hundreds. They are tiny elongated or globular creatures that hop if one takes a poke at them with a hair or a small plant fiber. Some species thrive in the soil of house plants, and may be mistaken for some kind of pest. Most species feed on soil fungi.

Springtails get their name from a tail-like appendage that is carried underneath the body, held in place by a catch on the underside of the abdomen. When the springtail needs to leap, it puts pressure on the tail and then suddenly releases the catch. The tail strikes the ground and flings the springtail into the air. This unique escape mechanism, along with several other peculiar features of springtails, distinguish them from all other insects. Many entomologists believe that springtails are not insects, but one remnant of an ancient group that preceded insects.

Like silverfish, springtails have external fertilization. The males leave little packets of sperm on small stalks where the females can find them. In some species, the male deposits a row of these packets in front of the female, then gently pushes her forward until she comes into contact with his offering.

Nobody has methodically studied the springtails of Florida, but there are probably more than 100 species.

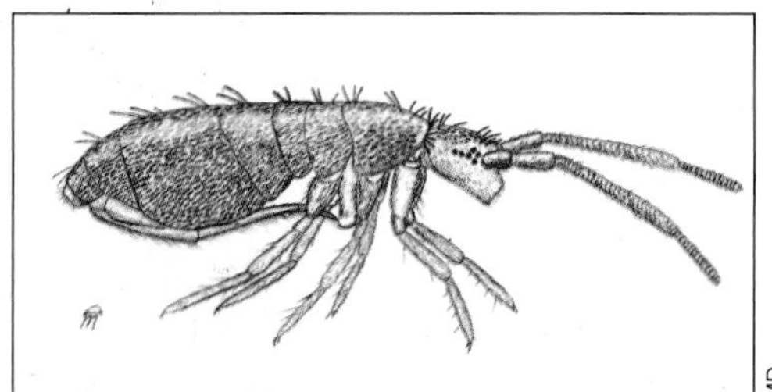
MD

VENERABLE INSECTS

Why is it that incredibly ancient types of animals, such as silverfish and springtails, are able to persist for hundreds of millions of years, surrounded by more advanced, more recently evolved groups of animals? The answer must be that the important thing in life is the ability to make a living, not the position of one's body plan on some scale going from primitive to advanced designs. There are no fads in nature. The new only replaces the old when the new has an advantage. A number of ancient animals have specialized representatives living in harsh environments. This may help explain why these creatures have survived through so many changes in the world's climate. If the world should end in fire, the silverfish are ready for a desert planet. If the world should end in ice, snow fleas (a kind of freeze-resistant springtail) are already sitting on glaciers awaiting their inheritance.

ORDER EPHEMEROPTERA

The Name. Mayflies are named for the month in which they begin to appear in the northern US and Europe, although May is not the only month they appear. As the scientific name for the order implies, adult mayflies have ephemeral (short) lives, usually only a day or two, but there is no need to feel sympathy for them. Mayflies are adapted for a hasty adulthood and most of their lives are spent as aquatic larvae. When the formerly aquatic mayfly leaves the water for its brief aerial fling, it jettisons its systems for feeding, digestion, walking, running, and swimming, becoming completely specialized for reproduction. For this reason, in order to study the ecological diversity of mayflies, one must look at the different habits of the larvae. The diet of Florida mayflies is usually algae and organic detritus filtered from the water, scraped from a surface, or sifted out of sand and mud. A few species are predatory.

Habitat. Each species has its own definition of desirable underwater real estate, based on the movement, depth, temperature of the water; the amount of dissolved oxygen available; and the type of soil, rocks, or submerged wood on the bottom. A large number of mayfly species require cool, well-oxygenated water, so the ranges of many eastern species do not even extend into northern Florida. There are fewer species of mayflies in all of South Florida than might be found in a single New England brook.

Importance in Florida. About 70 species of mayflies live in Florida. Most of these occur in the north, especially the western Panhandle, in the many streams and rivers running out of Georgia and Alabama. However, even in peninsular Florida, a few species of mayflies may be abundant and ecologically important. Many of Florida's upland sand-bottomed lakes have huge populations of the golden mayfly. The larvae of golden mayflies serve the invaluable function of stirring and cleaning the sandy bottom, helping to keep the lakes healthy. These larvae are also important food for fish.

Mass Emergence. When the larvae of large mayflies, such as golden mayflies, swim to the surface and change into their aerial form, they leave masses of larval skins floating on the water. Although sometimes mistaken for indications of a die-off of aquatic life, these are actually signs of renewal. Mass emergences of these mayflies are usually considered a nuisance because they are attracted to lights and pile up around floodlit restaurants and car lots near water. From the mayfly point of view, lakeside lights distract the adults from their all-important reproductive duties.

Thousands of mayflies fly about in huge swarms, performing an aerial mating dance consisting of up and down movements. The male seizes a female and mates with her. Within an hour, the eggs are dropped in water or attached to water plants.

A Very Unusual Natural History. A peculiar feature of the mayfly's natural history is that it is the only insect to shed its skin *after* its wings are fully developed. This is probably because the changes that a mayfly must make to go from an aquatic larva to a sexually mature adult are too radical to be accomplished in the hasty transformation that takes place on the surface of the water.

During this change of skin, the mayfly is floating helplessly, surrounded by aquatic and aerial predators. A complete transformation into adult under these circumstances would be like changing from a wetsuit into elaborate party clothes on a surfboard circled by sharks. After their almost explosive emergence from the water, most species of mayflies flutter to a nearby tree or rock, where they leisurely molt into a more brightly colored, sexually mature adult, ready to join the swarm of mating dancers rising and falling silently on the still air.

BK

BK

BK

ABS

Top: the extremely long tail filaments function as sensory devices, like rear antennae.
Above: **the wings of the mayfly are pleated like a fan, making them much stronger than if they were flat.**
Left: **a group of tiny mayflies with wingspreads of only 1/4 inch have been attracted to a light near the ditch from which they emerged.**
Far Left: **a golden mayfly emerging from the subimago or intermediate winged stage of its development.**

JLC

***Above: Callibaetis*, the little southern minnow mayfly, also called the helmet-headed mayfly. The male has two sets of eyes, one of which looks up, and overhangs the eyes on the sides of the head like a helmet. This species is more widespread in Florida than the golden mayfly. The larvae can live in almost any situation, including ponds, ditches, and even brackish canals. The slender green larvae perch inconspicuously on aquatic plants, grazing upon the algae that grow on plant surfaces. These larvae can even live in temporarily filled ditches, completing their development in one or two months, unusually fast for a mayfly. They get a special boost toward speedy growth; the female, unlike other Florida mayflies, releases fully developed eggs which hatch into larvae as they are being laid. Adult, little southern minnow mayflies usually have their mating swarms over open clearings, not over water.**

THE BENEFITS OF MASS EMERGENCE

Why is it that thousands of mayflies emerge from the water all at once, on the same day? Why don't they emerge gradually, a few at a time, over a period of weeks or months? Among other things, mass emergence ensures that short-lived adults, such as mayflies, will find mates before dying. Other Florida insects that have mass emergence include ants, termites, and midges (blind mosquitos).

Where there is a mass emergence of mayflies or other insects, the rich bounty naturally attracts predators such as birds and dragonflies, which seem able to spot swarms of flying insects from some distance. In spite of this, there is some safety in numbers. If the swarm is large enough, the predators quickly stuff their bellies while the vast majority of the swarmers continue their activities unharmed. If the emergence was spread over a long period of time, predators could eat a much larger proportion of the emerging insects.

DANCE SWARMS

Dance swarms are a way of bringing the sexes together. The members of dance swarms are almost all males. Females visit the swarm only briefly, pick up a male, then retire with him to a safer, more secluded spot. For males, participation in the dance swarm means that they are more easily found by females.

Dances occur in predictable places. For some species, it might be the topmost twig of a small tree, for others it might be the area above a light-colored rock, or the lee of a dense bush or wall. A shaft of sunlight appearing through trees is a common site for a swarm. These little landmarks are called "swarm markers." On windy days, swarm-ing insects fly lower to stay out of the wind and remain closer to their markers. If a swarm appears at a certain time of day in a certain place, it likely can be seen again at the same time and place the next day. Some insects swarm twice a day.

The significance of dancing in insects is not so far removed from that of traditional dancing by humans in earlier centuries when dancing was an opportunity to show vigor and skill in complex group activities, and to initiate or strengthen bonds between couples. This comes across clearly in a poem by Sir John Davies.

"This wondrous miracle did love devise,
...dancing is love's proper exercise."

SWD

***Above:* a dancing mayfly. Mature male mayflies can hover for several hours. Females fly up into the swarm to find a mate.**

ORDER ODONATA

Dragonflies and damselflies are active, bold insects, whose rapid movements are guided by excellent eyesight. They often behave as if they were curious about the things they see, and they are definitely intensely interested in each other, showing a wide variety of interactions. In these characteristics, this oldest group of flying animals seems to connect with the very newest member of the aerial club, ourselves. This connection is reflected in the popularity of the group. There are many fans of dragonflies and damselflies, and even some odonate-watching societies, especially in Japan and northern Europe. In Florida, there is enough interest in dragonflies and damselflies to support field guides to the Florida species. There are more than 150 species that breed in Florida, and some additional species that appear as strays.

Tricky to ID. Learning to recognize Florida dragonflies and damselflies is much like learning Florida birds. There are some highly distinctive species, some variable species, and some that are downright tricky and confusing. The Halloween pennant is a good example of a common, never-changing, distinctive species that flies throughout the year and occurs throughout Florida. Anybody can instantly learn to recognize this species; it is the dragonfly equivalent of the blue jay. The ebony jewelwing is an an easily identified species among the damselflies. The scarlet skimmer is a bit more difficult because males and females look very different, like the cardinal. There are also dragonflies and damselflies that are like warblers, having bright colors that vary with age and sex.

Breathing Through the Anus. Dragonfly and damselfly larvae are unique among animals in their realization of the full potential of the rectum and anus. The rectal chamber is enlarged and lined with gills, and water is pumped in and out through the anus. The water is exhaled with more force than it is inhaled, setting up small currents that bring fresh water to where it will be sucked in. Damselfly larvae have a set of three leaf-like appendages at the end of the abdomen that may also function as gills. A larva that is under attack can contract its rectum and shoot away from danger, propelled by a jet of water.

Danger at the Water Surface. When a dragonfly or damselfly falls into the water, it can become doomed if the long, narrow wings become trapped in the surface film. The many species which lay their eggs in or on plants below the water surface risk death when laying eggs. The female might be more likely to survive to lay several batches of eggs in different places if the male is holding the female as she dips into the water, and can help haul her out.

The danger that the water surface poses to adult dragonflies and damselflies may help explain why so many species spend most of their adult lives away from their breeding areas. Another factor is the abundance of predators such as birds, frogs, and even other dragonflies around the places where dragonflies and damselflies congregate to breed.

RFS

Above: **the final phase of the dragonfly life cycle. A dragonfly larva has climbed out of the water, and while holding onto reeds, discarded its larval skin and emerged as an adult. It is waiting for its new skin to harden. During this period (about an hour) it is in great danger from predators because it cannot fly. The strange-looking "creature" this dragonfly is holding is its own empty, larval skin. Another skin, that of a mayfly, is clinging to the green leaf on the left.**

Dragonfly Larvae. All dragonflies and damselflies have larvae that live underwater in ponds, streams, pools, and ditches. These larvae are fierce predators. They often eat mosquito larvae, and are important in controlling mosquitos that breed in seasonally flooded marshes and ponds that lack mosquito-fish.

Among several features peculiar to larval dragonflies and damselflies is the extendible lower lip, that can shoot out under hydraulic pressure in a small fraction of a second to seize a passing insect or crustacean. The victim is gripped by spiny lobes at the end of the lip, and dragged back to the waiting jaws. The lower lip is elbowed so that it can fold under the body, while the lobes clasp the front of the face like a mask. The best way to examine this strange but effective lip of death is to collect the larval skin left by a dragonfly that has crawled out of the water to transform into an adult. These skins are common on emergent reeds and dock pilings on the edges of ponds and lakes.

Dragonflies disperse so effectively in Florida that even the driest habitats, such as scrub and sandhill (elevated, well-drained, pine woods), miles from any water, are patrolled by dragonflies. Damselflies do not move so far, but even they often appear in Florida gardens many blocks from the nearest water.

RFS

Above: **a view of the lower lip partially covering the face of a dragonfly larvae. It has a serrated edge for grasping and holding prey. In the upper right corner, a reckless fish is seen approaching.**

RFS

Right: **the old skin of a dragonfly larva shows the hinged lower lip that can be extended in a flash for trapping prey.**

Below: the eyes of the dragonfly larva are set far apart, allowing the creature to triangulate for a precise strike from the lower lip.

RFS

Below: **the young larva of a dragonfly clinging to underwater plants. Depending on the species, the larva spends between one month to several years underwater.**

Bottom, right: **a dragonfly larva captures a small fish.**

RFS

RFS

GM

Dragonflies

SUBORDER ANISOPTERA

Dragonflies as a group are technically defined by the difference between their front and hind wings. The hind wings are much broader near the base than the front wings. The name "Anisoptera" means "unequal wing."

Dragonflies are among the fastest fliers in the insect world, hitting speeds up to 35 mph, with fantastic maneuverability as well. They capture their insect prey by seizing them in flight with their jaws, sometimes with an assist from the feet. The approach of a dragonfly is probably the last thing many mosquitos see.

Dragonflies perch at the top tip of reeds and grasses for a good view of their surroundings and often return to the same perch after a patrol. On the Indonesian island of Bali, children apply a sticky substance to the tips of long poles and erect these poles in rice fields. Dragonflies are caught when they perch on this trap, and are eaten, stir-fried with spices, minus their wings.

Above: this close-up of a darner dragonfly shows the attachments of the wings and the intricate veins in the wings.

This photo also shows the remarkable compound eye of a dragonfly. Up to 25,000 individual facets, each consisting of a tiny lens and sensory apparatus, probably form a fine-grain, mosaic image. The eyes of some dragonflies are so large that they touch each other at the top of the head. The black and yellow bullseye in front of the eyes is characteristic of common green darners and is probably used by the insects themselves to identify a member of their own species.

THE WING VEINS OF INSECTS

The delicate and complicated pattern of wing veins seen in dragonflies is a good example of the more primitive vein arrangements found in fossil insects from the Carboniferous Period, 300 million years ago. The wings of dragonflies and damselflies are so strengthened by this network and by the pleats in the wing that they do not bend excessively, even though the wing is long and narrow, and the power stroke is from the wing base. The blood is circulated through the wing veins by a special auxiliary pump, like a small heart, located at the base of the wings. On warm Florida nights, tiny nocturnal gnats, related to sand flies, take advantage of the exposed veins, and stealthily fly in to suck blood from the wings of resting dragonflies.

In less primitive insects, the system of wing veins is much less complicated, and becomes a series of flexible struts with specific points of weakness that allow the wing membrane to bend and flip in precisely controlled ways. This greatly increases the efficiency of the wing.

The pattern of wing veins of each species remains constant, even when quite complex, so the pattern is useful for identification. Artists who are not entomologists often make mistakes when drawing the wing veins of insects. It is easy to think of wing veins as lines, rather than as features of aeronautical engineering. The pattern of wing veins is like the pattern of cables that hold up a suspension bridge, or the pattern of girders that support a skyscraper. If these lines are not properly placed, something falls down.

RFS

COUNTERSTROKING: THE ULTIMATE FLIGHT CONTROL

Counterstoking is the normal pattern of wing beating in dragonflies and damselflies. The wings do not beat at the same time. The forewings almost complete a stroke before the hind wings start the same movement. By changing the pitch of the wings and the counterstroking pattern, hovering, backwards flight and extremely rapid flight are both made possible.

RFS

THE OBELISK POSITION

Some dragonflies may perch on a stem with their abdomen angled high into the air in order to reduce the surface area exposed directly to the rays of the hot sun at midday. When the air is cool, dragonflies warm their bodies by positioning themselves at a right angle to the sun, thus capturing as much heat as possible. Temperature control through behavior, such as tail-hoisting, occurs in a few other species, but most insects avoid excess heat by different means.

DRAGONFLIES IN FLORIDA: IMPORTANCE OF HABITATS

There are 108 species of dragonflies that live in Florida. The habitat requirements of the larva generally determine the presence or absence of a species in a region of the state. Some species breed in large lakes, others in ponds; some in clear streams, others in ditches.

The type of bottom (sandy or muddy), the presence or absence of particular water plants, the exposure of the water to sunlight, the permanence of the body of water through the year—all of these things are important to dragonfly larvae. Most species require fresh water, but some can live in brackish water, and one species (the seaside dragonlet) lives in salt marshes and mangrove swamps around the coasts.

There are seven families of dragonflies in Florida. The most common and conspicuous species belong to the families of darners and skimmers.

DRAGONFLY WINGS

Note the dark spot at the tip of each wing in the photo at right and the long, yellowish spots near the wingtips of the species below. These are blisters of blood, found in all dragonfly wings, called stigmata, meaning a mark or brand in Greek. It is believed that the weight of the stigmata may reduce vibration of the wings and thus improve the efficiency of flight. Another possible function may be to help control the angle of the wings during flight.

GM

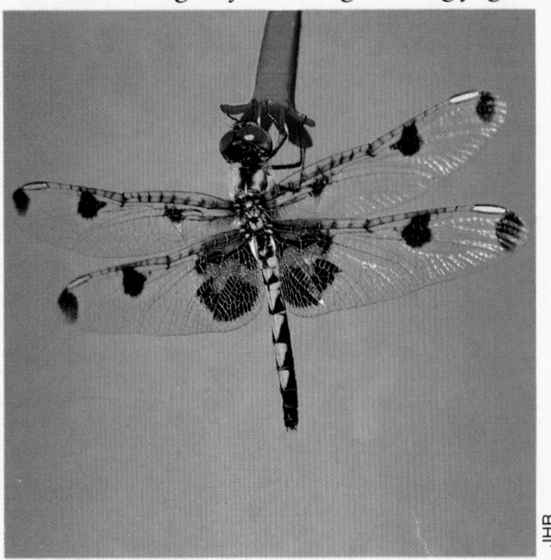

JHR

Although the veins carry blood and consist of living tissue, the wing membrane is composed of cuticle. There are tiny hairs along the veins which may sense and collect information about air flow over the wings, helping to control flight.

Note the large color patches at the base of the hind wings in the photo of a calico pennant dragonfly at left. These colorful areas are called the basal wing markings and are a common feature of the wing patterns of many species. Identification is sometimes achieved by noting the color of these markings and what portion of the wing they cover.

GM

Darners

Family Aeschnidae

The darners are large dragonflies, many with a wing span of about 4.5 inches. Their long, slender bodies are said to resemble darning needles. The older larvae are correspondingly large, and a menace to minnows and other small fish. Dragonfly larvae are most unwelcome in fish hatcheries.

Adult darners feed on flying insects, and appear to be able to spot a small moving insect at a distance of up to several yards. When darners are cruising overhead, one can test their ability to see small moving objects by tossing a small pebble into the air and watching to see them lunge, then swerve away.

The common green darner and the regal darner usually hunt near the ground, and are often most active in the dim light of evening. These are the Florida dragonflies that best earn the old name of "mosquito hawk." Perhaps early southern settlers, catching the evening breeze while sitting on the edge of a porch with bare feet dangling, noticed the dragonflies hunting the mosquitos that had gathered for a meal of human blood.

Darners often fly back and forth along the edge of a driveway or hedge at dusk, and if one stands nearby when mosquitos are out, one can see them detour to snap up a mosquito. They may use the edge of a country road to mark their patrolling territory, and in the morning there may be birds picking up the bodies of the dragonflies that were hit by cars.

Other darners may fly high in the air, often in large numbers, near the edges of lakes where midges and mayflies swarm. Here these dragonflies face a less modern threat than speeding cars: the swooping attacks of birds. John Audubon was the first to write about this in the southern US, in his 1840 account of the swallow-tailed kite. "In calm and warm weather, they soar to an immense height, pursuing the large insects called Musquito Hawks, and performing the most singular evolutions that can be conceived..." Audubon painted a "musquito hawk" in his notebook in the 1820s.

In Florida, darners and some other dragonflies appear in flocks or swarms, which may seem surprising for such aggressive and predatory animals. In their mass movements, dragonflies might be compared to tree swallows, which quickly gather where there is a mass emergence of prey, or where there is an especially attractive roosting place.

Above: **the common green darner. Note the distinctive bullseye spot on the forehead, green thorax, and blue abdomen. The scientific name, *Anax junius*, means "Lord and master of June." This name is not as appropriate in Florida as in northern states because there is a resident population found in Florida all year. The green darner is most common in South Florida in spring and fall because many individuals migrate northward in summer. The green darner preys on many kinds of insects and is ferocious enough to chase hummingbirds.**

Below: **the swamp darner, or heroic darner, has blue eyes as well as green stripes on its brown abdomen.**

DL

BK

BK

BK

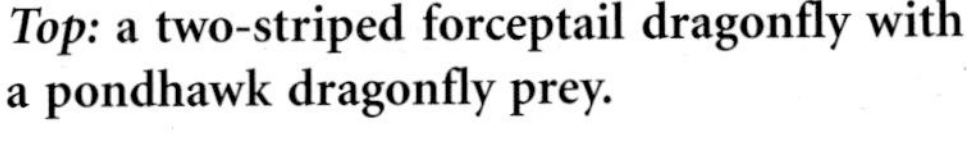

Top: a two-striped forceptail dragonfly with a pondhawk dragonfly prey.

Above: the forceps-like appendage at the end of its abdomen is used for grasping the female during mating.

Above: a Georgia river cruiser dragonfly resting on a pine twig. These large dragonflies are found patrolling rivers and streams as far south as Lake Okeechobee during the summer.

BK

Skimmers

Family Libellulidae

The skimmers are Florida's most common and most colorful dragonflies. They can be identified by the markings on their wings and bodies. As with birds, it is often necessary to learn more than one pattern, because males and females may have different markings, and young, non-breeding individuals may have yet another pattern of colors on the head and body. The immature coloration may be just as showy (at least to human eyes) as the mature coloration.

Most species spend their larval life in still water, such as lakes, ponds, and slow-moving ditches. These are usually the first dragonflies to colonize a newly created pond in a Florida garden, or even a neglected swimming pool.

Many dragonflies have highly specific requirements for their larval homes, and a number of them are rare or endangered in Florida. The purple skimmer is only found in Florida, where it lives around very clear, sand-bottomed lakes. As more lakes develop a muck layer due to runoff, this species grows steadily rarer. Most of the dragonflies that are rare or endangered in Florida require clear streams and rivers, and live in only a few places in North Florida.

BK

The scarlet skimmer is an Asian species, now abundant through South Florida. It was first seen in Florida in 1975. It is not known yet whether the scarlet skimmer is displacing any native species.

Top: **a female scarlet skimmer on a sedge.**

Above: **a male scarlet skimmer. The color difference between the sexes is striking. Males threaten each other by raising their abdomens to display the startling red color.**

Right: **a juvenile, male scarlet skimmer on a lotus seed pod. Note the abdomenal stripe.**

PC

JHR

JHR

Top and above: male roseate skimmers of the pink form. This is Florida's only pink dragonfly. There is also a red form of male roseate skimmer. Roseate skimmer larvae can live in pools and ditches filled with dirty water in summer, making this one of Florida's most adaptable species. The female, like some other skimmers, uses the tip of her abdomen to flick droplets of water into the air as she hovers over the surface laying eggs. This tactic may confuse some egg-eating predators.

Right: a male common whitetail skimmer. Note the black bands across the wings and the whitish abdomen. This species is usually found north of Ocala, and adults are present from March until November.

GM

GM

Top: **a halloween pennant dragonfly. Note the stripe on the lower segments of its abdomen, and the distinctive, large, orange wings which, unlike those of various similar species, are not clear or transparent. This dragonfly is sometimes mistaken for a butterfly.**

Right: **an Amanda's pennant. The color bands or stripes on various segments of the abdomen are often useful in distinguishing similar species of dragonflies.**

BK

MASTERS OF UNSTABLE FLIGHT

Aircraft designers always strive to reduce turbulence over an airplane's wings, but wind tunnel tests show violent turbulence around the wings of dragonflies. This unstable design allows explosive changes of direction. Dragonflies can out-maneuver almost every other flying creature. In addition, a dragonfly can lift double its own weight, an achievement that no man-made aircraft can match. However, this ability is related to the fact that small creatures are proportionately stronger rather than to the aerodynamic design.

GM

BK

Above: Amanda's pennant dragonfly on a tickseed flower. This insect is found as far south as Lake Okeechobee.

Left: a group of calico pennants, which have recently emerged from the larval stage, clinging to rushes while their skins harden.

GM

GM

GM

DRAGON AND DAMSELFLY LIFE CYCLE

This photo series shows an adult calico pennant emerging from its larval skin and expanding its wings. The life cycle begins with an egg laid in or near water. The egg hatches into the immature form, previously called a nymph or naiad, but now usually called a larva. The larva lives for a period underwater, breathing through gills in its rectum, while undergoing several growth stages. It finally crawls up onto some reeds or grasses and transforms into the winged, air breathing adult seen in these photos.

BK

GM

Above: cannibalism! Eastern pond-hawk dragonflies devour one of their own kind. Cannibalism is rare among adult dragonflies of most other species. The pondhawk is sometimes described as the most ferocious of Florida's dragonflies for its willingness to take on a variety of insects including many as large or larger than itself. These pondhawks are beginning their meal with the head of the prey. Predatory insects often attack the head and neck first to partially disable the prey. The legs and wings may continue to move reflexively, however, because the nerve centers that control complex movement are mostly in the body, not the head.

Left: a maturing male eastern pond-hawk eating a pearl crescent butterfly. The mature male is all blue with a green face. The dragonflies in the top photo show the green thorax and dark abdomen typical of immatures and females.

Right: a male dragonlet dragonfly. Note the typical blue color with black face. As dragonlets are very small, other dragonfly species may prevent male dragonlets from hunting over a wide area. Typically, males defend a territory only a few meters in diameter.

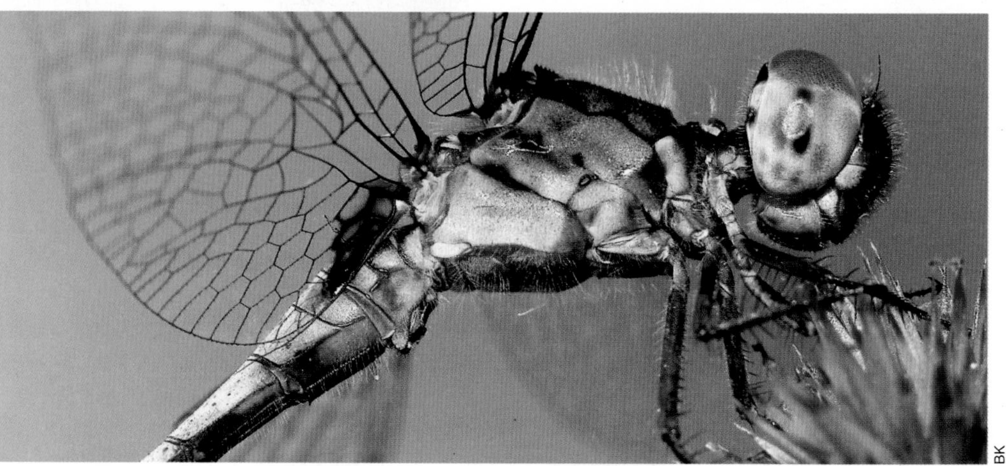

BK

Above: **a blue dasher dragonfly feasting on a fly. This species is known to capture around 300 insects per day, although most are much smaller than the fly shown in this photo. The distinctive white face and green eyes indicate a mature male of this species. The compound eye has bigger lenses in the top third, a feature found in some other insects. The small, round, silvery structure above and between the compound eyes is one of three simple eyes found in dragonflies and most other insects. Their function is not clearly known.**

GET THOSE INSECTS IN FORMATION! HUP! HUP! HUP!

Insects are too fantastically diverse and numerous to cover in any book. But it is possible to get around this problem. Entomologists have arranged insects in groups of species which have similarities in structure and natural history, so if one can recognize these groups, one can say a lot about the species that they contain. There are, for example, 71 species of mayflies found in Florida, and a comprehensive book on Florida insects cannot afford the space needed to illustrate and discuss all 71. But if one knows something about the group that includes the mayflies (the Order Ephemeroptera), one can understand many interesting and useful things about any mayfly one sees, without ever knowing the name of a single species. This book makes use of these official groups. From the largest to smallest, they are as follows:

The Order. *For example, the Order Coleoptera (beetles), is a massive order with more than 5000 species in Florida. There are perhaps 29 insect orders in Florida, but some are not covered in this book because they are rare, or the insects they include are too tiny for most people to notice.*

The Family. *For example, the Family Culicidae (mosquitoes) has about 79 Florida species. A couple of hundred families of insects occur in Florida. This book only mentions those families that are most conspicuous or have the most ecological importance.*

The Genus. *A genus contains one or more species. The genus* Periplaneta *includes several undesirable, large species of cockroaches which were accidentally imported into Florida. The genus name is underlined or italicized. The plural of "genus" is (confusingly) "genera." There are thousands of genera of insects in Florida.*

The Species. *This is a group of individuals which can interbreed and produce fertile offspring. The "cow killer" velvet ant (Order Hymenoptera, Family Mutillidae) is an example of a species. It's scientific name is* Dasymutilla occidentalis. *The first part of the scientific name, in this case* Dasymutilla, *is the genus. No other species is allowed to share this combined name: only one species can be called* Dasymutilla occidentalis. *Species are described and given names by specialist entomologists who have a profound understanding of the patterns of variation in a particular group, knowing what kind of differences are likely to occur within a single species, and what kind of differences are likely to signify distinct species. However, these specialists occasionally make mistakes, and this is one reason why the scientific names of insects are sometimes changed or updated in the light of new information.*

It is easy to get the impression that new species of insects pop up overnight, because one is always hearing that scientists have discovered a "new species." Such a new species has not suddenly evolved, but has been around for a long time (like a few million years). It has simply been overlooked by scientists.

BK

GM

Above: the eastern amberwing is one of the smallest dragonflies in Florida. There is generally more brown color in the wings of individuals found in South Florida.

Several Florida naturalists have commented on the striking similarity between the amberwing and paper wasps. Paper wasps are often seen in the same places as amberwings, flying over low vegetation in open areas. One would never guess this resemblance by looking at the photograph above, but in flight, the yellow wings with their dark spots flutter in just the right way to create the illusion of the distinctive wing movements of a wasp, while the dark brown abdomen with yellow accents is held in a wasp-like way.

When observing an insect that has conspicuous markings, it is fun to speculate on the ways these markings may be used to communicate, perhaps to members of its own species, or to warn or confuse predators. In many cases, nobody has actually tested the effctiveness of this communication. In a few cases, scientists have changed the color or markings of individuals to that of the opposite sex and observed the resulting confusion.

Left: an eastern amberwing dragonfly has just hatched from its larval stage. It will no longer live underwater and is expanding its wings in preparation for its new aerial life. The discarded skeleton from its larval form can be seen at the right side of the photo.

BK

Above: a red saddlebags eating a bee. This dragonfly is often found in swarms.

Right: the photo clearly shows the brownish color patch decorating about one quarter of the base of the hind wings, a color pattern typical of this species. One possible purpose of this kind of wing marking is to make the dragonfly appear larger. Or it may contribute to a wasp-like appearance when the dragonfly in flight is viewed from below.

The violet-masked dragonfly belongs to a genus called dancing gliders, a reference to their flight behavior during egg-laying. Flying low over water, the male holds the head of the female, which dips down to lay an egg, then bounces back up.

SWD

BK

Damselflies

SUBORDER ZYGOPTERA

Florida has 46 species of these dainty relatives of the dragonflies. As with dragonflies, it seems that there are even more species because males and females often differ in color pattern, and non-breeding individuals may have a third pattern.

Highly Variable. For damselfly watchers, this variability reaches crisis proportions in the very common Rambur's forktail: the males have two color forms (one immature), and the females have three. Some other species in the same genus (*Ishnura*) are almost as difficult to identify. This probably caused considerable cursing among early specialists working on Florida damselflies, though they only published their more restrained sentiments, for example: "The problem of coloration in the females of *Ishnura* is one fraught with great difficulties and surrounded by much controversial literature."

Damselflies as Prey. While damselflies may seem to lack the verve of dragonflies, they are every bit as predacious. Damselflies are themselves prey to many other animals, including frogs, lizards, birds, spiders, and dragonflies. Early-rising canoeists know that newly emerged damselflies are often found in large numbers in early morning on reeds and grasses lining the lake shores. Birds also know this, and make special trips to lakes and marshes to capture damselflies when they are most vulnerable. The larvae are eaten by fish, and some species of damselflies are unable to survive in water where there are fish and live only in seasonal ponds.

Three Families. Three families of damselflies occur in Florida. The broad-winged damsels (Family Calopterygidae) have only a few species, all of which breed in streams. These damselflies are distinguished by their iridescent bodies (usually green); the commoner species have dark wings. The spreadwings (Family Lestidae) include seven Florida species. Spreadwings rest with the wings partially open, the only damselflies to do so. All the rest of the Florida species are pond damselflies (Family Coenagrionidae) which perch with the wings held together over the back.

THE ODONATA AS A HOBBY

Dragonflies are attracting devoted followers. Some are birders who find dragonflies just as beautiful as birds, but more interesting, because less is known about them. Since dragonflies are harmless insects, little funding is available for their study. Much of the existing knowledge is the work of serious amateurs. A new dragonfly species is discovered almost every year. The Cape May Bird Observatory in New Jersey holds dragonfly workshops and New York's Central Park has a dragonfly preserve. There is also a Dragonfly Society of America.

BK

Left: a pond damselfly. Note that the front and rear sets of wings are similar in shape. They both are slender where they attach to the body and are wider at the tips.

GM

Above: the front and rear wings of the black-mantled glider dragonfly show a great difference in shape. The rear wings are much broader at the point of attachment to the body. This illustrates a major difference between dragonflies and damselflies and explains why they are classified in separate suborders called "unequal wings" and "similar wings."

DRAGONFLIES VS. DAMSELFLIES

Few people confuse dragonflies with damselflies because the dragonflies are bigger, faster, more robust, and zoom along with the wings held horizontal most of the time, like an airplane. Damselflies are slender, much more delicate creatures, and their flight is slower. Damselflies maneuver through vegetation, and can pick prey off a blade of grass. To small, fugitive insects, damselflies must seem like the highly maneuverable attack helicopters almost always featured in American action films, while the dragonflies are the jet fighters. Dragonflies race by, snatch an insect out of the air, and land on a perch to dismember it quickly and effectively.

Both dragonflies and damselflies belong to the order Odonata. Odonata means "the toothed-ones," a reference to the relatively large jaws which are equipped with long, sharp teeth. There are two suborders: the unequal wings (Anisoptera), which includes the dragonflies, and the similar wings (Zygoptera), which includes the damselflies.

Right: this close-up of a spreadwing damselfly shows the arrangement of damselfly eyes. They are widely separated, allowing for excellent binocular vision and depth perception. Compare this to the closeup photo of a dragonfly's eyes (see page 8). The difference is striking. The eyes of the dragonfly are so close together in many species that they actually touch each other at the top of the head.

SWD

BK

DAMSELFLY REPRODUCTION

The style of mating of dragonflies and damselflies is unique among insects. Before he mates, the male deposits his sperm in a specially modified structure at the base of his abdomen. At the tip of his abdomen, he has a set of claspers, with which he holds the head of the female, supporting her during copulation.

With both insects facing the same direction, the pair can even fly about during mating. Pairs of dragonflies and damselflies can often be seen flying about in tandem, the male continuing to hold the female, even though mating is no longer occurring.

In some cases, this is probably a form of "mate-guarding," keeping the female from the attentions of other males. In other cases, the male is actually supporting the female while she lays eggs.

SWD

Above: the tandem position. The male holds the female behind the neck with claspers located at the tip of his abdomen. Once the female is in the male's grasp, the pair will proceed to a safe place.
Top: the famous wheel position, also called a mating circle. The male (at the left) is still holding the female. The male has already transferred his sperm from a pore near the end of the abdomen to a pouch under the body. The female (at the right) extends her abdomen forward between her legs to receive the sperm from this pouch (called the accessory, or secondary genitalia).

JLC

***Right:* the duckweed firetail. Males, such as this specimen, have a showy red abdomen. Although other Florida damselflies have some red on their abdomens, this is the only species whose abdomen is solid red, without black markings. Notice also the red eyes, distinctive of the male. Females have brown bodies and brown eyes. This damselfly is found over matted aquatic plants, like the namesake duckweed, and also water lettuce and water pennywort. The duckweed firetail is the only firetail damselfly found in Florida**

BK

Damselflies

Forktails are among the smallest of the Florida damselflies. All the Florida species (except the lily pad forktail) have a projection from the male abdomen which is used to clasp the female during mating. However, this structure is a bit too small to see in these photographs.

Above: **a male Rambur's forktail. The male is easily identified by the striking blue final segment of the abdomen, the green stripes down the back, and the green sides. Different colors for different ages and sexes are useful for animals that use color patterns when looking for mates. In Rambur's forktail, however, one of the female forms is similar to the male. This similarity may save the female the bother of too much attention from eager males, which can be time-consuming. However, she must somehow be able to signal prospective mates at the right time.**

Opposite page, top: **male and female Rambur's forktail damselflies. The male is as described on this page. The female has three forms. In the first form, she is colored like the male; in the second, she has an orange-red thorax; and the third (shown here) is the olive form.**

SWD

The lily pad forktail spends it life in association with water lilies. The adult perches on the lilies above water and the larvae live their life in the water under the lily pads.

Above: **a female lily pad forktail. Mature females can be either blue or orange. This is another species in which some females apparently mimic males.**

Right: **the male lily pad forktail is always blue.**

SWD

BK

BK

JHR

Bluets, such as the ones above and left, include one third of Florida's damselfly species, a total of 17 species. The species identification of a bluet male is usually accomplished by examining under a microscope the shape of the tiny appendage at the tip of the abdomen.

***Above:* note the wide placement of the eyes in this close-up photo, typical of damselflies. Note also the numerous small hairs on the face and head. These hairs are also found on other parts of the damselfly and may be used for sensing air movement.**

JLC

Damselflies

Above: a spreadwing damselfly resting on the underside of a composite flower. The spreadwings are known for the way they hold their wings when at rest. Rather than folding them together above the back like most damselflies, they hold them partially open. Most spreadwings, and a number of other damselflies, are not found in permanent water where there are predatory fish. These damselflies are typical of a whole group of native insects and frogs that are completely dependent on ponds and marshes that are flooded only during Florida's summer rainy season. Few Floridians realize the importance of seasonal wetlands in maintaining the biolgical diversity of the state.

NT

Above: a sparkling jewelwing damselfly.

Left: an ebony jewelwing damselfly. Note that the wings of both the ebony and jewelwing damselflies are not very narrow, as they belong to the family of broad-winged damsels. Also of interest, broad-wings have a distinctive flight pattern due to a hesitation in their wingbeat.

Jewelwings have iridescent bodies that show green and blue colors when the light strikes them at the proper angle. The males lack the stigma (a small blister of blood—see page 9) in the wings common to other dragonflies and damselflies, but the females have a stigma which appears as a pure white spot at the tip of the wing, a striking contrast to the black wing color.

BBB

RFS

Above: **this damselfly is resting on a reed after hunting insects across the surface of the pond. It will soon take off to hunt again and will likely return to its same resting place when it tires.**

RFS

Right: **the variable dancer is not as variable in Florida as its name implies, although there are peninsular and Panhandle subspecies. The bluish tip of the abdomen, and the violet markings on the thorax, indicate a male. In the female, the abdomen and thorax are both dark. Most species of dancers lay their eggs in flowing water. The larvae cling to rocks to keep from being swept away. The variable dancer is an exception to this rule, and prefers still water for reproduction. It is the only small damselfly with dark wings and is common in gardens near breeding sites.**

WHY THERE ARE NO BUTTERFLIES IN THIS BOOK

Butterflies and moths are also insects, but they have their own book in this series, which is entitled Florida's Fabulous Butterflies. This book also shows many of their caterpillars which are surprisingly colorful and interesting. Butterflies have been extensively studied, so unlike this book, in which it is frequently stated that "little is known about...," it may be said that quite a lot is known about the 160 or so species of butterflies in Florida. And what is known is very interesting: migration, courtship, metamorphosis, and more!

WHY THERE ARE NO SPIDERS IN THIS BOOK

Spiders, mites, ticks, scorpions, centipedes, millipedes, and pillbugs are all missing from this book because they are not insects. Insects by definition have six legs, no more, no less. All the creatures mentioned above have more than six legs. Also, most insects have wings while these other creatures do not. However, spiders and the others are very interesting and are covered in this series with their own book, Florida's Fabulous Spiders (to be published in 2000). It would be impossible to do them justice in this book which is already straining just to give an overview of Florida's insects.

Spiders in particular are wonderfully diverse and numerous in Florida with many beautifully patterned species. Their shapes, colors, and habits are fascinating, especially their amazing bag of tricks for capturing prey. Some common jumping spiders have iridescent green fangs and huge eyes fringed with "eyelashes." Other spiders have crimson fur or tiger stripes. There are also many web-spinners with a great variety of ingenious traps, some involving rather advanced engineering.

ORDER ORTHOPTERA

Orthoptera means "straight wings." The wings of some orthopterans are small (sometimes entirely lost). Those with wings have two pairs, and the front pair is relatively straight. The front pair usually covers and protects the hind wings when the creature is at rest.

Members of the order Orthoptera are athletic leapers, agile, and alert. They may be either brightly colored or ingeniously camouflaged (or both). Collectively, they make up the most grand insect orchestras. Their sounds bring to mind lazy summer afternoons and warm moonlit nights. Almost none of the Florida Orthoptera can be considered pests, except for the huge, colorful lubber grasshopper, that sometimes attacks ornamental plants, and bird grasshoppers, which sometimes occur in large enough numbers to damage small trees. Orthoptera are a major source of food for Florida song birds and game birds (such as quail and turkey), exceeded in importance only by caterpillars. About 250 species of grasshoppers, crickets, and their relatives are found in Florida.

Music Makers. The songs of Orthoptera have attracted particular attention. Males of most crickets, katydids, and mole crickets sing to attract females, as do some grasshoppers. Crickets, katydids, and mole crickets sing by rubbing a set of tiny pegs on one forewing over a file set in the other forewing. The sound resonates on a specially constructed smooth membrane on the base of the wings. The singing grasshoppers produce their soft ditties by rubbing the bases of their hind legs across the leading edges of their front wings. None of the Orthoptera sing by rubbing their hind legs together, as is sometimes supposed.

Risky Songs. Singing is risky business because the sounds of the gifted insect musician may not attract an agent with a lucrative recording contract, but a hungry predator. There are even species of predatory insects that are specialized for tracking the songs of singing Orthoptera. Female Orthoptera, which carry the eggs of the next generation, are generally silent. Since only one sex needs to do the attracting, it tends to be the duty of the males, because males are more expendable. They can mate with more than one female and thus can afford the dangerous, exhibitionist behavior that attracts the opposite sex. This principle explains why male band-wing grasshoppers leap into the air and flash their yellow or red underwings to attract females. The songs and flashy colors of male birds have a similar function.

Unique to Florida. Florida is home to a surprisingly large number of grasshoppers, crickets, and katydids that live nowhere else in the world. About 20 of these Florida specialty species have been scientifically described so far, but this number is likely to double. The landscape of Florida has changed tremendously in the last 50 years, but the land itself is ancient, old enough to have its own species, which have evolved in Florida's natural habitats during many hundreds of thousands of years.

Classification. The jumping Orthoptera, distinguished by their hugely developed hind legs, are closely related to several other groups of walking and running insects: mantids, roaches, termites, and walking sticks, all of which have sometimes been included in the order Orthoptera. The classification of these groups will probably be unsettled for some decades. This book ignores the controversies of classification, and proceeds directly to the interesting features of these insects.

Above: **a short-winged meadow katydid on a flower of stick-seed daisy. This species is common and widespread in Florida. Grasshoppers and katydids often eat flower petals.**

Right: **the dramatic face of a half-winged cone-headed katydid. Note the cone at the top of the head. The black jaws of this species are strong and sharp enough to draw blood if the animal is handled carelessly.**

PC

Top: a short-winged bush cricket perches on a grape leaf above flowers of rattlebox. This species often spends the day on palmettos.

Above: a male tree cricket showing the wide forewings used for singing, overlaying the folded hind wings used for flying.

Crickets

Family Gryllidae

Crickets are just bugs like any other bugs. They haven't all gone to charm school. Still, these perky songsters, with their plump hind legs and long delicate antennae seem to exude charm. Florida is especially rich in cricket diversity, from the gangly, graceful, pale-green tree crickets, to the tiny, rotund, ant-loving crickets that live in ant colonies. Of the 75 species listed for Florida, several have not yet received formal scientific names. These unnamed species are clearly distinguished by differences in the songs that the males use to attract females. In these species, it is difficult to find the differences in structures that are normally used to identify insects. Scientists are not eager to name species that can only be identified when alive and singing, and would prefer to find some little difference that is also useful for identification of dead specimens in museums and other collections. There are probably more such species to be found, especially in the Panhandle.

The songs of crickets are produced by rapidly running a ridge on the underside of one wing across a file on the upper side of the other wing. The type of sound depends on the spacing of the teeth of the file, the speed of wing movement, and the characteristics of special resonating areas of the wings. Many species of crickets can create more than one kind of song: there may be a calling song, a courtship song after a female arrives, and an aggressive song if another male appears.

The songs of crickets are often included in the sound tracks of movies in pre-smooch scenes set in moonlit gardens. These scenes are sometimes punctuated with owl hoots on a lonely woodland path just before the menace-music announces that something bad is about to spring from the shadows. Often, the cricket song used does not occur within a thousand miles of the scene of movie action, but this does not matter, for the mood is set.

Floridians can enjoy the romance of cricket songs through most of the year, with different singers during different seasons and in different habitats. The repetitive nature of cricket songs allows them to quickly fade into background sounds, like the tick of a clock, of which we have no awareness. With a small effort, however, one can snap out of this auditory sedation. Then, a walk through a Florida habitat suddenly becomes enlivened by a changing chorus of chirps and trills.

BK

JHR

CRICKET LORE

Crickets are the subjects of many legends and superstitions. The Cherokee Tribe of Native Americans was especially fascinated with crickets. When a warrior was feeling weak, a cricket was placed in a bowl of water and left there overnight. If, in the morning, the cricket was still alive, it was released and the water consumed by the warrior who wished to build up his fighting spirit. Apparently, the odds were against the cricket surviving the night, so it might take a number of days before such a remedy could be ready. World-wide, interest in crickets has been recorded throughout history. For example, children in ancient China amused themselves by keeping crickets in special, ornate containers, and pitting them in battle against each other.

BM

Top: a little green bush cricket on an ixora flower. In spite of its small size, this species produces a song that can be heard at least ten yards away. When singing, this cricket usually remains hidden in dense vegetation. The female has a flattened, egg-laying tool that can split leaves and deposit eggs between the layers.

Left: a female field cricket. This individual is shortwinged and unable to fly. Many species of crickets have both flightless forms and long-winged forms that can fly to new areas. The sword-like structure on the rear of this cricket is for depositing eggs in the soil.

Right: a female camel cricket. These strange crickets are always wingless, and do not sing.They spend most of their lives underground, but sometimes wander into garages. One Florida species lives in the burrows of gopher tortoises.

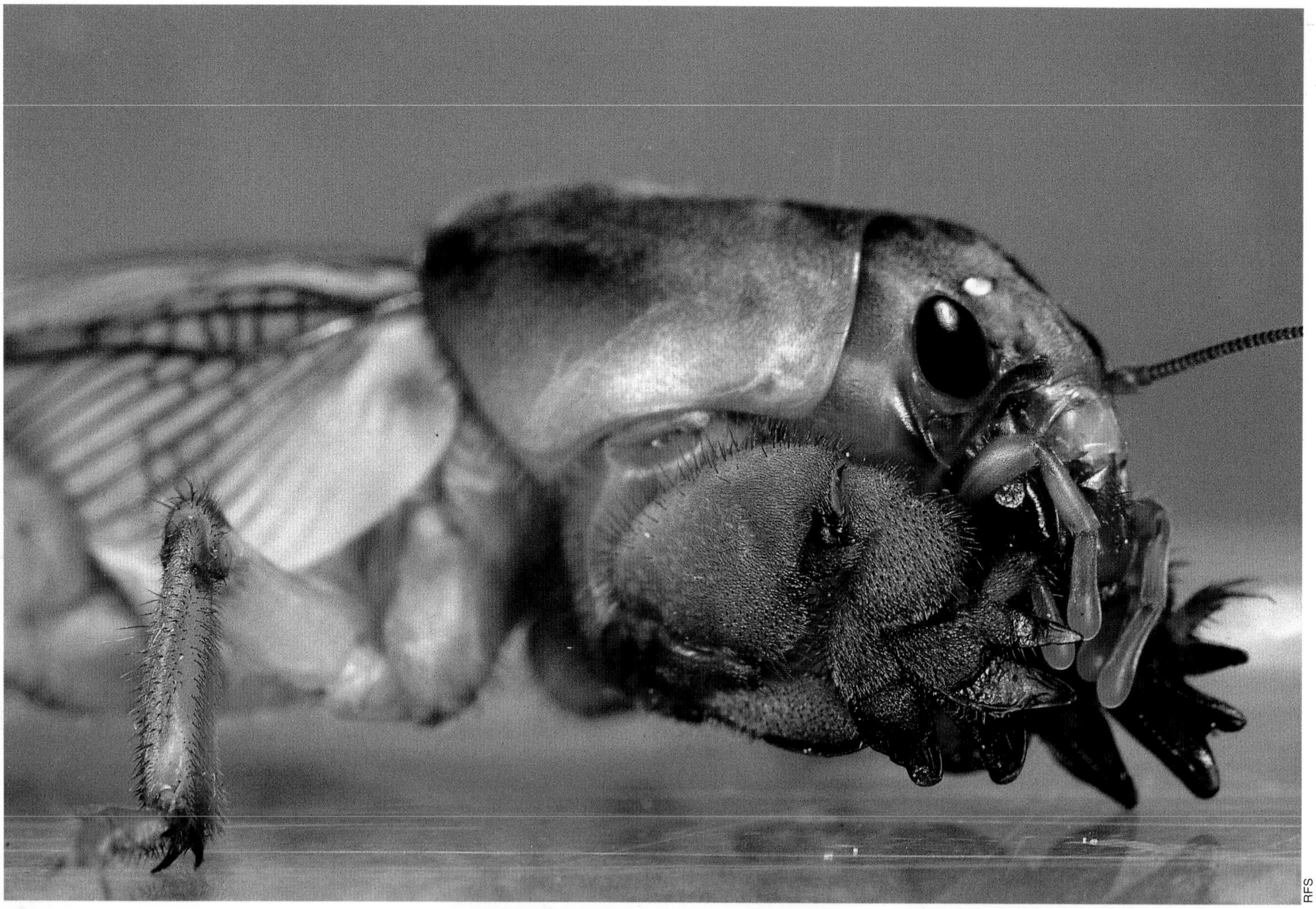

RFS

Mole Crickets

JLC

Top: **note the flat claws which the mole cricket uses for digging.**

Above: **a predatory wasp invading the tunnel of a mole cricket.**

JLC

Above: **the tawny mole cricket.**

Right: **the mole cricket's name is derived from its burrowing habits and the enlarged front feet with strong claws, like those of a mole.**

Family Gryllotalpidae

There are only four species of mole crickets in Florida, but they are familiar insects, large, active, and destructive. Three of Florida's four species were accidentally imported from South America. Mole crickets feed primarily on roots of grasses and other plants. Their front feet are enlarged, with blade-like "fingers" used for digging. Mole crickets prefer sandy areas where the ground is easy to dig. They are not deterred by wet soils, as they are covered with a dense velvety nap that repels water and sticky soil.

The imported species of mole crickets have become major pests in Florida, especially in lawns and golf courses. In 1980 alone, about $11.7 million was spent on insecticides for the control of mole crickets in Florida. But how can a dollar value be put on the loss of status for the man whose lawn has brown spots? In Biblical times, mole crickets might have been seen as an omen. It might now be said, "Into that land, which was more concerned with the greenness of its lawns than the education of its children, was sent a great plague of mole crickets."

Researchers in Gainesville have made an effort to bring in natural enemies of mole crickets. There is some evidence that the imported and native enemies of mole crickets may be having some effect, especially in pastures, where drenching the ground with insecticides is not economically justified.

Mole crickets are miracles of mobility. They burrow, jump, and swim with equal ease. They can run rapidly, both forward and backward, with a peculiar scuttling motion. They fly well for such bulky insects, and may be attracted to lights in great numbers during a few nights of the year. On one occasion, their large numbers forced the shut-down of some of the night events at Disney World.

Male mole crickets attract females with a low-pitched but penetrating call. The calling is usually made from an open burrow, where the male is somewhat protected from natural enemies attracted to the call. At least one Florida species modifies this open burrow as an underground sound chamber, with the opening flaring to the surface like the mouth of a horn. As the mole cricket digs this burrow, it periodically pauses and utters short chirping sequences that allow it to judge the acoustical quality of the burrow and modify the burrow accordingly.

BK

BWM

Grasshoppers

Family Acrididae

The Evasive Grasshopper. Most hunters locate their prey by movement, so an alarmed grasshopper alternates between moving extremely fast and remaining absolutely still. Naturalists who pursue grasshoppers know that in the second after it lands from an evasive jump, while the hunter is still tracking the trajectory, the grasshopper usually runs a short distance through the grass and turns. When the pursuer approaches, the next leap is from an unexpected place and in an unanticipated direction. In spite of these escape mechanisms, great numbers of grasshoppers are devoured by their natural enemies.

Courtship Displays. Males of several common Florida grasshoppers leap into the air and display their pink or yellow wings, while making a loud rattling noise, rather like the buzz of a rattlesnake. Some species signal with striped or banded hind legs. All this is done with the caution of an animal that is highly edible, but also needs to be seen by the opposite sex.

Top: **a short-horned grasshopper. Members of the family Acrididae are often called short-horned grasshoppers to distinguish them from the katytids and their relatives (page 38) which have extremely long antennae.**

BK

Above: **a Cuban anole captures a short-horned grasshopper.**

THE DANGEROUS LIFE OF GRASSHOPPERS

In the miniature Serengeti of a grassy Florida clearing, grasshoppers are the antelopes, constantly ready to leap away from a horrifying series of hazards. There is the monstrous curved beak of a swooping kestrel, and the skink stealthily working its way through a cover of tussocks. By a small seep, a frog is crouched, with its great, muscular, sticky, enveloping tongue. Right in the line of leaping, there may be a spider's invisible trap cables that can send a hopper tumbling out of control down onto the sheet of webbing, a trampoline of death where the spider awaits, all legs and fangs. This explains why almost all of Florida's 75 species of grasshoppers are beautifully camouflaged, and among the most alert insects.

SWD

Top: **a red-winged grasshopper posed to show "flash-coloration." The colored hind wings are used for display to the opposite sex. Also, the grasshopper presents in flight a striking image to any predator, an image that vanishes when the grasshopper lands and shuts its wings.**

Above: **two male short-horned grasshoppers attempting to mate with one female. As with most grasshoppers, the female is larger than the male.**

HOW A GRASSHOPPER GROWS

This photo series shows the immature forms of the American grasshopper as it molts from one stage of growth to another. Each stage is called an instar and there may be from four to eight stages before the adult form appears. A. First stage (or first instar) B. Third instar. C. Since the outer skin of a grasshopper is inflexible and cannot grow, it splits open to allow the grasshopper, with its newly formed shell underneath, to emerge. The old skin is left behind. D. The mature form, or adult grasshopper.

The outer skin of an insect also serves as an external skeleton. When it molts, the insect has the enviable opportunity to replace worn parts such as teeth and leg joints. Even legs and antennae lost in accidents may be replaced. Only a few insects, such as silverfish, continue shedding as adults.

Grasshoppers

Grasshopper Song. Unlike the crickets and the katydids, which are night-singers, most grasshoppers sing during daytime. Grasshoppers sing to attract mates. There are even species in which males and females both sing, moving carefully toward each other through the weeds, guided by a soft duet. So much for the rather sexist saying, "Happy are grasshoppers' lives, for they all have noiseless wives!"

PC

PC

GRASSHOPPER EYES

The world is filled with creatures that eat grasshoppers. The resulting need for camouflage often determines body shape and color. Some species have bands that break up the visual outline of the body, while others have stripes that blend with grass blades. Even the coloration of the eyes follows the pattern. Some Florida grasshoppers and katydids have more than one color form as an adult. One of the benefits of this diversity may be that it makes predators less effective, as they must search for several different models simultaneously.

THE HAPPY GRASSHOPPER AND THE POET

Among the classical and romantic poets, the grasshopper has the reputation of a happy and carefree animal. This attitude is most beautifully expressed by John Keats in his poem, "On the Grasshopper and the Cricket."

"The poetry of the earth is never dead:

When all the birds are faint with the hot sun and hide in the cooling trees,

A voice will run from hedge to hedge about the new-mown mead—

That is the grasshopper's. He takes the lead in summer luxury;

He is never done with his delights, for when tired out with fun,

He rests at ease beneath some pleasant weed."

Aesop, the ancient Greek author, is credited with the famous fable in which the grasshopper sings all day while the ants work laying up food for the winter. When winter comes, the grasshopper freezes and starves while the ants gloat in comfort.

The story of the grasshopper and the ants is based on natural history observations. Most grasshoppers in temperate climates really do spend the end of summer singing among the weeds, and the ants really do spend this same season providently working on nest construction and laying in supplies. The fable omits the fact that the survival strategy of grasshoppers dictates that at the end of summer the last part of life must be spent in a great burst of reproduction, a concept foreign to perennial species like ants and humans.

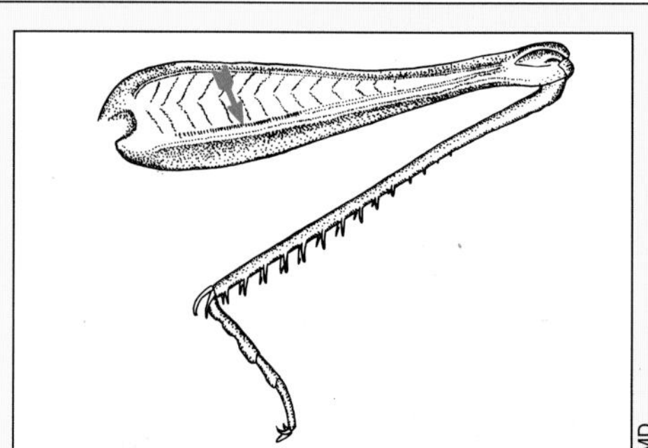

MD

GRASSHOPPER SONG: THE MECHANISM

This drawing shows the rough portion of a grasshopper's leg which is rubbed against a special area of hardened veins in the forewings to produce sounds. Katydids have a different method of sound production. They rub the rear edge of the right forewing against a special area of the hind wing to produce their sounds.

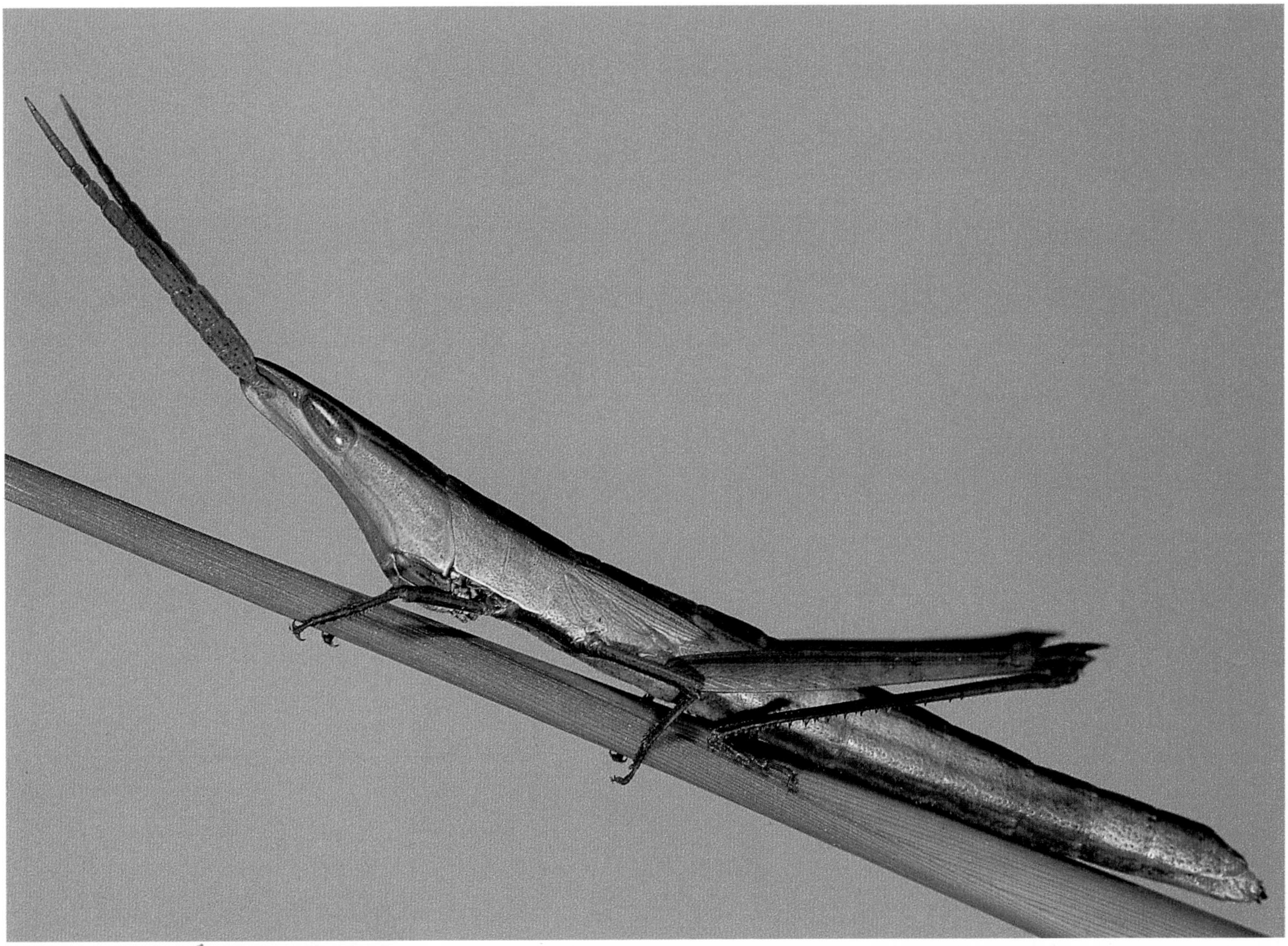

BK

BK

Top: **a long-headed toothpick grasshopper. The flattened antennae resemble new shoots of grass.**

Above: **short-horned grasshoppers mating. Note the striking difference in the appearance of the male and female (sexual dimorphism). This short-winged species is unable to fly, but gets around anyway.**

This is one of the most common species found in lawns, along roadsides, and in other disturbed areas. Males of this species can make soft noises by rubbing the hind legs against the wings. they do so not to attract females, but to repell other males.

PC

A PLAGUE OF LOCUSTS

Plagues of locusts (which are a kind of short-horned grasshopper) appear in the records of ancient Assyria and Egypt, as well as the 10th chapter of Exodus. The larger swarms may cover up to 1,000 square kilometers and contain billions of individuals. Swarms travel by day and rest at night, with a constant fallout of masses of hoppers that refuel by eating all the vegetation along the way, including crops.

These grasshoppers usually begin their journey in large grassland areas where the rains have ended and travel in search of areas where the females can lay their eggs in wet soil. In the 1800s, there were great plagues of grasshoppers in the American Midwest, but these migrations are now much reduced.

There are occasional population explosions of certain grasshoppers in Florida, but there are no great plagues in the state because there are no large grasslands to serve as breeding grounds. The grasshopper shown above is a Florida species related to the plague locust (same genus).

BK

Grasshoppers

Lubber Grasshoppers. Most grasshoppers are exceptionally well camouflaged, but, in any large group of insects, there are exceptional species. The huge, clumsy, brightly-colored lubber grasshopper is the exception among Florida grasshoppers. This species may raise its colored wings defiantly and bubble out a poisonous froth when threatened by a bird. It not only manufactures poisonous and repellent chemicals, but it can also shunt poisons from the plants it eats into its own toxic secretions.

Florida gardeners are familiar with the lubber grasshopper's special fondness for amaryllis leaves, and might wish for more natural enemies to control this species. There is some help at hand: the larvae of certain flies attack lubber grasshoppers, consuming them from within. A Florida bird of fields and pastures, the loggerhead shrike, also preys on lubber grasshoppers, impaling the grasshopper corpse on a thorn or a spike of barbed wire until the grasshopper's poisons have evaporated or decomposed. Some specialized wasps and flies attack the eggs of grasshoppers, even though the eggs are buried in the ground.

BK

JLG

Top: **the adult lubber grasshopper.**

Above: **a lubber enjoys the fruit of beauty berry, a native plant. Florida gardeners are very familiar with this grasshopper because it is so visible in the garden, and capable of biting large chunks out of plants.**

Left: **this photo shows the bright red wings of the lubber which are usually hidden when the grasshopper is at rest.**

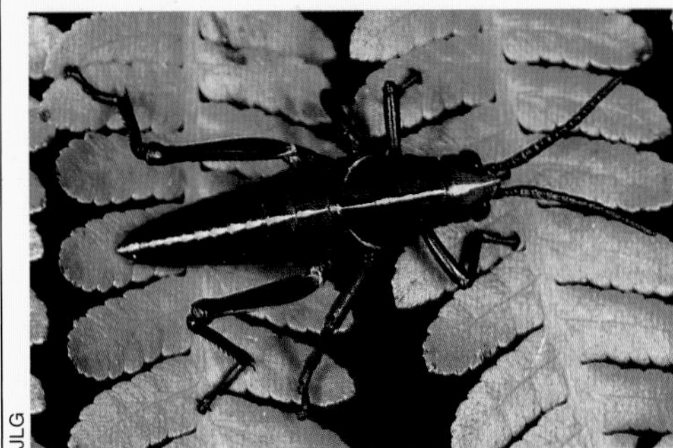

JLG

PC

JP

BK

BK

THE IMMATURE LUBBER

The photo above shows the mature lubber emerging from the skin of it's immature form. The white threads on the side of the emerging hopper are linings of the breathing tubes. Immature lubbers are usually black with yellow markings. The photo at top shows the distinctive yellow stripe down the back. Immature lubbers go through a number of stages before the adult form appears. The lubber third from top in the left column is one of the last stages of the immature (or larva) form. It will turn black a few hours after emerging from its old skin (photo, above right).

When lubber grasshoppers are very young, they tend to gather in groups, expecially when they are resting at night. Certain other brightly-colored insects with repellent chemicals occur in similar groups for resting or feeding. It may be that if one nasty-tasting or stinky grasshopper is repellent, a group of them is even more so, thus it is beneficial to congregate. It is also possible that young and inexperienced predators must learn which insects are inedible, so it is better to be part of a group of inedible individuals, because the chance of being injured as part of a taste test is less if one is in a group of individuals, any one of which can provide the lesson to naive predators in the immediate vicinity.

Katydids and Their Relatives

Family Tettigoniidae

On a Florida evening, when crickets are tuning up their bird-like chirpers, katydids give the impression of rummaging through the toy box up in the attic. From the sounds, one would think they had pulled out raucous kazoos, small vehicles that click and tick, rhythmic maracas filled with small round seeds, a dry stick that is run over a cheese grater, while in the background an old radio is lisping soft, repetitive static. The Katydid Toy Orchestra of Florida is one of the largest in the country, with at least 64 species. Each species has its own sound.

Most species sing at night, but the meadow katydids, most of which live in open damp or marshy areas, sing quietly through the day from perches on the swaying blades of grasses and sedges. The best way to find a singing katydid, either by day or night, is to follow the sound to the clump of plants where the insect is hidden. His long antennae stick out and wave gently as he sings.

In northern states, katydids sing at the end of summer when they become mature; their sounds are often associated with the coming of fall and the ripening of corn. There is always debate whether their calls sound more like "katydid" or "katydidn't." Actually, their sounds are far more varied than this narrow choice.

The katydids appearance is as varied as their songs; some green, some brown; some with broad wings like leaves; some with narrow wings like grasses. In many species the head is extended forward between the eyes—these are the cone-headed katydids. All these insects have very long, fine antennae, and rather slender jumping legs. Species of katydids, like other Orthoptera, tend to be confined to one habitat, such as pine flatwoods, marshes, or areas of low shrubs. The diet of katydids, like that of many other Orthoptera, is largely unknown. Some species feed on leaves.

Supreme Court Justice Oliver Wendell Holmes liked katydids enough to write a poem about them. His knowledge of insect biology, however, did not match his legal abilities. Today, his tone seems sexist and his aversion to tea parties antiquated.

Thou art a female, Katydid!
I know it by the trill
That quivers through thy piercing notes,
So petulant and shrill.
I think there is a knot of you
Beneath the hollow tree,
A knot of spinster Katydids,
Do Katydids drink tea?

Top: **a gladiator katydid.**

Above: **a young meadow katydid on a tasselflower, a Florida wildflower.**

Top: a very young katydid on a skyflower.

Right: the eggs of an angular-winged katydid.

Far right: the eggs have hatched into baby katydids.

Bottom left: one of the true, or broad-winged, katydids.

Bottom right: a pink katydid. Pink color forms are rare. It appears to be a regularly appearing mutation that seldom survives because it is so obvious to predators.

BK

JLC

Top: note the ovipositor of this katydid used for placing eggs. It indicates that this is a female. Also, note the special katydid ears, which are small openings just below the first joint on the front legs. These auditory slits help distinguish katydids from grasshoppers, since the ears of grasshoppers are located on the sides of their bodies.

Left: the beautiful yellow phase of the oval-winged katydid. Usually green, it is one of the most common Florida katydids. Its familiar buzz-click song can be heard from low shrubs and weeds. The dark spot in the eyes of these katydids (also in many other photos in this book) is not a pupil, but the part of the eye directly in front of the camera lens where it is possible to see the eye's dark center.

Katydids and Their Relatives

Right: a broad-tipped conehead katydid on pickerel weed. This species may be green or brown in Florida, but brown seems more common for males, green for females. The song is a raucous buzz, and, although loud, it is difficult to pinpoint its location.

Opposite page: the eastern thread-legged katydid is found only in Florida and Georgia. It is the most slender katydid in Florida and is usually found on narrow-leaved grasses such as wiregrass (here it is on sedge).

BK

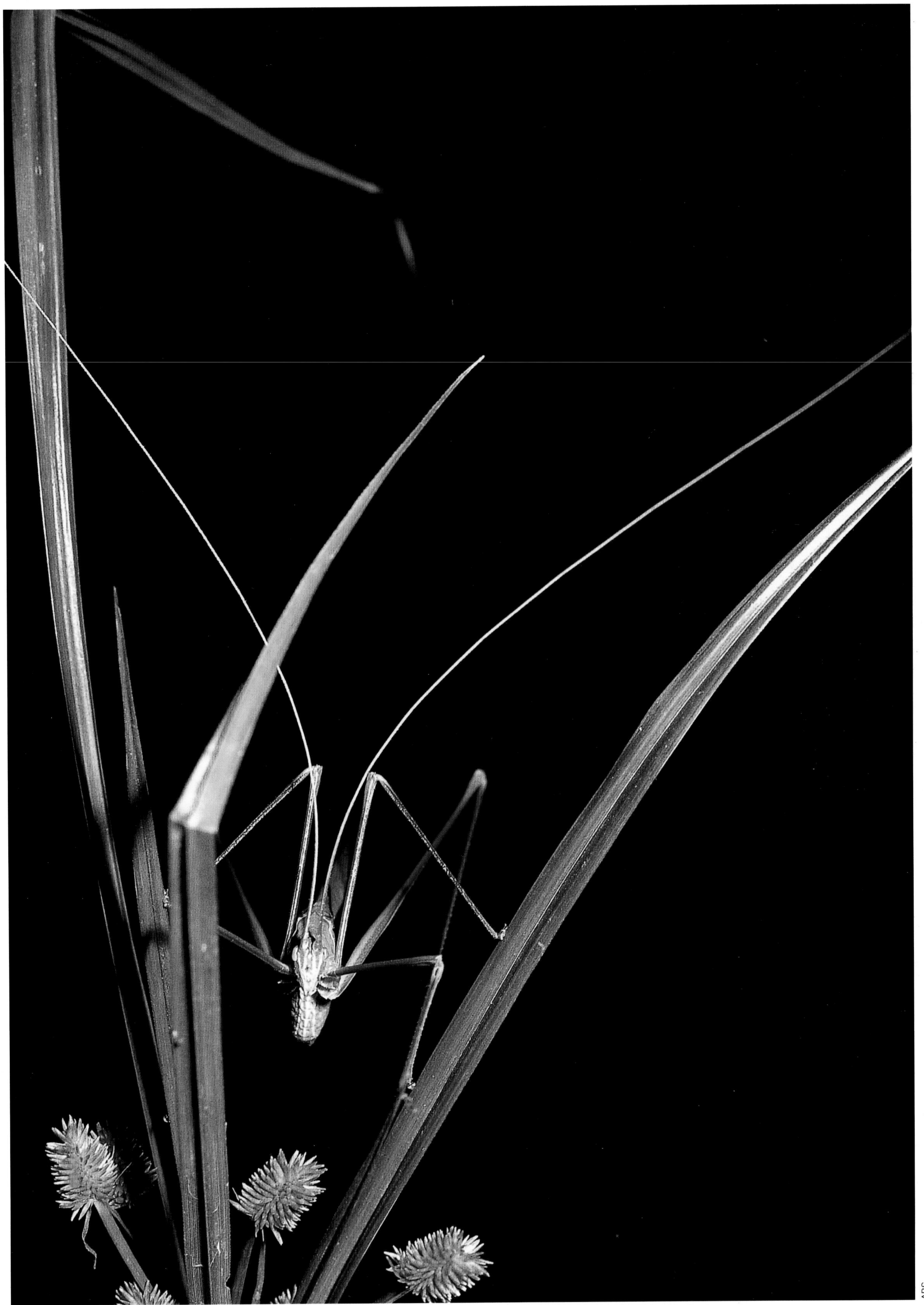

ABS

JHR

ORDER MANTODEA

Mantids are commonly called "praying" mantis because of the prayer-like way they hold their front legs, but "preying" mantis might be more accurate because this insect is a cannibal that even consumes members of its own family.

Praying mantids are the most familiar examples of insects that lie in wait and grab their victims with a quick strike of the front legs. The spined joints of these legs then clamp around the struggling prey. Assassin bugs, ambush bugs, and several groups of flies use the same highly effective technique.

The strike of the mantid is both fast (3/100-6/100 of a second) and precise. The prey is targeted along the line of sight of a special sensitive area in each eye. When the prey appears in this spot in both eyes at once, it is exactly in striking distance. An extra calculation allows for the position of the head, which is relayed by sensitive hairs at the neck. The triangular head of the mantid separates the eyes to provide great depth perception.

While stalking, mantids try to appear as a harmless bit of the scenery by swaying smoothly from side to side as they advance, like a leaf or grass blade moved by the breeze. The movement of the head allows the eyes, which are incapable of independent movement, to scan the prey and its surroundings, giving a more detailed view and allowing a more accurate estimation of distance.

REC

Top: a praying mantis parent with her egg mass. The heavily spiked forelegs are used to capture and hold prey.
Left: praying mantis hatchlings emerging from an egg mass. The egg mass of this species is covered with a quick-hardening foam.
Below: a human finger shows the small size of the baby mantid.

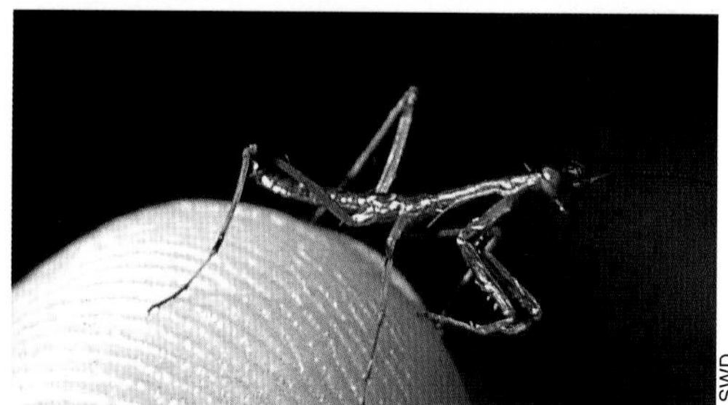

SWD

EATING THE HUSBAND

There are only about seven species of mantids in Florida, and most are not very common. Weirdly enough, the relative scarcity of mantids, and their rather poor mobility, may help explain why some female mantids show a tendency to eat their mate (this also occurs in some spiders). When a male mantid eventually encounters and mates with a female, he might do more to ensure the success of his offspring by serving as the female's prey and providing nutrients for their eggs, than by leaving that female and conducting a long and dangerous search for another mate. Thus natural selection, which cares nothing for the shocked stares of biologists, may actually select for males that do not defend themselves effectively against a hungry mate. This may be considered as an unusual male counterpart of a very common type of parental sacrifice among female insects and spiders. Many females, including female mantids, break down their own vital organs and reprocess them into nutrients for the eggs, so that by the time the last egg is laid the female is hardly more than an empty husk that dies within the next few hours or days.

BM

BK

JHR

Top, left: **a praying mantis has captured a skipper butterfly. Predatory insects often wait on flowers to ambush visiting insects.**

Top, right: **a mantis eating a katydid.**

Above: **a Carolina mantid spreads its wings.**

Right: **a mantid photographed in the Florida Everglades.**

Mantis is a Greek word which is often used interchangeably with mantid. Mantis means "prophet" or "soothsayer" and indicates the respect mantids receive in some cultures, especially in Africa. It may be that mantises are considered special because of their alert and intelligent appearance, patience, and boldness around humans.

JHR

BK

MANTIS CAMOUFLAGE

Mantids are amazingly well camouflaged, which probably helps them ambush prey, and avoid becoming dinner themselves for a bird. Two common Florida mantids have contrasting, but equally dramatic methods of concealment. The grizzled mantid is flat and mottled gray, like the tree bark where it lives, and the slender grass mantid is invisible in grass. Both are often attracted to lights, and end up on the walls of buildings, where they are suddenly conspicuous.

BK

JHR

BK

ORDER PHASMATODEA

Walkingsticks belong to a small order of slender, flightless insects that seem most closely related to the mantids, and are sometimes combined with them in one order. In habits, however, the two groups are as different as the leopard and the lamb: the mantids are all fierce predators while the walkingsticks are all shy vegetarians.

Walkingsticks are not uncommon in Florida, but usually achieve their goal of remaining completely unobserved among the stems and twigs of their host plants. Only six species are found in Florida, but there could easily be two or three additional species living their retiring lives in the tops of trees or shrubs in the Panhandle.

THE DEVIL RIDER

Florida does have one maverick walkingstick that breaks the rules of normal behavior among the group. This is the two-striped walkingstick, which is decidedly plump relative to the skeletal standards of walkingsticks. It also runs about in a lively manner when disturbed, and sports orange racing stripes on a dark brown background. This common species can afford to be noticed, because it is able to squirt a defensive liquid produced by glands on the thorax. The repellent chemicals, called terpenes, deployed by the two-striped walkingstick, smell terrible and are highly irritating. They can cause temporary blindness if they are squirted into the eye of a bird or mammal. The male of this walkingstick is much smaller than the female, and spends much of its adult life mating and riding about on the female. Since each female lays many eggs over a period of at least several weeks, the male has a better chance of fathering many offspring if he stays with a single female, rather than roving about looking for additional females. These might be difficult to find, since the male must travel everywhere on foot. This riding behavior of the male two-striped walkingstick is reflected in two local Florida names for the species: the "devil-rider" and the "musk-mare."

ORDER DERMAPTERA

The earwigs are a small group of insects, with fewer than ten species in Florida, but some are quite common, and all are quite peculiar. The most striking characteristic of the adult earwig is the pair of pinchers at the rear, useful for defense in the dark alleyways under logs or the bark of dead trees, where any number of predators may approach from behind. When danger strikes in the open, the pinchers can be raised up over the head to assist the jaws in repelling a frontal attack. Like scorpions and skunks, earwigs don't need to cover their rear; their rear covers them. No Florida earwigs are able to pinch a human hard enough to hurt, but a predator such as a spider might be driven off.

Some Florida earwigs have a pair of wings (intricately folded like advanced Origami) under short wing covers. The pinchers are sometimes used to help tuck the wings back into place. The males of some species of earwigs have larger pinchers than the females, which suggests that the pinchers are used in courtship, or in combat with other males. Earwigs tend to show well-developed maternal care. The female guards and licks the eggs until they hatch (in some species the female assists her babies to emerge), and watches over the young after they are born.

The name earwig is an old term for the common European species, perhaps derived from the supposedly ear-like shape of the hind wings when they are unfolded; or from the resemblance of the pinchers to an antique device for ear-piercing; or from rare instances, multiplied in folklore, of earwigs seeking shelter by crawling into the ears of sleeping humans. The last explanation seems most likely.

There are only a few documented cases of earwigs crawling into ears, but the notion of an insect with long pinchers tiptoeing into a human ear is exactly the kind of vivid image that could carry a name into universal usage. Earwigs do not feed on earwax, but they eat almost anything else, including flowers, and insects, such as aphids and scale insects.

BK

PC

TR

***Top:* the riparian earwig, often found along the Florida coast, but also inland.**

***Bottom right:* the European earwig, one of many examples of insects accidentally imported from the Old World.**

***Bottom left:* the gold-winged earwig lives in wet areas, hiding by day in clumps of grasses and sedges, especially sawgrass. It is often attracted to lights.**

BUGS AND THE GREAT CYCLE

Gold is useless to life, while some common elements, such as sulphur and carbon, have worth beyond all price. Life itself can persist because each generation holds its essential elements only on loan, and a host of organisms ensures that the dead do not carry their treasure into an eternal grave. Insects play a very large role in this recycling of the materials of life. The final release of elements is achieved through chemical breakdown, but this usually requires that the dead tissue (for example, a dead twig) be ground up so that bacteria and digestive enzymes can get at the stored nutrients. Innumerable insects make their living by scavenging, and are especially valuable in breaking down dead plants, whose durable tissues need special treatment. Thousands of species of insects consume dead leaves. Many of these actually get their sustenance from bacterial films on the leaves, or the threads of fungi that move into dead leaves, but the effect of these creatures is to chop the leaves into tiny fragments so that chemical decomposition can occur. Thousands of species of beetles bore into dead bark and wood. Some of these beetles can actually digest cellulose. Others have internal pouches, like the rumen of a cow, where microorganisms break down the wood. Still others introduce fungi into the wood and feed on the produce of their fungus gardens.

In Florida, termites are among the most valuable decomposers, removing and recycling enormous quantities of tree trunks, branches, and twigs that would otherwise clutter up the landscape, even consuming much of the cardboard and paper that litter Florida's roadsides, the tracks and droppings of the ill-bred. Termites take longer to deal with waxed paper, and, unfortunately, draw the line at styrofoam. Termites are not at all the chittering, house-wrecking imps shown in the television ads for pest control companies. The truth is even worse: termites are completely unable to tell the difference between our elegant homes and any other big heap of dead wood. Nothing adds insult to injury like the foe that does not even acknowledge our existence. Our pride demands cartoon termites with little horns, pitchforks, and evil grins.

BK

ORDER BLATTARIA

Blattaria in Latin means "insect that shuns the light," an appropriate name for the household species. However, some native outdoor roaches, like many other nocturnal insects, are attracted to light.

Roach Headquarters. Few Floridians would be surprised to hear that their state is a center of cockroach diversity in the US, with at least 38 species. The good news is that most of these species are outdoor creatures, at home only in rotten logs, native grasses, or forest leaf litter.

The Household Species. Of the 38 Florida cockroaches, three species are most commonly found in houses: the American cockroach (probably introduced from Africa in the 1600s), the Australian cockroach (also African) and the German cockroach (Asian in origin). The first two are large species often called palmetto bugs.

Cockroaches have seldom been implicated in the transmission of diseases (more than can be said for visiting grandchildren en route to Disney World).

Ancient Animals. Cockroaches are interesting animals, if only because of their remarkable resilience in the face of their numerous natural and unnatural enemies. Cockroaches are a very old group of insects whose body plan has scarcely changed since the Carboniferous Period, more than 300 million years ago. They are among the few creatures whose future looks bright if humans continue overpopulating the planet.

Survival Skills. The life skills of domestic cockroaches include speed, agility, nocturnal activity, resistance to dry conditions, an attraction to hard-to-reach crannies as resting places, and a willingness to eat a great variety of substances. There are also a couple of more unusual abilities. Cockroaches have a pair of terminal abdominal appendages, called cerci, which have a series of long, erect hairs. These long hairs can activate giant nerve fibers that conduct impulses at unusual speed to the nerve center that controls the legs, so a cockroach can be running from the air displaced by a stomping foot before a warning signal has even reached its brain. These giant nerve fibers in cockroaches, which also occur in crickets, have been useful in research on nerve function and growth. Domestic cockroaches also have the ability to negotiate a complex, frequently changing environment in the dark; this talent is not clearly understood.

Florida's outdoor cockroaches are almost unstudied. Wild cockroaches are usually described as "omnivorous," which really means that if they are brought into the laboratory they seem content with bits of apple and crumbs of peanut butter sandwiches. Nobody knows how they actually make a living or what their habits are.

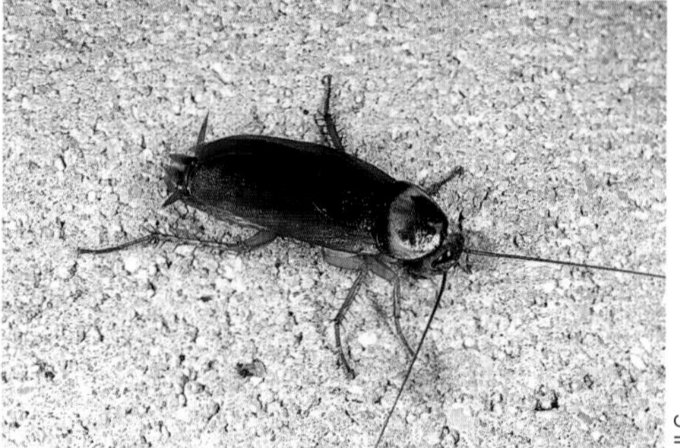

JLC

JLC

Top: **the Cuban or green cockroach, a species that lives outdoors.**

Center: **the American cockroach.**

Bottom: **the nymph or larva of the American cockroach. Note that the larva does not have wings.**

JLP

JLC

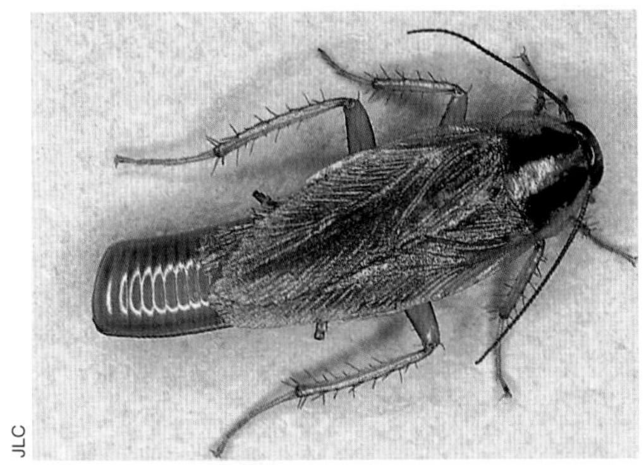

JLC

BK

Above: **a native Florida stinking roach.**

Left, top: **a roach egg case opened and the young exiting. A newly hatched roach can sustain itself for about a week until it finds food (an adult can survive six months or longer if it has access to water).**

Left, middle: **the Australian cockroach carrying an egg case.**

Left, bottom: **a German cockroach carrying an egg case.**

ROACH EGG CASES

A special feature of the cockroach is the egg case, a tough, watertight, purse-shaped structure secreted by the roach around two neat rows of eggs. Some species bury the egg case or hide it in rotten wood or leaf litter. Then it becomes vulnerable to parasitic wasps. The German roach avoids these wasps by holding onto the egg case until it is just about to hatch. The green roach and the Surinam roach keep the egg case inside the body and give birth to active young.

COPING WITH ROACHES IN THE HOME

Roaches flourish in Florida despite the most determined efforts of householders. Roaches are fast, secretive, and resistant to some insecticides. Cleanliness reduces their numbers, but will not eliminate them because there are always a few stray crumbs that roaches detect with their sensitive antennae. Australian and American roaches can live outside and re-invade a roach-free home. The small, German cockroach does not readily live outside, however, and once eradicated, usually does not re-occur unless re-introduced from another building. However, since the mid-1980s, Florida has been home to the Asian roach, which looks just like the German roach but is an outdoor species which sometimes wanders into the house. Unlike the German roach, the Asian roach is attracted to lights at night. If one is pursuing what seems to be a German roach and it flees with quick dashes and short flights, it is an Asian roach.

THE PALMETTO BUG

Just as airline officials might refuse a carry-on bag stuffed with open packages of Limburger cheese, many people refuse to use words with too many negative vibes. In Florida, the larger species of cockroaches are called "palmetto bugs." This name subtly suggests that these insects do not really live in the house, but are wild, outdoors animals which are just visiting, like racoons which have learned to use the cat's door to enter the kitchen. There is, in fact, a native, palmetto-inhabiting, Florida species that casually invades from the outside, a large, clumsy, flightless species officially known as the Florida stinking cockroach. No homeowner ever uses that common name. While the Florida stinking cockroach really does occur regularly in the leaf bases of cabbage palmetto, the more common "palmetto bugs," when found outside, are more likely to be in a pile of boards near a compost heap or in a stack of plastic flower pots. The four species of large exotic roaches in Florida all belong to the same genus, Periplaneta, *which appropriately means "all over the planet."*

ACCIDENTAL ARKS

The old-time sailing ships, while romantic in retrospect, had living conditions that would be totally unacceptable today, even in a prison. These ships had a rich variety of vermin, including fleas, lice, flies, grainweevils and other stored-food pests, and roaches. Some of the natural enemies of these insects followed their prey on board the floating ecosystems. Early traders and explorers quickly spread roaches to the most remote parts of the world, to such a degree that it has required considerable modern detective work to figure out the origins of household roaches. Along with these roaches came some of their natural enemies, including the wasps that parasitize egg cases and the huge huntsman spider. This spider, which is common in South Florida, is fast enough to run down a speeding roach. It is considered the cheetah of spiders. Many Floridians recognize this spider as a specialized roach-eater, and welcome it as an ally in garages, porches, or even indoors.

NT

ORDER ISOPTERA

Termites are among the most destructive insects, costing Floridians millions of dollars every year. The most expensive problems are caused by termites gobbling up the wooden structures of buildings, but termites also readily attack furniture, fence posts, outdoor signs, wooden walkways–anything wooden that is not protected with termite-repellent chemicals. Included in the termite expense bill are all the chemicals and treatments needed to prevent termite attacks. One can fairly blame termites for the addition of all these pesticides into our homes. The useful side of termites in the wild is that they recycle dead wood and other forms of cellulose.

Recognizing termites in the home. Once termites are established in a house, the current treatments for eliminating them are generally inconvenient and expensive, involving replacement of some wooden structures, or tenting the house and treating it with toxic gases. New termite baits may soon be used instead of tenting in some situations. It is important for homeowners to be able to recognize termites and their damage. Termites are often first discovered when the winged forms emerge to start new colonies. It is common for some of these future queens and males to emerge indoors. There are also ants that frequently inhabit attics and wall voids in Florida, where they cause little, if any, damage. These also may emerge indoors as winged queens and males. The homeowner encounters a little swarm of winged insects running about on the floor; are these pesky ants, or are they sinister termites?

Termites vs winged ants. Termites lack the narrow waist between the second and third sections of the body, and the winged forms of termites have two pairs of almost identical, paddle-shaped wings. Ants have a narrow waist, and the front pair of wings are like long, narrow triangles, and much larger than the hind wings. Worker termites of the species that live in Florida are pale, grub-like insects which, unlike worker ants, never come out in the open.

Termite damage. The damage termites cause is usually concealed under a thin layer of wood, sometimes little more than the coat of paint. Termite inspectors often use a thin screw driver to probe into hollow woodwork. Termites may also make tell-tale covered pathways over cement areas to get to wooden structures. Although most pest control companies are responsible and have competent field operators, there are always a few people who are poorly trained or who are a bit too eager to sell an expensive termite eradication treatment. One should never agree to a costly treatment program without seeing actual live termites and viewing the extent of the problem.

Termites outside the house. The occurrence of termites outside the house, for example, in a tree stump in the yard, is not an ominous sign that the house is about to come under attack. There are termites everywhere in Florida, from mangrove swamps to sandhills, from the heart of the Everglades to the heart of Miami. The practical control of termites is not based on eliminating them from the environment, but rather on maintaining a defensive perimeter between the termites and any edible wooden structures.

Social insects. Termites are social insects, like honey bees and ants, but are more closely related to cockroaches than to these other social insects. They have their own way of doing things. Among the termites, both males and females can be workers or soldiers, not just the females, as in the ants, bees, and wasps. Much of the work in a termite colony is done by young termites, while the young of ants, bees, and wasps are helpless grubs. The male termite stays with the queen throughout her life. This is not the case in other social insects. Termites pair up soon after flying. An endearing sight, as long as it is not in your living room, is the male termite devotedly following his queen as she searches for a place to begin a new colony.

Division of labor. When a termite queen dies, or when the colony becomes excessively large and spread out, some workers can develop into supplementary queens. Young workers can also develop into regular, winged, dispersing queens and males, or into soldiers. One can sum this up by saying that the individual termite has many more career options than the adults of other social insects. While the termite enters the work force at an early age, decisions on its adult role can be postponed until it is nearly mature. These decisions are not made by the termites themselves, but are determined by the balance of hormones circulating through the colony.

Processing wood into sugar. Termites are able to break down the cellulose of wood into sugars, thanks to a large intestinal chamber populated with many kinds of microorganisms that carry out the chemical decomposition. Termites have their own groups of digestive microorganisms, found nowhere else, and this mutual-benefit system is apparently extremely old. Thanks to this cooperative arrangement, the termites have gained access to one of the largest resources in nature—dead wood and other dead plant material. Most Florida soils are sandy, and termites move through these soils easily. This allows Florida termites to expand out of large pieces of dead wood to feed on fallen branches, twigs, pine cones, even dead leaves, and accumulations of dead grass.

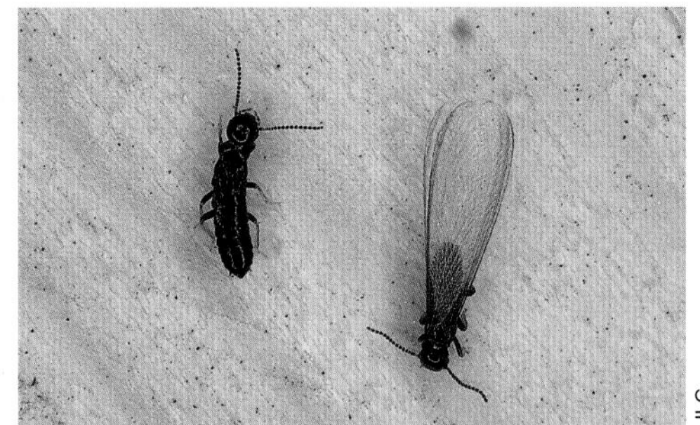

Opposite page: **adult drywood termite.**

Left: **a reproductive termite (with wings), soldier, and worker.**

Top: **reproductive termites before and after their wings have broken off.**

Above: **the subterranean termite soldier has a large head and pincer-like jaws.**

WHY NOT MORE SPECIES?

There are 17 species of termites in Florida. To most Floridians, this would seem like more than enough. However, scientists ask themselves why there aren't even more species, considering that termites have made such a breakthrough in the efficient consumption of cellulose. There are at least ten times as many species of wood-eating beetles in Florida as there are termites. This is a good reminder that there are disadvantages to being a social insect, and one of them is that the colonies require a lot of food and are unable to move long distances. Logistics prevent termites from becoming specialized to take advantage of small resources, such as a dead twig at the top of an oak tree. There are many specialized wood-eating opportunities that termites are unable to exploit, and a huge group of wood-eating beetle species has evolved to take advantage of these resources.

THE PHILOSOPHER AND THE TERMITE

The Nobel laureate, dramatist, and poet Maurice Maeterlinck had a special interest in social philosophy, and early this century, turned his attention to the honey bee and the termite. He reviewed most of the natural history then known about these insects, and published two books: "The Life of the Bee," and "The Life of the White Ant" (at the time, termites were sometimes called white ants). The termite book became a natural history bestseller.

Maeterlinck's judgement of termite society shows how a highly intelligent person, in possession of a large number of facts, can still come up with some strange ideas. Here are a few bits from his view of a termite's life.

> *"Blackness prevails: constraint, oppression. Year follows year in unrelieved darkness. All the inhabitants are slaves; and nearly all blind. None but the victims of the great genital frenzy ever climb to the surface of the earth, breathe the pure air, or glimpse the light of day. Everything, from beginning to end, takes place in perpetual gloom....In the termitary the gods of communism become insatiable .... The more they are given, the more they require; and they persist in their demands until the individual is annihilated and his misery complete...By night and day they exhaust themselves, without ceasing, in various defined and complicated labours. Isolated, vigilant, and more or less useless in the humdrum of daily life, the monstrous soldiers wait resignedly in their gloomy barracks for the hour of danger and self-sacrifice..."*

Where does Maeterlinck, and some more recent portrayals of the lives of social insects, go astray? Perhaps it is through an incomplete understanding of the genetics of social insects. All the termites in a nest are very closely related, so they are actually working for their own families. The young that they raise and defend are their own siblings, or possibly half-siblings. Working for the betterment of the family is not slavery in any strict sense. Moreover, termites are genetically adapted and programmed to labor constantly in perpetual gloom, and would rush frantically about and quickly die if taken out in the sunshine for a recreational picnic. Humans, in spite of Maeterlinck's gloomy assessment, are not likely to descend to a termite-like social system. It is true that humans seem genetically programmed to work cooperatively, but the individualistic tendencies seem just as strong. Whether at the tribal level, or at the level of a society more populous than a termite colony, cooperation and conformity are balanced by the ability of the individual to assume new roles, take advantage of new opportunities, and provide new services to the community. This is possible because the human brain can learn about a zillion times as much as the microscopic termite brain. Maeterlinck would not agree with this analysis. He suspected that the instincts of termites operated through a mystical, "collective soul."

ORDER PSOCOPTERA

The barklice and booklice are tiny insects—some of the giants are a quarter-inch long. They occur everywhere in Florida, often in large numbers. They are small enough to escape notice most of the time, but small children, who generally have sharp eyes and a fascination with tiny things, often point them out to their parents. Barklice and booklice are not actually lice (they are not parasites), but have this common name because a few species superficially resemble true lice.

They live on a scale so small that a few fungal spores are a good snack, and a pinhead-sized portion of a lichen is a banquet for the whole family. They are "snappers-up of ill-considered trifles," to use a disparaging phrase from Shakespeare.

One would certainly say this about the domestic Psocoptera, the booklice, which often live in large numbers among the books in old houses, feeding on library paste laced with mold spores, with perhaps a nice little flake of dandruff for dessert. Many of the outdoor barklice live in big aggregations, and some of these spin silk in quantities sufficient to cover sections of branches or patches of bark.

None of the outdoor species cause any damage to plants. There are about 80 Florida species listed so far, but as there are only a few people in the world who study barklice, there are probably many additional species not yet discovered.

TE

JLC

JLC

***Top:* a tiny bark louse that lives on palmettos.**
***Left:* a branch covered with silk produced by barklice. They are probably feeding on lichens and fungi.**
***Above:* a larger species on oak.**

SO MANY FLORIDA INSECTS, SO FEW MICROSCOPES

This book on Florida insects and their relatives is one in a series of books that deals with various groups of Florida animals. The book on reptiles and amphibians, for example, covers almost every species found in Florida; if this insect book were to do the same, its length would be over twenty thousand pages. Some book stores have shopping carts for big books, but for twenty thousand pages we're talking forklifts. There are so many kinds of insects in Florida that there aren't enough experts even to catalog them. There aren't enough microscopes in the whole state to even begin looking at all these bugs. Why are there so many? The answer is related to size.

At one level, it is easy to see that everything depends on size. There is clearly more standing room in the back yard for ants than for elephants, and standing room is the least of the problems of large animals. As human parents often point out, one can't make a living by lounging about all day: it is necessary to get up, go out, and do things. This takes a lot more than standing room, so large animals can only occur in relatively small numbers, and this means not only small numbers of individuals, but also small numbers of species.

The other way in which size influences everything is in the quantity of food and shelter that an animal needs. A large animal cannot make its home in a hollow twig, nor raise a whole family on the food provided by a single palmetto seed. Small animals can take advantage of these opportunities. A particular resource, such as a palmetto seed, which is hard, chemically protected, and only available in the fall, is most efficiently used by an animal that is specialized to find and consume it. The advantages of efficiency and specialization have led, over many millions of years, to a huge number of tiny animals with highly specialized professions.

Leaping from the size scale of a tiny insect to that of a natural community, such as a lake or a forest, it is easy to see that the overall efficiency and stability of these systems are derived from the professionalism and the diversity of the thousands of species and millions of individuals that use and recycle resources, and respond to small changes in the system. It has never been very necessary for our own species to understand the value of having large numbers of small species that keep the biological world working, because we have always lived in a world rich in biological diversity. Now, however, we have the ability to drastically simplify large parts of the Earth, so it is suddenly very important to understand the roles of small organisms.

Even with the shortage of microscopes, and the lack of the twenty thousand page version of Florida's Fabulous Insects, *we now know that this much is true: big things always depend on small things.*

ORDER HEMIPTERA

The Hemiptera, or true bugs, are a large group with about 800 species found in Florida. It is also an extremely diverse group, including creatures as different as rotund burrower bugs, fantastically slenderized marsh treaders, perfectly camouflaged pine stink bugs, and the gaudy milkweed bugs. There are a few key hemipteran features, however, that allow the naturalist to recognize a member of this group despite its diversity. These key features are not designed for the convenience of naturalists; rather, they represent major adaptations that appeared early in the history of Hemiptera, before the Hemiptera had achieved its present diversity. Here are three key feature.

1. The Wings. The wings of true bugs can be folded out of the way, flat over the back, with the hind wings protected by the forewings. The forewings of most species are divided into two sections, one of which is thickened and protective, the other a thin membrane. This explains the order name "Hemiptera" which means "half-wing." Seen from above, the wings of Hemiptera seem divided into triangles, an easy way to recognize a member of the group.

2. The Mouth. The mouthparts are adapted for piercing and sucking. They do not resemble a simple soda straw with a sharp tip, but are a complex structure that fits together to form two channels, one for saliva, the other for sucking, each with its own pump. The mouthparts are hinged and can be folded back under the head and body when not in use. The whole apparatus is extended forward for operation by means of blood pressure, which is controlled by valves.

This piercing-sucking system is used by some true bugs for sucking plant juices, while others prey on insects. The true bugs that feed on plants are sometimes described as sap-suckers, but the feeding of these bugs is usually more brutal than the delicate tapping of the vein of a leaf. The vegetarian bugs usually destroy plant tissue, primarily by the action of their salivary secretions, and suck up the liquid contents of plant cells. This usually leaves a conspicuous scar on the plant, or the shriveling of shoots and young leaves.

3. Stink Glands. A third characteristic of the true bugs is the stink glands, found on most species near the bases of the middle pair of legs. Some true bugs, such as squash bugs, can spray repellent, while others emit chemicals which flow out onto textured, evaporative areas surrounding the glands. To a predatory insect or spider at close quarters, this defense amounts to intense chemical warfare. Many insect-eating birds avoid true bugs. The reason is easily understood by anyone who has popped a berry into his mouth without first noticing a stink bug clinging to the fruit.

BBB

Above: **a leaf-footed bug showing the triangular markings which are typical of the entire group of true bugs. The point visible between the antennae is not the beak, but a simple spine. The beak is long and fine, folded down along the underside of the body when not in use. This species feeds on various plants. Males defend a space on a flower, repelling rivals with their spined, hind legs.**

TRUE BUGS: THE BUGS TAKE ON THE WORD POLICE

The word "bug," in Old English, referred specifically to the bed bug, a small, repulsive, blood-sucking insect that used to be common in homes. Bed bugs lurk in cracks in sleeping chambers and, after wooden beds became popular, in the cracks of beds. These insects, which are now hard to find, creep out at night to feed on the blood of sleeping humans, and it is not surprising that the word "bug" is related to "bogie," as in "the bogie man." Over time, the word bug became a more general term for small crawling creatures, and is now popularly used not only for insects, but also for spiders, pillbugs, millipedes, and most other arthropods.

When scientists needed English names for the orders of insects, they used "the bugs" as the common name for the order Hemiptera, which includes bed bugs, as well as thousands of other insects with quite different habits. Since "bug" was commonly used for a huge variety of other arthropods, entomologists began calling the Hemiptera the "true bugs." For many years entomologists have avoided using the word bug to mean all insects and other crawling things, but this is a hopeless struggle. There is no way that the very popular, appealing, Old English word "bug" will ever be replaced by its accurate, but clumsy, scientific equivalent, "terrestrial and freshwater arthropods." Some day there may be an edition of this book simply titled, "Florida's Fabulous Bugs."

PC

Seed Bugs

Above: a milkweed seed bug, commonly found on milkweed and oleander in Florida. Remarkable among the seed bugs for its large size and bright colors, milkweed bugs sit about in groups on milkweeds. Young milkweed bugs feed on milkweed seeds, whose contents they are able to liquify and extract through their slender mouthparts. The orange-and-black color is a warning to birds that these insects should not be eaten. The plant in this photo is milkweed.

Family Lygaeidae

The seed bugs are one of the larger groups of true bugs in Florida with 115 species. They include several inconspicuous but destructive species, chief among them the southern chinch bug, which can reach densities of 1000 per square meter in lawns. Most species of seed bugs however, live an obscure existence and cause no economic damage.

A brightly colored seed-eating bug in a related family (Rhopalidae) is the golden rain tree bug, which often occurs in immense numbers where there is a golden rain tree. The adult bugs are black with red trim, and the young bugs have a bloated red abdomen that makes them look as if they had just had a big meal of blood (although they are not bloodsucking). Hundreds of these sinister-looking bugs may congregate on the walls and lawns of houses near a golden rain tree, prompting panicky calls to the local agricultural extension agent. These insects cause no damage, as golden rain trees are not grown for their seed crop.

A TALE OF A TOXIN

"Dangerous if swallowed," proclaim the bright colors of milkweed bugs, milkweed beetles, milkweed butterflies such as the monarch, and a batch of insects living on poisonous plants other than milkweeds. Milkweeds and some other plants produce poisons called cardiac glycosides that can cause heart failure in vertebrates. Insects that feed on milkweeds hoard the poisons for their own protection. The very defense that saves the plant from vertebrate grazers and browsers becomes the armor of its insect enemies. There are certain insects that can still attack the milkweed-eating insects, and milkweeds are not overwhelmed by their insect enemies.

Hidden in the human brain are vestiges of the time when our species was dependent on wild plants. When humans eat plants with cardiac glycosides, a chemical mechanism induces nausea before a lethal dose has been ingested. This usually leaves a lasting impression, causing a permanent aversion to the toxic plant.

Many thousands of years ago, most humans lived like the inhabitants of the remotest rain forests do today, surviving only through an encyclopedic knowledge of the natural history of the area. It would have been easy and useful to make the connection between orange-and-black insects, and the poisonous nature of the plants on which they feed. These insects announce that their host plants must be avoided, or prepared in some special way to remove the poison. Orange-and-black is a combination used today on signs warning of danger. Orange-and-black is the color combination associated with Halloween, and invokes both alertness and unease. It is the message of the milkweed bug and the monarch butterfly to predators: death lurks here.

Leaf-footed Bugs

Family Coreidae

The leaf-footed bugs are a group of vegetarian true bugs that often have their hind legs flattened and expanded into a leaf-like structure. The function of these leaf-like legs is unknown; perhaps they are camouflage or involved in courtship. There are about 40 species of leaf-footed bugs in Florida.

Leaf-footed bugs can defend themselves with chemical sprays, but still have natural enemies that are able to deal with this defense. When a golden silk spider catches a leaf-footed bug in its web, it allows the odor of the defensive spray to dissipate before feeding. Meanwhile, this odor attracts tiny flies that wait for the spider to feed, then land near the jaws of the spider to sip up the bug juice that oozes out where the spider is feeding.

Some leaf-footed bugs are specialized in their diets. One common Florida species, which feeds only on cactus, was exported to Australia to help control prickly pear cactus, which had taken over huge areas of rangeland.

Above: **a leaf-footed bug, showing the enlarged hind legs which are the "leaf-feet."**

Below: **eggs of leaf-footed bugs on a rose leaf. The eggs may be pearly or gold.**

Above: immature leaf-footed bugs often gather in large groups.

Left: a leaf-footed bug on a thistle, a favorite food plant for several species. The stink glands are found on the sides, just in front of the white band on this species.

BK

Stink Bugs

Family Pentatomidae

Stink bugs have a characteristic broad-shouldered look as adults, and also have their famous stink. Some species are camouflaged as leaves or bits of bark, while others are brightly colored, probably advertizing that they are especially bad-tasting. Stink bugs include a few crop pests, such as the harlequin bug, which attacks collards in Florida. Some Florida stink bugs are predatory, with caterpillars prominent on their menus. Florida is one of the outstanding states for stink bugs with about 80 species, although Arizona offers some competition.

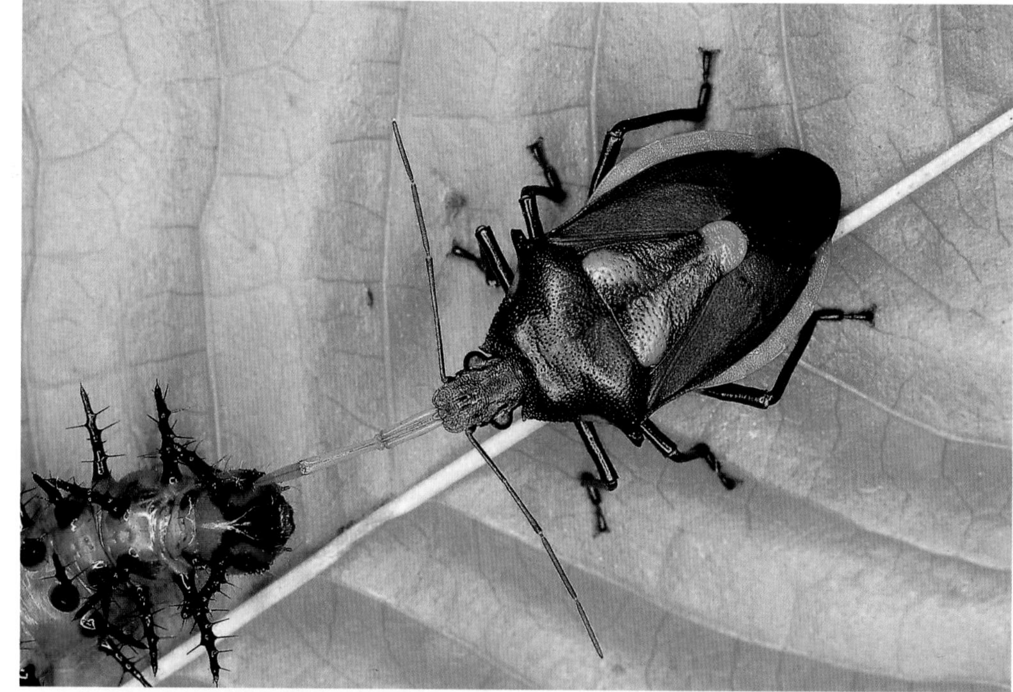

JLC

BK

BK

Top: **stink bug nymphs on southern fleabane. Young stinkbugs often have more colorful markings than adults.**

Middle: **a predatory stink bug impales a gulf fritillary caterpillar and sucks its juices through its siphon tube. Most stink bugs suck plant juices, but some prey on insects.**

Right: **the face of a green stink bug showing the typical triangular shape.**

Far right: **a white-spotted stink bug, a plant-feeding species. The sharp points on the thorax may be additional protection against birds or frogs, which usually swallow their prey whole.**

DL

Top: feeding stink bug nymphs share a honeybee.
Below: a harlequin stink bug and its colorful eggs.

JLC

JLC

Right: this view of a green stink bug shows its long siphon tube piercing the surface of a plant, allowing the bug to suck juices. Note also the two sets of eyes, one compound (many lenses) and one simple. The compound eyes form images, while the simple eyes probably sense some aspect of the light, such as intensity or day length.

JHR

Giant Water Bugs

Family Belostomatidae

Giant water bugs can grow to be two or three inches long, big enough to feed on minnows and tadpoles. Their prey is seized by clamp-like front legs and injected with a powerful paralyzing venom that causes death and liquifies the tissues. Giant water bugs readily bite in self-defense when handled; the bites are said to be very painful, but nobody volunteered to verify this for this book. Giant water bugs are sometimes called "toe-biters," though the aquatic bugs that seem to most frequently nip the feet of Floridians are the much smaller creeping water bugs (Family Naucoridae).

Like most aquatic bugs, giant water bugs disperse at night, and are often attracted to electric lights. In the old days in Florida, when the native wetlands had not been extensively drained, and when electric lights were few and far between, enormous numbers of these formidable bugs might appear at lights several times a year. "Electric light bugs" is an old common name for the giant water bugs. It seems odd to name an insect for an aberration completely outside its natural way of life, but as the hemipterist William Blatchley wrote in 1926:

"When electric street lights were first installed our larger species were attracted to them by the hundreds, and for the first time the average human learned that such bugs were denizens of the earth. To them he gave the name of "electric light bugs," and their uncouth shape and sprawling motions, when on the ground beneath the lights, usually caused him to regard them with a holy terror. They are, however, harmless, but when picked up incautiously can inflict a severe wound with their stout beak. This is very painful for a time, but seldom produces a swelling or numbness."

Four of the six Florida species of giant water bugs have the interesting habit of depositing the eggs on the back of the male. The female covers most of the male's back with neatly arranged eggs, which are thus never left unattended, and also benefit from aeration as the male moves about, or waves his legs over the eggs. After the eggs hatch, the empty shells fall off, or they may be scraped off by the next female.

BK

GM

Top: **a toe-biter clinging to a cattail stalk with its minnow prey. Protruding from the rear is a short snorkle that conducts air to the breathing openings on the sides of the body.**

Right: **a male toe-biter. Eggs have been attached to its back by its mate, thus converting the male into a swimming incubator. Some of the eggs have already hatched.**

Water Boatmen

Family Corixidae

Water boatmen resemble backswimmers, but do not swim on their backs, so the color pattern is reversed, with the pale color (seen against the water surface from below) on the underside. Although backswimmers and water boatmen are similar in general appearance, they are only distantly related.

A feature that distinguishes water boatmen from backswimmers (and all other true bugs) is their ability to eat solid food. They have a relatively wide mouth opening, and can slurp up ooze from the bottom or filaments of algae from the leaves of an aquatic plant. These are the only vegetarians among the aquatic true bugs, and even they sometimes eat mosquito and midge larvae. The front legs of male water boatmen have one or two rows of small teeth that can be run across the sharp corners of the head to make a chirping sound.

Backswimmers

Family Notonectidae

The streamlined backswimmers shoot through the water like submarine skiffs, propelled by oar-like hind legs. A dense row of long hairs on the legs spreads out to catch the water on the back stroke, and folds back along the leg when the oar is brought forward on the return. The back of the backswimmer is mottled silvery white to blend better with the silvery, rippling surface of the water viewed from below, perhaps by a predatory fish. Adult backswimmers fly at night to disperse and colonize seasonal ponds and seasonally filled ditches. Backswimmers are predators and help control mosquito larvae, especially in seasonal pools. There are 11 species in Florida.

GM

RFS

GM

Top: a water boatman. The finely banded pattern is typical of the family. Huge numbers are sometimes attracted to lights.

Left: a backswimmer renews its air supply. This supply is carried both on the underside of the body and beneath the wings.

Lower left: a backswimmer. Some species have clusters of hemoglobin-containing cells associated with the respiratory system.

INSECTS INVENT THE AQUALUNG

Many aquatic insects are really amphibious. A major problem for the truly amphibious organism is air supply. The closed breathing system of gills is generally unsuitable for breathing in the open air, but an open respiratory system (like our own) which brings air to the tissues, cannot extract oxygen from water. Aquatic insects in many groups have independently evolved a solution that allows them to use a single respiratory system to breathe both in and out of the water. This mechanism takes advantage of physical properties of gases.

Aquatic insects, such as water beetles and true bugs, can carry into the water with them a bubble of air that is held so that the openings of the respiratory system are contained within the bubble. This may be a normal kind of bubble, such as the one carried down by diving beetles under the wing covers and seen as a silvery protrusion at the rear of the beetle. Often, however, the bubble is a thin layer of air trapped by a nap of fine, velvety hairs.

The amount of oxygen that an insect can carry down in a bubble is small, only enough for a short submersion, but this oxygen is replenished from the surrounding water. The rate at which carbon dioxide produced by the insect escapes into the water is extremely fast, so there is no buildup of this gas in the bubble. As oxygen is removed from the bubble, the physical laws that govern the movement of gases cause oxygen to move from the higher concentration in the surrounding water to the lower concentration in the bubble. The original bubble was mostly nitrogen, which makes up about 80% of the air, and this nitrogen does not easily dissipate out of the bubble, providing stability to the bubble.

The only thing that can prevent this system from working indefinitely on one bubble is an extreme scarcity of oxygen in the water, or the gradual escape of microscopic bubbles from the larger bubble. Most of the bubble-carrying insects must come to the surface periodically to renew their bubble aqualung. Some species, however, have a layer of hairs that is extraordinarily dense and fine, two million or so hairs per square millimeter; each hair is bent at the tip. These hairs hold air so securely that the insect almost never comes to the surface.

The efficiency of the bubble gill can be increased by moving through the water. Some insects, such as the water boatmen, may move their legs to direct a stream of more oxygenated water past the bubble gill.

Water Striders

Family Gerridae

The most modest of imperialists, the water striders have conquered a territory only a molecule thick, the surface layer between air and water. The water striders are not the only surface insects with the ability to walk and even jump on water, but they are the most highly specialized and most dominant.

The secret of the water strider is in its long, delicate feet, which are covered with tiny, erect, water-repellent hairs. These hairs allow the weight of the insect to depress the surface film without actually breaking it. In a shallow pond or lake shore, the impressions made on the surface by a water strider can be seen as shadows on the bottom—four oval shadows for the middle and hind legs and a pair of round shadows for the front legs.

This dimpling of the water surface is important for the water strider, because if its feet were not planted in their little depressions on the surface, the strider would go skittering away across the surface at the least little breeze. When the water strider wishes to move, this again is only possible because its feet are lying in what can only be described as shallow holes in the water. As the water strider skates across a pond, the power strokes are delivered by the middle legs, thrusting back against their toe-holds in the water.

Water striders live on the blood of other insects that have fallen into the water and are trapped in the film. Most insects are waterproof, to the extent that they can keep from drowning or absorbing much water for at least several hours. The typical prisoner of the surface film is an insect whose weight pushes its legs and body below the surface, while its wings lie spread on the surface. An insect trapped in this way can swim with its legs, but its wings create tremendous drag, and the insect is soon exhausted by the effort, especially if the openings that it uses for breathing are underwater.

When feeding on a dead or dying insect, the water strider is constantly alert for large fish that may burst up from below and gulp down both the water strider and its dinner. Water striders often choose to feed on very small insects, and skate off with the meal to the relative safety of a clump of reeds or a lily pad, away from fish and other hungry water striders.

Another feature of the surface film is that it transmits vibrations. Water striders have sensory hairs on their front feet that feel the vibrations set up by an insect struggling on the surface. Water striders signal to each other by surface wave signals generated by vibrating their legs. Males of some species have a special high-frequency signal that proclaims their gender as they skate along, in case any other strider is interested, rather like the teenage boy whose car goes by throbbing with the bass of his stereo.

BK

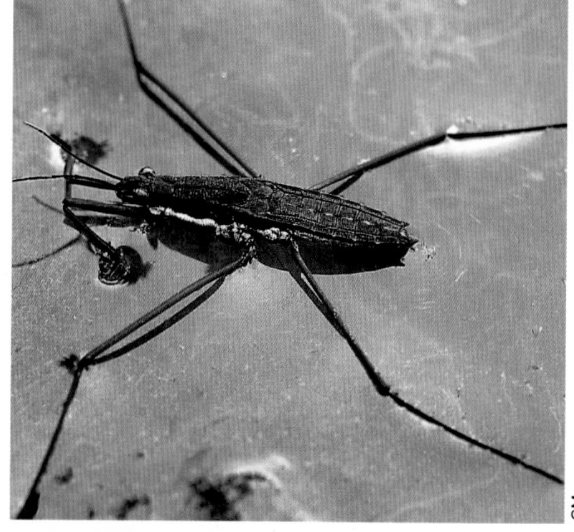

GM

Above: **an immature water strider feeding on a drowned long-legged fly. This strider's prey might be stolen by a minnow, but the strider is protected by secretions from a scent gland.**

Right: **adult water striders are usually dark above and silvery below.**

OCEAN INSECTS

In early October 1996, strong winds from the east battered the Atlantic Coast of Florida for day after day, with gusts exceeding forty miles per hour. These winds left along the beach thousands of water striders, hopping clumsily through the sand, half a dozen at a time trapped in the shallow pit of a footprint. These doomed bugs were blown in from the Sargasso Sea, a couple of hundred miles east.

Ocean-going water striders are almost the only truly marine insects, insects that can live in the open ocean. The marine habitats that one might expect to be occupied by insects are instead filled with crustaceans, such as crabs and innumerable species of shrimp. The crustaceans are a huge group, with many adaptations for life in the sea. The insects, for all their diversity and versatility, have not been able to displace a single species of crustacean from a single coral reef anywhere in the world. The empire of the insects ends at the beach, except for the sea-going water striders of the tropics and subtropics. They have found a place, not quite sea, not quite air, an undulating two-dimensional realm, for which they have their own adaptations. The water strider family is not particularly large: there are 27 species in Florida, perhaps a few hundred in the entire world. This little family, however, may occupy a larger portion of the globe than any other family of insects. Treading so lightly, they have found the world between worlds, until a great wind sweeps out of the east.

Bed Bugs

Family Cimicidae

Bed bugs are not very common in Florida, but it is worth knowing what they look like, so that other insects that happen to appear in the bedroom are not mistaken for them. In the old days, English inns were famous for their bed bugs, and the conditions in these hostelries may represent the ideal situation for bed bugs: a drafty bedroom with a heavy wooden bed, wooden floors, and paneling, all with cracks in which bed bugs could hide; a room inhabited by a succession of guests, each staying for only a few nights. The draftiness of the room encouraged well-prepared travelers to bring their own bedding, so even if the innkeeper eliminated bed bugs, they would eventually be reintroduced by guests. Bed bugs are unable to fly, and must be carried about by their hosts. This transportation system is quite effective, as expressed in a familiar rhyme:

The June bug has a gaudy wing,
The lightning bug a flame,
The bed bug has no wings at all,
But he gets there just the same.

The bite of a bed bug is almost unnoticeable, perceived as "a slight tickling sensation." Most people later get an allergic reaction from the saliva, due to the chemicals that it contains which keep blood from clotting. This reaction usually consists of a small, itching welt, with no spot indicating the site of the puncture. A few people have no reaction, and a few people get a large area of swelling. There is no evidence that bed bugs ever transmit diseases. Bed bugs are creepy and annoying insects, but not dangerous. They appear in early literature in humorous contexts, for example, in ancient Greek comedies. Bed bugs have always been considered a slightly ridiculous affliction, annoying by their numbers and for the penetrating smell they emit, but safe to joke about.

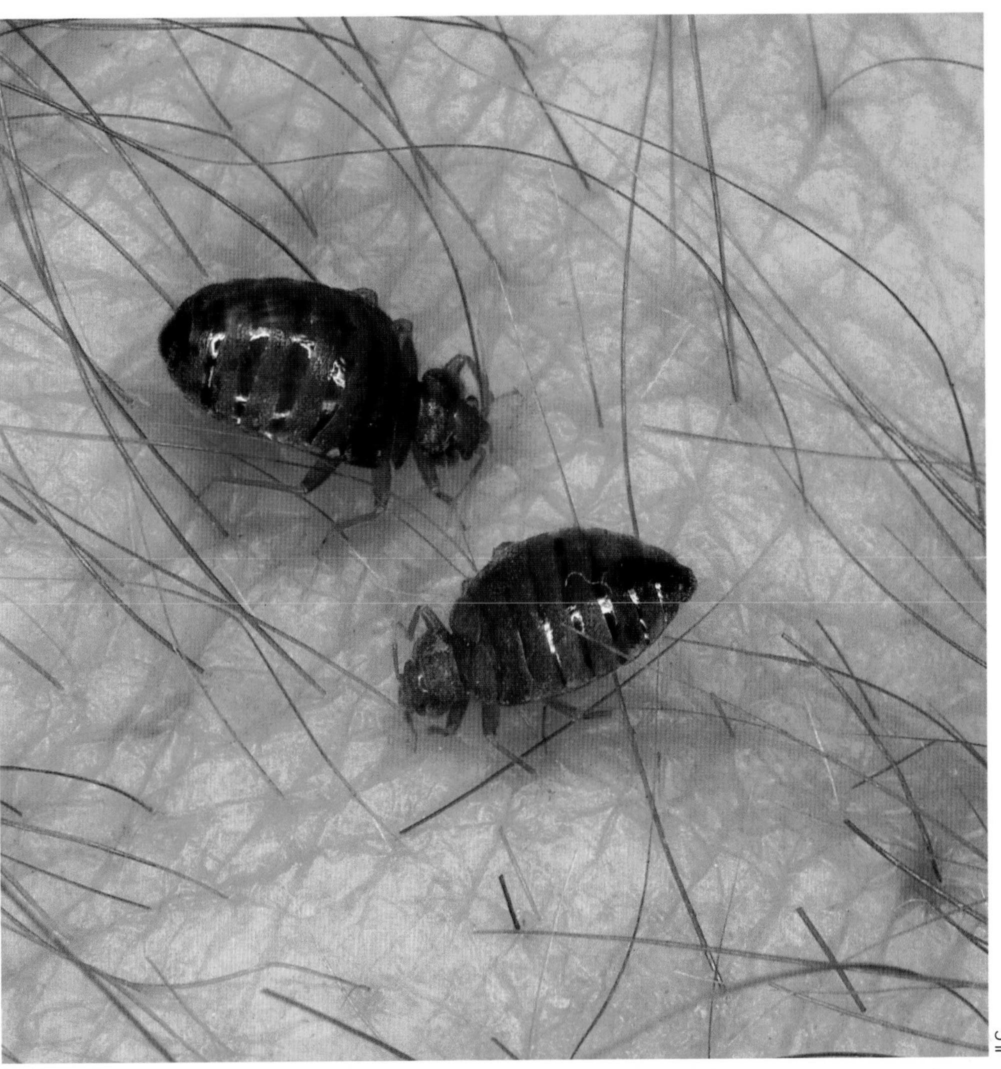

JLC

BUGS ON BIRDS

Birds have their own problems with insect pests. There are species of bed bugs that live in the nests of certain birds. Several species of bloodsucking maggots pester nestlings. The most prevalent of the insect parasites of birds are the bird lice, found on all species of birds thoughout the world. Most species of bird lice are very host-specific and none can be transmitted to humans who handle birds. Bird lice may be irritating to their hosts, but seldom do serious damage.

BIRDS AND BUGS

Insects are of tremendous importance to Florida's bird life. From a bird's eye view, the rich and abundant arthropod fauna of Florida is a flying, crawling, wiggling, burrowing feast. Imagine a world in which birds not only sometimes lived in houses, but a world in which birds could also think, read, and write the same as humans. In such a world, birds would receive one of the most notable products of civilization: junk mail. If birds could read and write promotional literature, junk mail would go out to tree swallows inviting them to spend the winter in Florida catching rays and flies. Wood warblers on business trips to South America would be advised to stop and sample the famous spiders of Florida's oak hammocks. Whip-poor-wills would get seductive flyers featuring live moths dancing nightly through the winter for their enjoyment. The resident songbirds, with the smugness of residents everywhere, would tell the visitors tales of June swarms of midges so thick that you spent a whole morning sitting burping on a telephone line after a single pass through the swarm. They would regale the snow birds with stories of August flights of queen ants and termites so succulent that the grease fairly dripped from your beak, of pines so full of beetle grubs and ants that you could stuff the stomachs of four nestlings with half an hour's tapping at the bark. The advertising weeklies that litter the front yards would have coupons for local eateries, for oaks with a caterpillar on every other leaf, for bushes thronged with cicadas calling you to dinner, for all the mayflies you can eat at the early bird special, for thick katydid steaks, spider surprise, hornworms by the pound, dragonflies with the dew still on their wings, mole crickets by moonlight.

The list of the visiting and resident insectivorous birds in Florida is long enough to horrify the most stout-hearted beetle: swallows, swifts, flycatchers, woodpeckers, wood warblers, nightjars, titmice, jays, vireos, wrens, thrashers, towhees, kestrels, screech owls, burrowing owls. In the nesting season, even the seed and fruit eaters turn their attention to arthropods. Sparrows, cardinals, and blackbirds cram their nestlings with insects and spiders.

The insects, of course, were they literate, would view the situation completely differently. If they were signposting their community, the notice "Neighborhood Bird Watch" would not refer to a recreational activity.

BK

Assassin Bugs

Family Reduviidae

Assassin bugs have a short, stout, curved beak that is used to stab and inject venom into their prey, which may be well-defended insects such as bees or beetles. The injected saliva of some assassin bugs seems to cause an almost instant paralysis of the prey. This venom does not cause paralysis in humans, but the bite of a carelessly handled assassin bug is not a happy experience. An entomologist who was bitten on the finger when he grabbed an assassin bug reported, "The pain at first was not so great as that from the sting of a bee or a wasp, but in a few moments it was much greater, continued unabated for over an hour and the spot was tender to the touch for two weeks."

The species of assassin bugs found in Florida are very diverse in color and form, but all have the short, curved beak, and a long narrow head. The most familiar assassin bugs are those that lie in wait on flowers, and on the tips of leafy plants where other insects often land to rest and survey the world around them. There are many less conspicuous species that hunt on tree trunks, under loose bark, or among tall grasses. About 65 species are found in Florida.

BK

JHR

Top: this assassin bug is waiting patiently on lantana berries. It is called a wheel bug because of the cog-wheel shape of its back.

Above: a smaller species of assassin bug dining on the blood and liquified tissues of a house fly.

Left: a wheel bug with a cluster of its eggs. The eggs of most terrestrial Hemiptera are barrel-shaped, with a cap that can be pushed up by the hatchling. There are also microscopic openings for air. Since the egg is already formed in the female at the time of mating, there are additional passages which allow the sperm to enter.

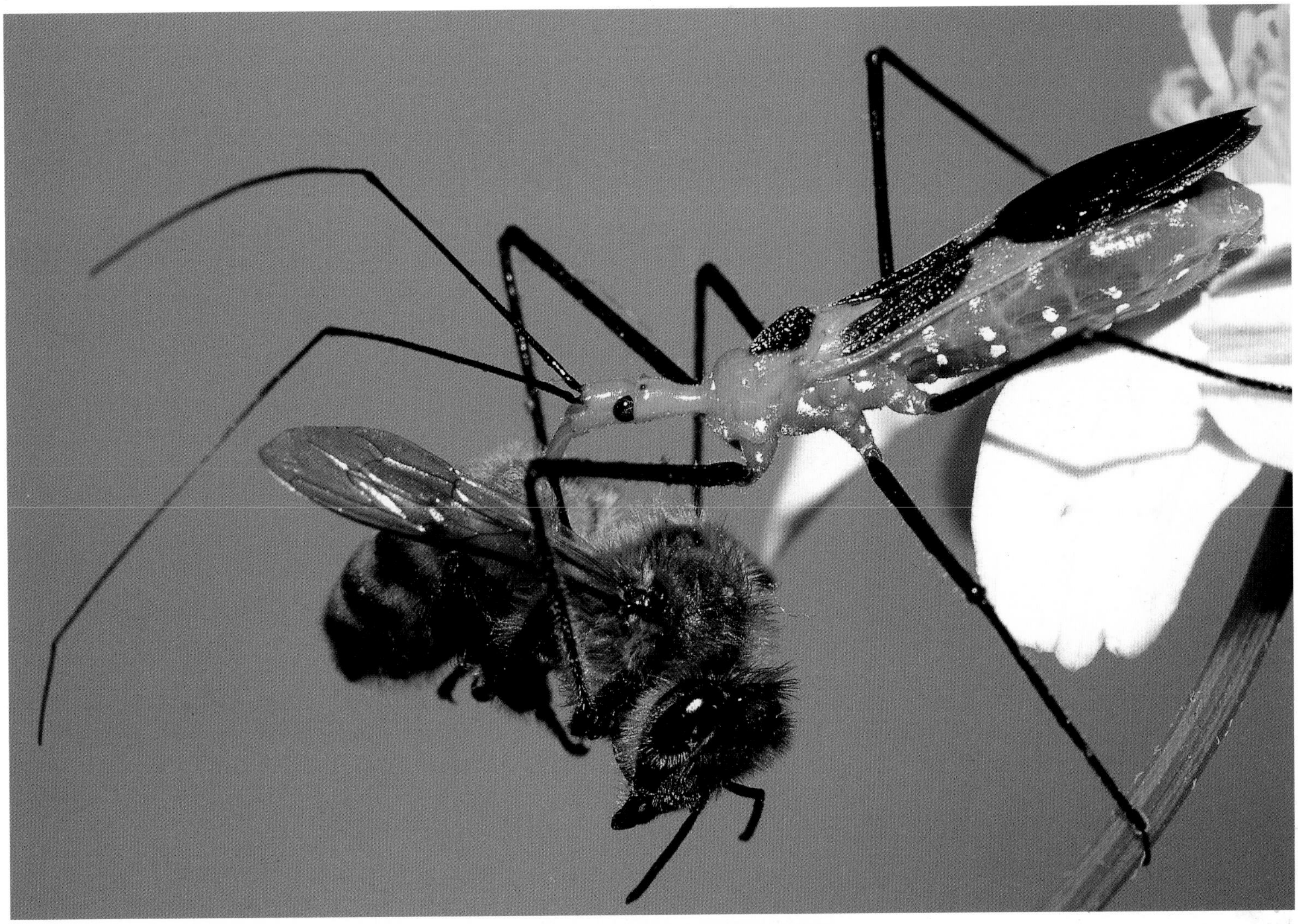

BK

PC

Top: this assassin bug has captured a honeybee. The assassin bug's coloring resembles the non-predatory milkweed seed bug also found on flowers. The strong jaws and powerful sting of the honeybee are no match for the paralyzing venom of the assassin bug.

Above: an immature bee assassin bug on a trumpet honeysuckle flower.

BK

THE KISSING BUG

One group of assassin bugs is adapted for sucking blood of sleeping animals. This includes the notorious "blood-sucking cone-nose," a red-and-black bug almost an inch long. This species is also known as the "kissing bug" because it often bites its victims on the lips. Its bite is painless, thanks to an anesthetic injected before feeding, but there can be swelling the next day. In parts of South and Central America, this species carries a dangerous parasite that causes Chagas disease, which has no cure. Fortunately, the conditions for transmission and spread of this disease do not seem to occur in Florida. The prevalence of window screening in Florida may be the reason, since the spread of the parasite depends on large numbers of kissing bugs moving freely from one host to another.

BK

Ambush Bugs

Family Phymatidae

The ambush bugs are a little group of small, compact, predatory bugs, closely related to assassin bugs. These bugs usually wait motionlessly on flowers, where they are well camouflaged as a discolored bit of dead flower.

Top: **ambush bugs are able to subdue remarkably large prey, such as this skipper butterfly.**

Right: **disruptive bands of color and a bizarre shape conceal this predator by making it look less bug-like.**

BK

PERIL AND PASSION AMID THE PETALS

When flowers attract insects that sip nectar and gather pollen, the stage is set for dramas that go far beyond eating and drinking. Many species of predatory insects and spiders waylay their victims on flowers. Some of these are professional flower-lurkers, seldom found anywhere else. Examples are ambush bugs, assassin bugs, certain crab spiders, the digger wasps known as bee-wolves, and thick-headed flies, which also attack bees. All these insects are probably genetically programmed to hunt on flowers. Then there are the predators without an instinctive attraction to flowers, but with the ability to learn that a particular patch of flowers is a good hunting area. Dragonflies, robber flies, and social wasps may stake out patches of flowers. The nectar-sipping insect flitting from flower to flower does not have such a carefree existence. It is taking risks that most shoppers would consider terrifying if these dangers threatened in the aisles of the supermarket.

On the other hand, a flower is a good place for a meeting of the sexes. Butterflies hang around flowers looking for mates. Male bees and wasps often patrol a series of flowers where females of their species do their shopping, like guys trying to pick up dates in the grocery store. Strangely enough, these cruising males may have an important role in pollination, even though they do not visit as many flowers as the females do. Many plants produce so many blossoms that there is no need for a female insect that is gathering nectar or pollen to fly to a different plant. When trying to shake off the attentions of would-be lovers, the female is likely to take evasive action that leaves her near a different plant, whose flowers she then visits. Cross pollination, therefore, may owe something to the passions of male insects.

ORDER HOMOPTERA

There is so much variety in this order of insects that no one English name can begin to encompass the group. The Homoptera includes such dissimilar insects as the leafhoppers, treehoppers, cicadas, planthoppers, aphids, whiteflies, scale insects, and mealybugs. The scale insects and mealybugs do not even look like insects, but resemble waxy blobs or pimples on plants. The features that unite the Homoptera are the fine, sap-sucking mouthparts, and the position of the wings (if any), which are folded slanted, rooflike, over the back.

Homoptera feed by piercing plant tissue and drinking sap, or less frequently, cell contents. Most Homoptera feed on plant sap extracted from the sap transport system, and the dilute nature of this diet demands that they spend their lives in almost constant feeding to extract the nutrients that they need. Plant sap averages 87-90% water and 10-13% sugar, with very small quantities of other nutrients; this is roughly equivalent to one of the popular soft drinks. Sap-sucking insects depend on symbiotic bacteria and yeasts in the gut to perform the miracles of biochemical synthesis needed to turn sap into a balanced diet, but nothing can compensate for the fact that these insects are feeding on lightly-flavored sugar-water.

The problem with a life of almost incessant feeding is that it forces homopterans to spend most of their time at predictable places, their feeding stations on plants. Here they can be easily found by their natural enemies. The diversity of forms seen in the Homoptera reflects different strategies of active and passive defense in the group.

Plant sap is one of the most abundant foods in the world, and the Homoptera have prospered accordingly. Not only are these insects common, but the number of species is large. There is no list of Florida species, partly because the order includes many species so difficult to tell apart that even the process of naming species is far from complete. There are probably about 800-1000 species of Homoptera in Florida.

The Homoptera include a number of significant pest species in Florida. Most of these are among the leafhoppers, aphids, scales, whiteflies, and mealybugs. These insects cause relatively little damage by the actual removal of sap, but the injection of saliva can injure the plant in several ways, often causing curling or browning. Even worse, some of these insects carry plant diseases. The great majority of these pests are species that are not native to Florida, but were accidentally imported on plants.

BK

Above: **a close-up photo of the dog-day cicada (*Tibicen* sp.) which is common in Florida. Note the tube extending down between the front legs which is used for sucking sap from plants. This type of mouth is common to all Homoptera. Above the beak can be seen a series of bands resembling the grillwork of a car. These are ridges of the external skeleton, to which are attached the powerful muscles operating the sucking chamber that pumps sap out of a plant. A much smaller pump injects saliva into the plant through a separate channel in the beak. In cicadas and most other Homoptera, there is an ingenious adaptation of the digestive system for a watery diet. A section of the hind end of the gut is closely bound to the anterior end, and water passes directly from the front of the digestive system to the rear, concentrating the sap that goes into the central chambers where chemical digestion occurs.**

Cicadas

Family Cicadidae

Symbol of the sultry dog days of summer, the cicadas are among the most conspicuous insects of Florida because of their noise (they may be the loudest of all insects). There are more than a dozen species of cicadas in Florida, each with its own song. There are other cicadas in other regions, whose songs are almost always associated with hot weather, as in this description by the great French entomologist J. Henri Fabre (1823-1915).

The road shimmers like a sheet of molten steel. From the dusty and melancholy olive trees rises a mighty, throbbing hum, a great flowing musical composition whose players have the whole sweep of the woods for their orchestra. It is the concert of the Cicadae, whose bellies quiver and vibrate with increasing frenzy as the temperature rises.

Cicadas are Florida's largest Homoptera, and achieve their size while underground, sucking juice from the roots of trees, a diet that is remarkably deficient even by homopteran standards. Their secret is having plenty of time; cicadas spend years in leisurely subterranean growth.

The number of years required for most Florida species to become adults has not been worked out. Some northern cicadas emerge synchronously, all the members of a species emerging the same year. In such cases, the historical record of emergences reveals how long it takes them to develop. In the Florida Panhandle, there is one species of periodical cicada which takes 13 year to reach adulthood. It is a variety of the better-known northern cicada, popularly, but inaccurately, called the "seventeen-year locust." Other Florida species seem to emerge in smaller numbers every year. The annual density of cicadas can be estimated by counting the larval skins left clinging to tree trunks after the cicadas have emerged. It is unlikely that cicadas ever occur in Florida in numbers sufficient to damage trees.

The male cicada sings by means of a muscle that deforms a stiff, convex plate until it suddenly snaps into a concave position with a click, like the click one might get by bending a stiff piece of tin. There is a second click when the plate pops back into its original form. This operation is performed about 100 times per second, or faster, to produce a buzz that is amplified by resonating air sacs in the abdomen. Small differences in construction and muscular tension on the plate can result in different sounds. Each species of cicada produces a distinctive song, even though they all have similar equipment.

Female cicadas have a set of little knife blades on their rear end, used for slitting twigs and inserting eggs.

***Top:* adult dog-day cicada of which there are several Florida species. These cicadas take several years to develop underground.**

***Opposite page, top:* the seventeen-year cicada common in northern states. It appears in Florida only in parts of the Panhandle where it takes 13 years to develop. Note the distinctive red eyes.**

THE CICADA AND THE WASP

Cicadas have many natural enemies, including any insect-eating bird large enough to take on a cicada. The most spectacular of its natural enemies is the huge, cicada-killer wasp. This wasp digs a deep burrow and stocks it with paralyzed cicadas on which its larvae feed. These are solitary, non-social wasps, but they may make groups of burrows in particularly good nesting sites. Although these wasps look scary, they do not sting people unless handled. Most Floridians who find clusters of these nests in their yard imagine that these harmless wasps are monstrous yellowjackets from Hell, and promptly douse the area with insecticides.

JHR

CICADA POETRY

Cicadas are prominent in the folklore, art, and tradition of many countries. The emergence of the insects is often taken as a sign of rebirth and resurrection. The Chinese poet Ou-yang Hsui many centuries ago described the song of the cicada in these words:

"A thing that cried upon a tree top,
Sucking the shrill wind, to wail it back in a long whistling note—
Now shrill as a flute, now soft as a mandolin, sometimes a piercing cry,
Choked at its very uttering, sometimes a cold tune,
Dwindled into silence, then suddenly flowing again,
A single note, wandering in strange keys,
An air fraught with undertones of hidden harmony."

BBB

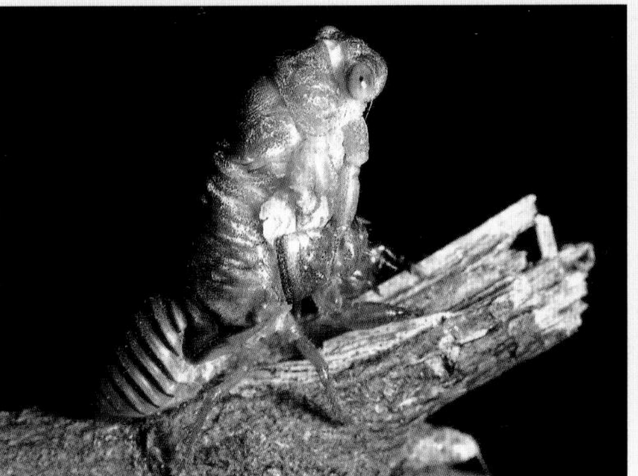

BBB

BBB

Above: **an adult cicada emerging from its larval skeleton. Note the white color and clear wings of the newly emerged adult.**

HOW INSECTS GROW

The hard, external shell of an insect is a remarkable structure. It serves as a skeleton for muscle attachment, protection against enemies and diseases, and a barrier preventing water loss. The appendages that an insect uses for walking, flying, grasping. eating, digging, and climbing are all part of its external skeleton. The lenses of the eyes and the sensory hairs and pits are all modifications of the external skeleton. It is ruggedly tough and versatile

There is a problem, however. As the insect grows, its body can only expand in certain membranous areas and joints, the external skeleton cannot itself grow. The logistics of growth in insects resemble building a large vehicle (for example a Ford Bronco), inside the body of a much smaller car (a Volkswagen Beetle).

The insects have solved this apparently impossible problem by a series of complicated steps. It is no wonder that most naturalists have little idea how insects grow. Here is a rough, simplified outline. The insect grows its new skin inside the old, but the new skin is soft and stretchable, and finely pleated in strategic places. At this stage, the insect is a little like a suit of armor with a partially expanded inflatable dummy snugly fitted inside. The muscles attach themselves to this new skin. Now there is a new problem. The thick external armor must be partially dissolved from the inside in order to make it weaker, to create a space between the old and new skin, and to remove for recycling most of the materials used in the old skin. The new skin develops a chemically resistant upper layer, then chemicals that can dissolve the old skin are passed up through channels in the new skin. These chemicals are only activated after they reach the zone between the protected new skin and the old. The thick lower layers of old skin are dissolved and absorbed. When all this is completed, the insect takes advantage of the weakness of the old skin and the elasticity of the new by shunting blood to areas where it can cause the new skin to expand and burst through the old. The splits occur along special lines of weakness in the old skin. The insect struggles out, and proceeds to inflate, primarily by moving blood to different areas of the body to increase pressure from within. All this must be done within a set time, before the new external skeleton begins to harden. The hardening is an irreversible chemical process, comparable to tanning leather.

Zillions of insects are shedding their external skeletons at any given moment, but it is a process that is seldom seen. This is because the time when an insect is changing its exoskeleton is a period of extreme vulnerability, so insects usually do their changing at night, or in hiding. Insects are as secretive about changing their skins as most mammals are about giving birth, and for similar reasons. Occasionally, one sees a large insect, such as a grasshopper or a cicada, changing its skin, or a butterfly emerging from the skin of its chrysalis. These observations are so rare, and the transformation so remarkable, that it seems a unique, almost miraculous experience.

BK

Leafhoppers

Family Cicadellidae

The leafhoppers are a big group of small sap-suckers that can usually be recognized by their slender, tapered shape, narrow forewings held slanted over the back, and leaping ability. A nervous leafhopper that is not quite alarmed enough to hop, is likely to show a characteristic behavior of scuttling sideways to the opposite side of a stem or leaf. Many species are beautifully colored and patterned, like tiny masterpieces of the enamel-worker's art, but their small size means that their beauty often goes unnoticed. There are several hundred species of leafhoppers in Florida.

Leafhoppers are like mosquitos of the plants, causing irritation of the tissues when many of these insects are sucking sap at the same time. Like mosquitos, the worst crime of leafhoppers is that they can carry diseases; in this case, the diseases are mostly viruses that attack plants. There is a long list of leafhopper-borne diseases, including curly-top disease of tomatoes, stubborn citrus disease, and corn stunt. There must also be complicated relationships between leafhoppers, plant diseases, and native Florida plants, but this has not been studied.

Many leafhoppers are highly specialized, and will feed on only one species of plant, or perhaps a few closely related plants. Some leafhoppers extend this fussiness to a preference for only a particular part of a plant, such as the upper side of the base of the leaf stem where it joins the twig. Several species of leafhoppers may coexist on the same plant. Some leafhoppers are confined to special habitats and may occur in only a small region.

On the other hand, some leafhoppers feed on many kinds of plants and are widely distributed. There are even some migratory species that travel long distances to feed on crop plants.

The world of leafhoppers is not only filled with exquisite color patterns too small for the unaided human eye to appreciate. It is also filled with complicated songs undetectable to the unaided human ear. Many leafhoppers sing, but an insect the size of a leafhopper cannot generate much volume through the air. Small insects produce songs that are carried through solids, much as the sound of a distant train is carried through railroad tracks. A plant that is host to several species of leafhoppers and treehoppers vibrates to the beat of unheard tom-toms and bongos. Both males and females can sing. "I am here, all alone," they call over the telephone lines of leaf and stem, "Where are you?"

PC

Top: **a large leafhopper species called a sharpshooter. It is common on citrus and other plants such as this St. John's wort.**
Above: **close observation of leafhoppers often reveals a mosaic of colors. This creature is the red-lined leafhopper.**
Opposite page, top: **another leafhopper.**
Opposite page, bottom: **a red-veined leafhopper usually found on vertical stems.**

PC

PC

Whiteflies

Family Aleyrodidae

Adult whiteflies look like microscopic moths, but unlike moths they often occur in large numbers on the undersides of leaves where they feed on sap. Several species are serious pests, including the sweet potato whitefly, which can severely damage squash and tomato crops in Florida. This species has also developed resistance to several commonly used insecticides. Whiteflies can also transmit plant diseases.

Immature whiteflies have reduced appendages and sensory organs, and from above they look like oval blobs, sometimes ornamented with fringes or tufts of wax.

In many situations, whitefly populations are kept under control by natural enemies; this is probably true for the small number of native species in Florida. The pest species in Florida were accidentally imported, and long-term control of these species may require importation of their natural enemies, or control methods that are less injurious to natural enemies already present.

THE MAJOR INSECT GROUPS

Insects, like other animals, are divided into major groups called orders. Florida has about 30 orders of insects, but the great majority of the most common and conspicuous insects belong to a small number of big orders. The first four listed below are sometimes called the "big four."

Coleoptera *(translation: sheath wings) includes the beetles. The front wings are hardened and meet in a straight line down the back. The hard shell of the front wings covers and protects the hind wings.*

Lepidoptera *(translation: scaly wings) includes the moths and butterflies. Two pairs of wings covered with tiny scales that are easily rubbed off. (not included in this book—see Florida's Fabulous Butterflies)*

Diptera *(translation: two wings) includes the flies. A single pair of membranous wings.*

Hymenoptera *(translation: membrane winged) includes sawflies, bees, ants, and wasps. Two pairs of membranous wings. The wings are missing in worker ants and some other female Hymnoptera. Females usually have an egg-laying apparatus, sometimes modified into a stinger.*

Hemiptera *(translation: half wings) includes the true bugs. Two pairs of wings, the forewings usually with the base area hard or leathery. Piercing-sucking mouth.*

Homoptera *(translation: same wings) includes leafhoppers, cicadas, scale insects, and their relatives. Two pairs of wings that usually meet at a slant over the back like a peaked roof. Piercing-sucking mouth.*

Orthoptera *(translation: straight wings) includes grasshoppers, crickets, and their rleatives. Two pairs of wings. The forewings are usually leathery or modified for singing in the male. Jumping hind legs, and chewing mouth.*

Odonata *(translation: toothed ones) includes dragonflies and damselflies. Two pairs of membranous wings, long abdomen, large eyes, chewing mouth. They are predators.*

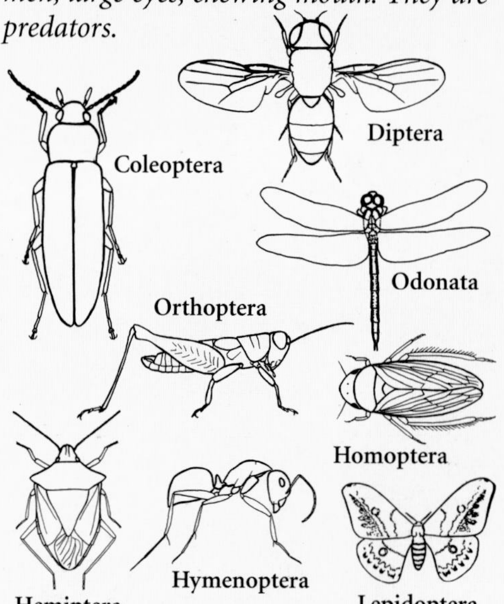

BBB

Spittlebugs

Family Cercopidae

The spittlebugs are a small group of sap-suckers whose best trick is the ball of protective froth produced by the young. Like many Homoptera, the spittlebugs can produce wax, but instead of allowing this to accumulate as a white powder or filaments, they dissolve it to form a waxy soap. The young spittlebug draws air into the tip of the abdomen, dips the abdomen into the pool of fluid, and quickly blows a small but durable bubble. Hundreds of these bubbles are produced in rapid succession, until the insect has completely disappeared in its bubble bath.

This airy refuge is not completely safe. Specialized predators, such as certain wasps, seem to know there is a bug in the bubbles, and haul it out. However, general predators such as ants, jumping spiders, or robber flies, are not likely to realize that an insect is concealed in the froth, nor would they be inclined to struggle through the bubbles.

In Florida, the only strikingly common spittlebug is the two-lined spittlebug, found mostly in the southern part of the state. The adults are often attracted in great numbers to lights. They have an unpleasant smell, and their red-and-black coloration is probably a warning that they are inedible.

BBB

Top: **the adult two-lined spittlebug is easily identified by its markings**

Above: **a nymph (immature) spittlebug hides in its protective bubblebath.**

Right: **this photo shows what a large amount of foam this little bug can create.**

BBB

WHO DOES BUG TASTE TESTS?

Many species of insects look or smell like they might be toxic, but in most cases, nobody has experimented to see if these insects are actually rejected by predators such a spiders or lizards. Many of the protective chemicals of insects may have properties useful to humans.

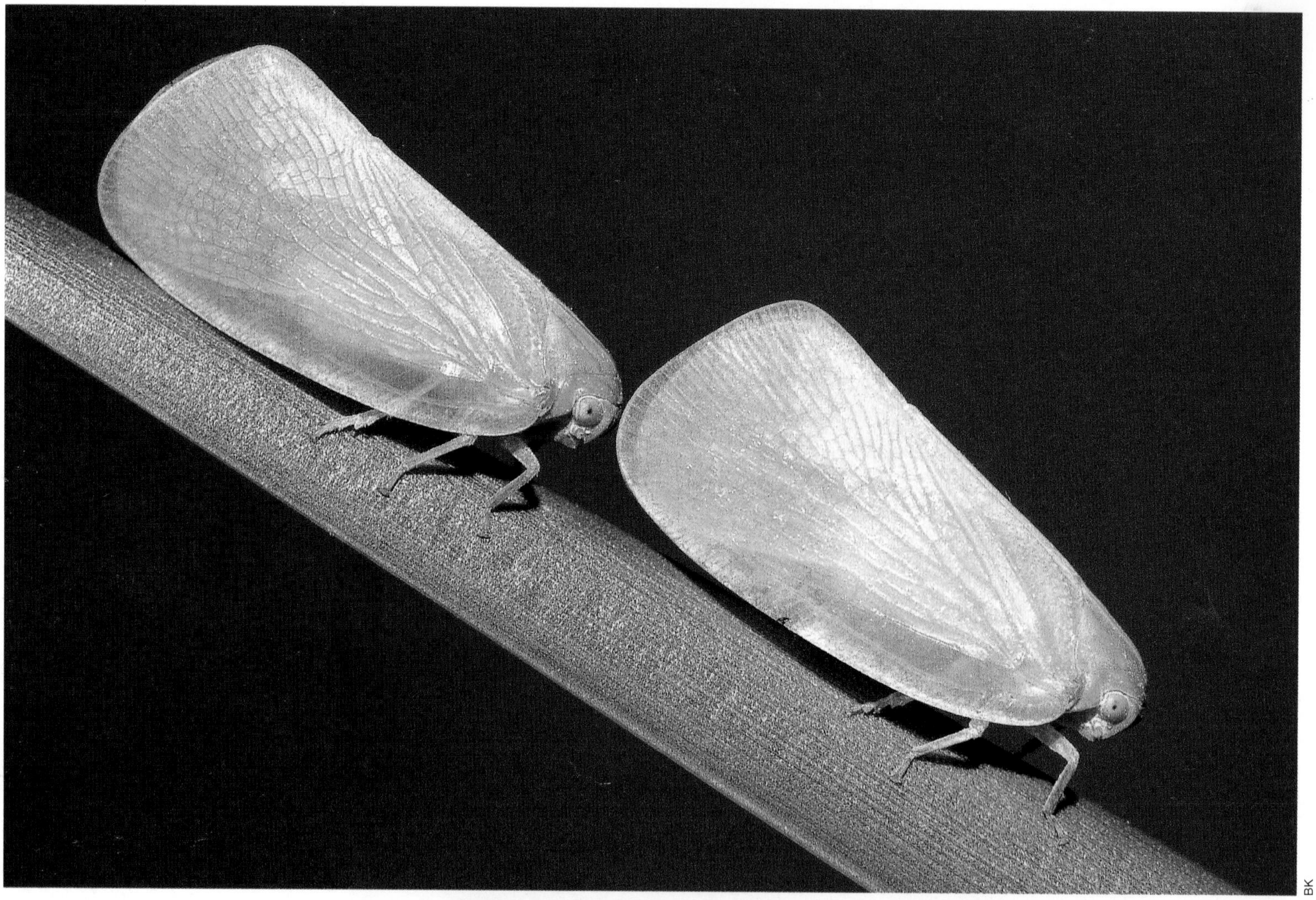

Planthoppers

Several Families of Homoptera

Planthoppers are small, attractive, jumping, sap-sucking insects that may resemble small moths, tiny cicadas, or leafhoppers with broad, clear wings. Few species cause economic damage by their feeding, but planthoppers serve as carriers of some plant diseases. A planthopper is a possible carrier of lethal yellowing disease of palms. There are 220 species of planthoppers in Florida.

Planthoppers usually stay hidden in vegetation, but there is a conspicuous species, the palmetto planthopper, that is easily found on palms and palmettos in spring and summer. (This is not the species that carries lethal yellowing disease.) The palmetto planthopper readily displays the most notable of planthopper talents: the manufacture of large quantities of wax. Young palmetto planthoppers live in groups on the undersides of palmetto leaves. Each planthopper produces a fountain-like tail of long, fine wax filaments. The ends of these are constantly breaking off and adhering to the waxy surface of the palmetto leaf. The planthoppers turn around as they feed, and the whole group of hoppers is soon surrounded by a broad carpet of powdery wax filaments.

Top: **a pair of palmetto planthoppers.** ***Above:*** **the larva of a palmetto planthopper. Tufts of wax filaments are produced by glands at the rear.**

Now the drama. Enter a predator, perhaps a ladybeetle or a lacewing larva. No sooner does this predator set foot on the carpet of wax, than its front is covered with bits of wax, like a person who has stepped out of the shower only to immediately tumble into a big box of tiny bits of Styrofoam. The bodies of insects are themselves covered with a thin layer of wax to keep in water; that is why the planthopper wax sticks so readily. The antennae, which are major sensory organs of the predator, and its jaws, are clogged with wax. It stops and cleans off the wax bits. It takes another step. The same thing happens. It turns around and leaves the scene.

Most planthoppers cut down on wax production as they become adults, when they are more mobile, and less involved in feeding than in reproduction. During their last molt they may change dramatically. The svelte adult palmetto planthopper, a tender jade color with orange trim, is no longer recognizable as its flat and shaggy younger self.

Right: a pair of dictyopharid planthoppers. The comical-looking, upturned "snouts" have nothing to do with breathing (insects have no noses), and may serve primarily to make the insect look like surrounding buds or leeflets when it is feeding. The whimsical shapes of planthoppers and their attractive colors should make them popular objects of study, but there are very few specialists (only one in Florida) who deal with this group.

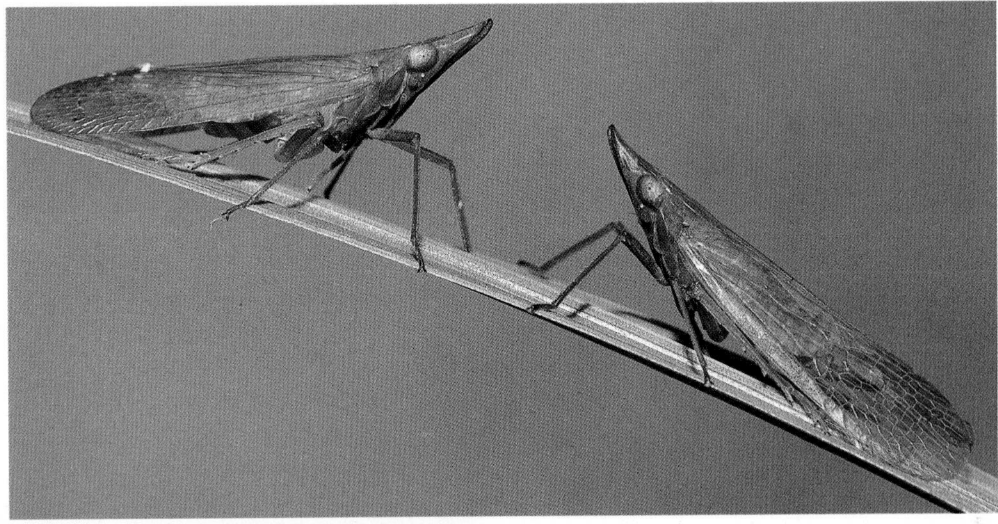

BK

BK

Left: an acanaloniid planthopper. Members of this group look like leaflets, and even the veins of the wings look like those of leaves. In flight this species looks like a small green moth, but unlike a moth, it gets a take-off boost from its powerful, jumping hind legs. The small knob with a long hair below the eyes is the antenna. The beak is tucked betwen the front legs.

HONEYDEW: NECTAR OF THE BUGS

Sap-sucking Homoptera spend hour after hour patiently processing large amounts of sap to get the concentrated sugars and other nutrients that they need for growth. As they stand there, plugged into their sap supply, they themselves are juicy morsels in a rough neighborhood. They are like fat merchants camped with their bulging wagons in the wilderness, while hungry nomads whet their knives in the surrounding hills. Many of the Homoptera do exactly what the merchants would do: they use their wealth to hire guards. These Homoptera release some of the processed, concentrated sap, called honeydew, to attract ants, which guard the honeydew producers.

This ant-attracting strategy is most common among treehoppers, aphids, and scale insects. Some species release drops of honeydew when there is an ant to receive it, while others squirt it onto the surrounding leaves and stems. The first method ensures more personalized attention from the ants, while the second attracts a greater number of ants and persuades them to patrol a much larger area of the plant. To use the wealthy merchant analogy, the first method is like paying bodyguards, the second is like spreading money through the community to hire a large number of agents and supporters. Large numbers of Homoptera produce noticeable quantities of honeydew droplets. Some people believe honeydew may have been the "manna from Heaven" mentioned in the Bible.

The honeydew made by Homoptera incidentally attracts a huge variety of insects. For example, a Florida sand pine infested with pine aphids can have over 100 species of insects coming to visit for the sake of free honeydew. Many of these insects are parasitic flies and wasps that attack leaf-eating and root-eating caterpillars and grubs. The Homoptera, therefore, may have far-reaching effects by attracting and supporting the natural enemies of plant-eating insects. When the sap-suckers are not too numerous, they are probably beneficial to their host plants and to neighboring plants.

The residue of honeydew that clings to the surface of leaves fosters the growth of a group of fungi called sooty molds. The fruit of unsprayed citrus trees usually have sooty mold on them. Sooty molds cause little damage to plants, and support yet another interesting community of insects.

JLC

Above: **ants tending their aphid "cows," and collecting honeydew.**

PC

Treehoppers

Family Membracidae

The treehoppers seem to peer out with beady red eyes from under the shelter of an outlandish hood. They are weirdly cute insects. The thorax of treehoppers is developed into a heavy shield, covering most of the head and body. This shield may be elaborated into a point, resembling a thorn, or it may be thin and sail-like, or swollen and notched. Some species are brightly colored. Treehoppers are generally harmless sap-suckers, causing negligible damage to plants. The young of many species produce a sweet fluid, called honeydew, which attracts ants. These ants guard the young treehoppers. There are about 65 species in Florida, but the Panhandle insects have not been thoroughly studied, and the real number could close to 100.

Many treehoppers, especially those whose young are not protected by ants, show some form of maternal care. In Florida this may be most easily observed in the two-lined oak treehopper, which is common on oaks planted as shade trees. The mature female is mottled brown, and when it presses its body close to a twig, it resembles a leaf bud or twig stub. The eggs are laid in slits in a twig, and the mother watches over them, refusing to be driven away, even by a naturalist poking at her with a grass blade. The young hatch in spring, and stick close together while growing up, their mother remaining on guard. The brightly-colored young are much easier to see than the dark female, so late spring is the time to look for this treehopper. The young adults have a distinctive pale coloration with red stripes, but this eventually darkens to brown.

JHR

Top: a young adult oak treehopper resting on a fern (which is not a host plant).

Above: buffalo treehoppers, whose big heads and heavy shoulder evoke the bison.

Nobody knows the significance of the dramatic markings of the immatures and young adults, but they may be chemically protected and advertising their inedibility.

BK

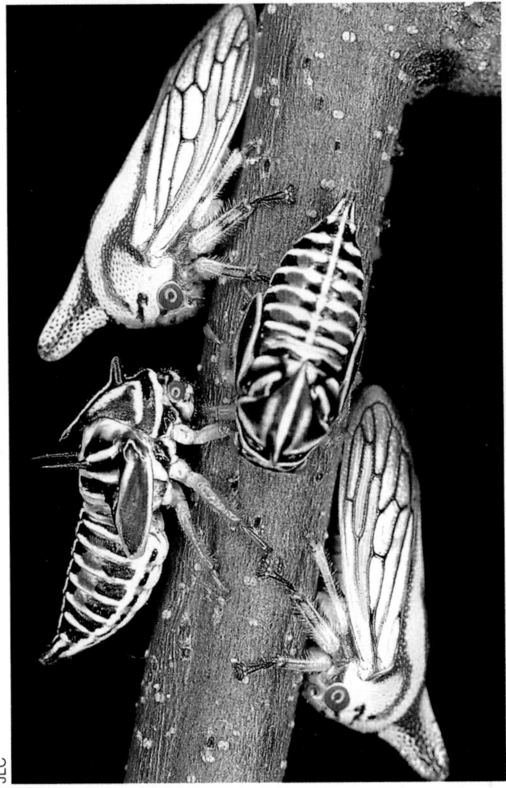

JLC

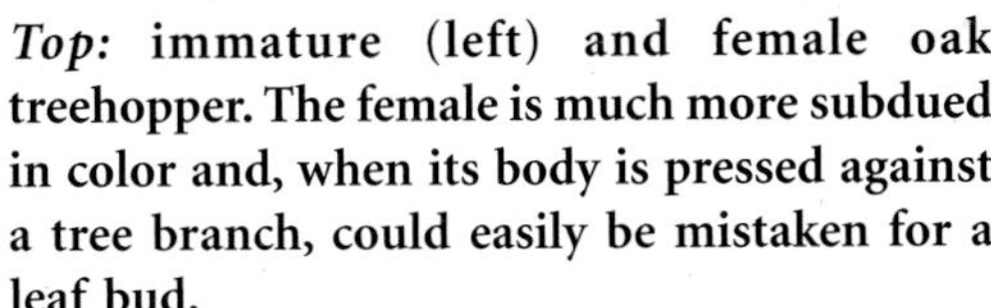

Top: immature (left) and female oak treehopper. The female is much more subdued in color and, when its body is pressed against a tree branch, could easily be mistaken for a leaf bud.

Above: young adult and immature oak treehoppers.

Right: young adult oak treehopper emerging from its larval skin.

BK

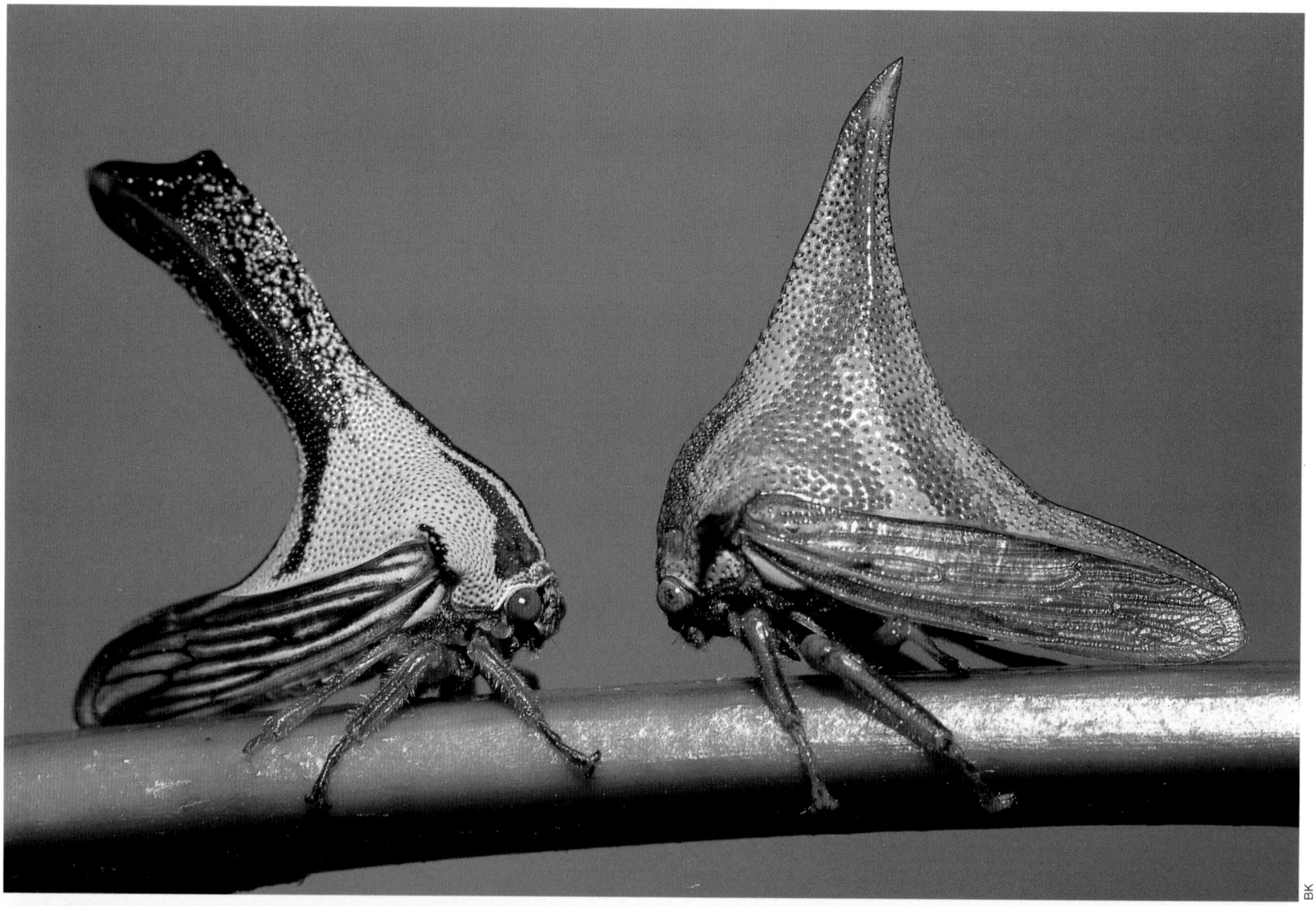

BK

REC

BK

BK

BK

Opposite page, top: male (left) and female thornbugs. Thornbugs are a type of treehopper. The fancy enlargements of the thorax of treehoppers have several functions: as a hard shield for the body, as camouflage, and as sharp protrusions that make the treehopper difficult to swallow. This species feeds on several tropical and subtropical trees in the legume family.

Opposite page, bottom: thornbugs can sometimes be seen feeding in thick clusters on a host plant.

Top: the immature form of the species of thornbug shown at the top of opposite page.

Above: a thornbug with a real thorn (of a rose bush) showing the camouflage possibilities.

Right: a front view of a thornbug reveals the triangular shape and striking coloration which even extends down the sides of the legs. Adult treehoppers are able to fly in a rather clumsy buzzing way, but their speed of escape from danger owes much to the jump start given by their powerful hind legs.

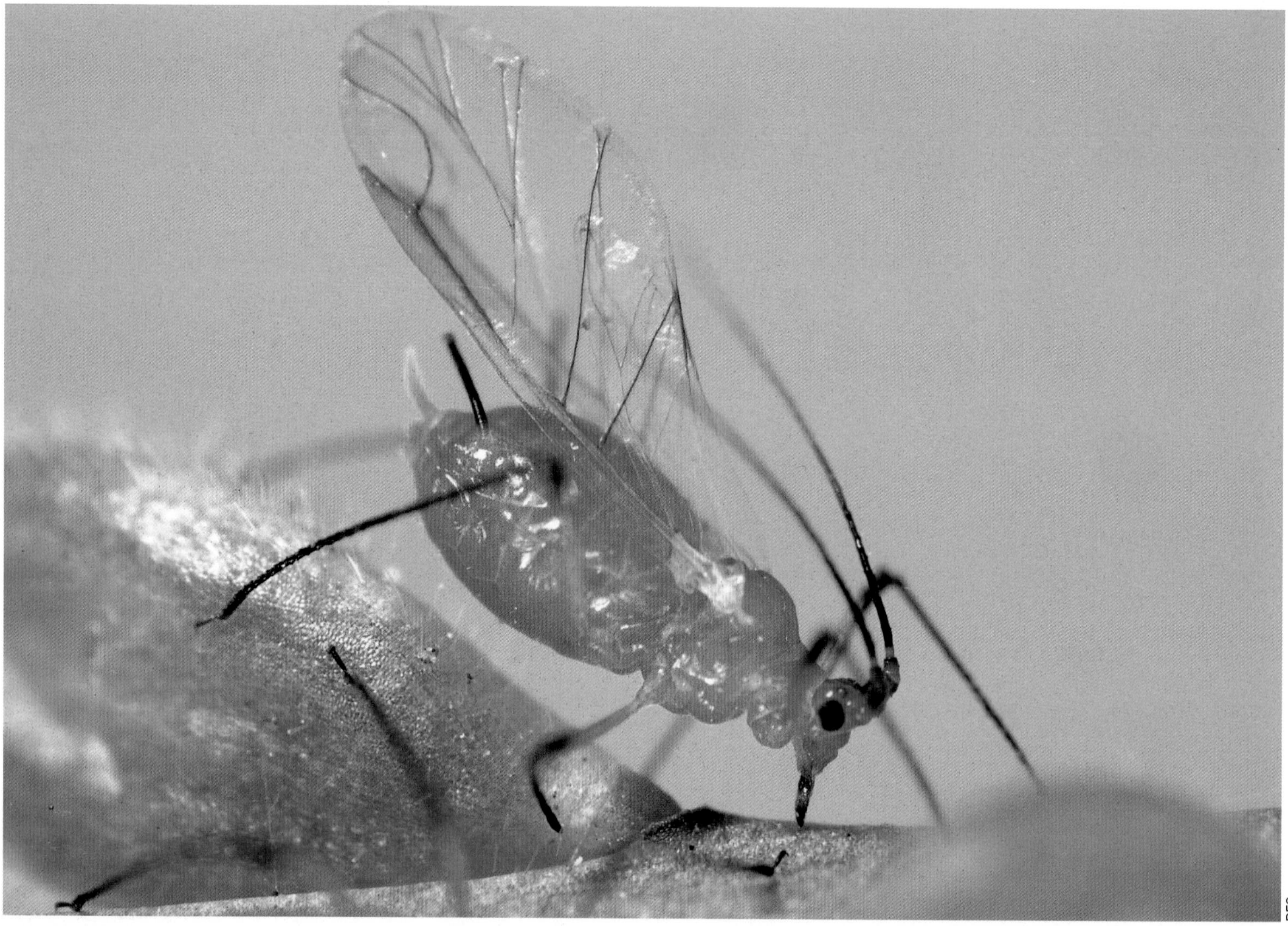

Aphids

Family Aphididae

Aphids are tiny insects, found on many plants in great numbers. They are often called "plant lice." They are small, pear-shaped sap-suckers, usually with long antennae and long legs. The long legs are not suited for running, but allow aphids to step carefully over the plant hairs usually found on the surfaces of leaves and stems. Some of these hairs may be sharp and barbed.

Most Florida species of aphids are green, but some are pink, yellow, brown, or black. The species found on both milkweed and oleander (which are poisonous) has a bright, orange-yellow warning color. The color of an aphid may indicate its age, the color of the sap it drinks, or the color of internal colonies of microorganisms that transform the sap.

Several species are pests of vegetables and fruits in Florida, and some may carry plant diseases. Florida has at least 75 species of aphids.

Aphids have a huge list of natural enemies, from opportunistic predators, such as crickets and earwigs, to all sorts of specialized wasps, flies, ladybeetles, and lacewings, whose chief goal is to gobble up as many aphids as possible. Protective ants may hold some of these predators at bay, but sooner or later, as more and more enemies show up, the aphid population begins to decline, and then it suddenly crashes. The rise and fall of a group of aphids on a plant often happens in a matter of a few weeks, presenting one of the most convenient and vivid examples of how natural enemies can control populations of insects. The aphids never completely disappear, because there are some individuals that move to new locations ahead of the feeding frenzy of predators.

Top: **an aphid sipping sap from the stem of a plant. A pair of short tubes, called cornicles, extends upward from the rear of the aphid's body. These tubes secrete a rapidly hardening, waxy substance used to fend off predators.**

Below: **a cluster of aphids bellies up to the bar, like football fans at halftime. Each aphid inserts a slender, flexible hypodermic that can thread its way between cells to the sap-transport tubes of the plant. Excess sugar and water may be excreted as honeydew, attracting ants and other insects that guard the aphids, and also guard the plant against caterpillars.**

Above: **the orange and black uniform of oleander aphids warns of the toxic sap they have drunk. Even these aphids have predators such as small wasps that develop inside the aphids. The shriveled remains in this photo are not victims, but the cast-off skins of growing aphids that shed in the midst of their drinking companions.**

Right: **this photo shows the adult aphid and the very small, but identical, immature aphids. This is an example of gradual, or incomplete, metamorphosis in which the young, called nymphs, closely resemble the adults. As the aphid grows, it must shed its skin. Aphids usually mature in two weeks or less with only three to four skin changes.**

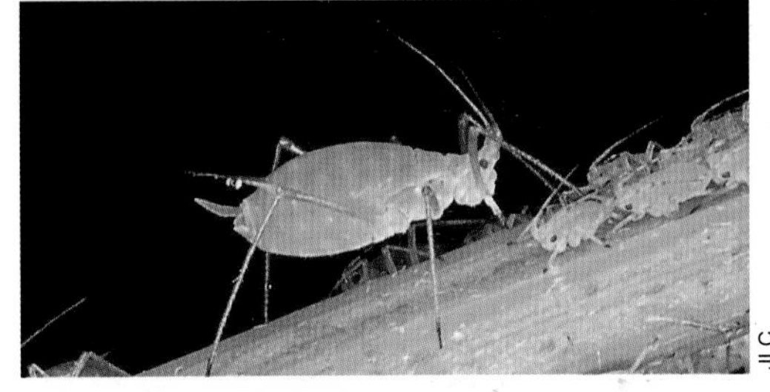

SECRET WEAPON OF APHIDS: THEIR ASTONISHING ABILITY TO REPRODUCE

Aphids can give valuable lessons in population biology. Aphids are usually found in clusters, and if one looks at a cluster when it has just started forming, there is usually a winged female surrounded by wingless offspring of various sizes. With a little patience, one can see this female giving birth, not to an egg, but to a fully formed little aphid, which almost immediately unfolds its awkward legs, takes a few steps, and inserts its beak into the plant. The larger offspring are also producing baby aphids, so it is clear that these larger wingless offspring are themselves mature. So rapid and efficient is this assembly line of aphids, that newly born aphids already have recognizable embryos of their own offspring. Even without seeing such embryos, early naturalists realized that female aphids kept in isolation from males could produce generation after generation without being fertilized.

This, therefore, is the great secret weapon of aphids: a winged female that settles in a new spot, such as a young shoot on an orange tree, can establish a population that grows extremely fast. In fact, this population grows twice as fast as that of a normal animal whose population is half males, since males do not give birth. If the aphid population affects the plant or plant shoot so severely that the flow of sap begins to dry up, some aphids produce (also without males), a generation of winged females that can disperse to set up their own little groups.

Observing this reproductive strategy, the naturalist might begin to ask himself or herself (especially the latter) whether males really serve any useful purpose. Reassuringly, especially to the male naturalist, somewhere in their annual cycle aphids usually dedicate a generation to winged males and females, which fly about and mate. This provides the genetic diversity and the opportunity to accumulate beneficial genetic traits that almost all animal species seem to require.

At some point in their annual cycle, most aphids produce a generation of eggs. This is a resting stage that gets them through an unfavorable season. This is particularly important for aphids living in cold climates, but may also occur in some Florida species. Some aphids play other reproductive tricks, such as producing a different-looking generation that feeds on a different host plant.

Aphids are a reminder that reproductive strategy, not just the ability to attack and defend, can be an extremely valuable weapon for survival.

JHR

Scale Insects and Mealybugs

Ten Families of Homoptera

The scale insects and mealybugs are a peculiar group of sap-suckers that have lost or reduced most of the external features usually associated with insects. They precisely fulfill the darkest predictions of human parents about their children who spend all their time lounging in front of the TV drinking soda pop. Bloated and almost immobile, their muscles atrophied, oblivious to the dangers and opportunities of the world around them, the scale insects and mealybugs seem little more than enlarged digestive systems. A similar fate, of course, does not really await human children: human behavior is such that today's couch potato may be tomorrow's Navy Seal, or computer software engineer and weekend marathoner. The scale insects and mealybugs, in contrast, have degenerated to fit a truly parasitic way of life. In spite of this, they are not featureless blobs, but may have elaborate shields or waxy coverings, rows of tubercles, and patterns of small hairs. There is no doubt, however, that they bear little resemblance to a normal insect.

There is one time in the lives of scale insects and mealybugs when they resemble real insects rather than plant pimples or waxy warts. When the young first hatch, they have functional legs, antennae, and eyes, and they move about actively to find a place to settle on the plant. They are small and light enough to be occasionally picked up by the wind, and it is by wind dispersal of newborns that scale insects and mealybugs are most likely to get from one isolated plant to another. This neonatal adventuring is an extremely chancey mode of dispersal, and successful individuals among the scale insects and mealybugs are likely to be those that remain on the plant where they were born. This means that annual plants, which must be colonized each year, are unlikely to be good hosts for these insects. The great majority of species in Florida and elsewhere are found on perennial plants. A special feature of many Florida habitats hostile to these poorly-dispersing insects is a high frequency of fire, which can remove all the above-ground vegetation, including scale insects and mealybugs.

Not surprisingly, humans provide the best travel opportunities for scale insects and mealybugs. These insects are usually so inconspicuous that they are regularly transported on plants, even cuttings. Many Florida species are not native to the state. In the soft scale family, for example, there are 44 Florida species, of which 30 were accidentally imported from other places.

Scale insects and mealybugs are sitting ducks for their natural enemies, including a wide variety of wasps, flies, and beetles. Waxy coverings, or hard shells, or protective ants attracted by honeydew provide some defense. The enemies, however, take full advantage of the poor mobility of scales and mealybugs, and their consequent tendency to build up dense populations that are easy to find and exploit. Native species of scales and mealybugs, therefore, are usually controlled by natural enemies, while introduced species (often imported without their specialized enemies) may become serious pests. Some of the most successful examples of biological control of insect pests have been the introductions of natural enemies of scale insects.

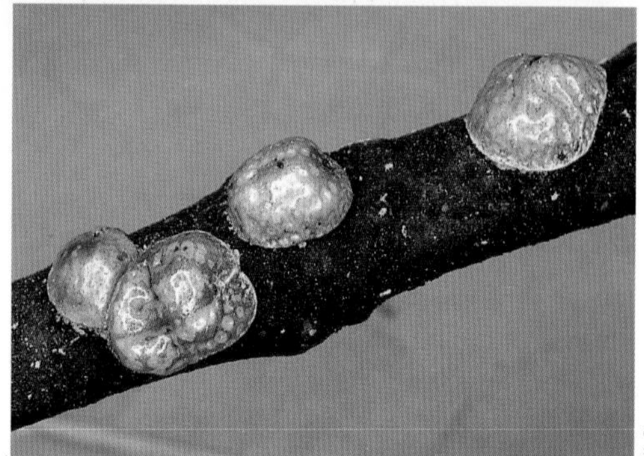

JLC

Top: **cotton cushion scale. This species is a stowaway from Australia, arriving in California in 1868. Aftr 20 years as a major pest, it was brought under control by the introduction of natural enemies from its homeland, particularly the vedalia lady beetle. Both the scale and its predator were introduced to Florida long ago.**

Above: **tuliptree scale.**

Upon maturity, male scales and mealybugs again become recognizable insects with wings, legs, and eyes. They fly about looking for females, and are able to move from one plant to another, reducing the amount of inbreeding in the populations.

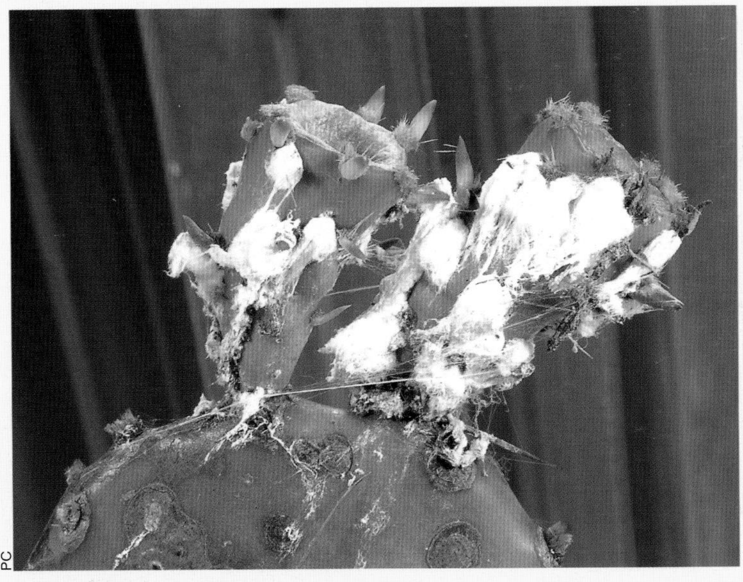

PC

PC

AN INSECT TO DYE FOR

Among the most easily observed of the Florida mealybugs is the cochineal insect, which makes messy blobs of waxy strands on prickly pear cactus. Hidden within this protective fluff is a plump insect, that is further protected from predators by its ability to synthesize a red chemical, called carminic acid, which the insect stores inside its body.

Early inhabitants of the Americas, from Mexico to Peru, discovered the cochineal insect as a source of dye. When Spaniards conquered Mexico in 1518, they found an already established cochineal industry with plantations of cactus. The insects were carefully brushed from the cacti into baskets, killed by heating, and dried to make a powdered dye. The Spaniards immediately recognized cochineal as one of the most valuable and easily traded products of the New World. For the next 350 years, cochineal was the best available scarlet dye. Particularly after 1630, when a method was perfected for dying wool a permanent, vivid red with cochineal, it was used for everything from the carpets of the wealthy to the uniforms of the British Redcoats.

Cochineal insects were raised in big cactus plantations not only in Mexico, but also in Spain, North Africa, India, South Africa, the West Indies, and the Canary Islands. In 1868, about 6,000,000 pounds of cochineal were produced in the Canary Islands alone, at the rate of about 70,000 insects per pound. Soon after this date, the much cheaper red aniline dyes were invented, and the cochineal industry collapsed.

Cochineal is still sometimes used as a food coloring and in lipstick, but its day as a major commodity is over. Few Floridians, observing the fluffy white patches stuck here and there on a prickly pear pad, would think of the fierce Dutch pirates of the Caribbean swooping down on the returning Spanish fleet to snatch their treasures of gold, silver, gems, and cochineal.

PC

Top, left: **the white, protective covering made by the cochineal bug is often found on native cactus in Florida.**

Top, right: **a cochineal bug exuding the red body fluid which was used as dye by Native Americans. The cochineal bug produces the red chemical as a defense against predators, but there are specialized predators which are undeterred. In Florida, a small moth feeds on cochineal insects. It even stores some of the chemical and spits it out at attackers.**

Above: **a cochineal bug with its white covering removed.**

Leaf Miners

Some blotches and trails of damage on leaves are not caused by sap-suckers, but by small insect larvae that feed between the upper and lower layers of the leaf. These leaf-mining larvae include species of flies, beetles, and moths.

For a small, vegetarian insect, this is a great way to make a living, burrowing through a nutritious sandwich, never exposed to the weather. The only drawback is that there is only a tissue-thin layer separating a leaf-mining larva from enemies stalking about on the surface of the leaf, and there is no way to escape. For this reason, most leaf miners do not survive to maturity.

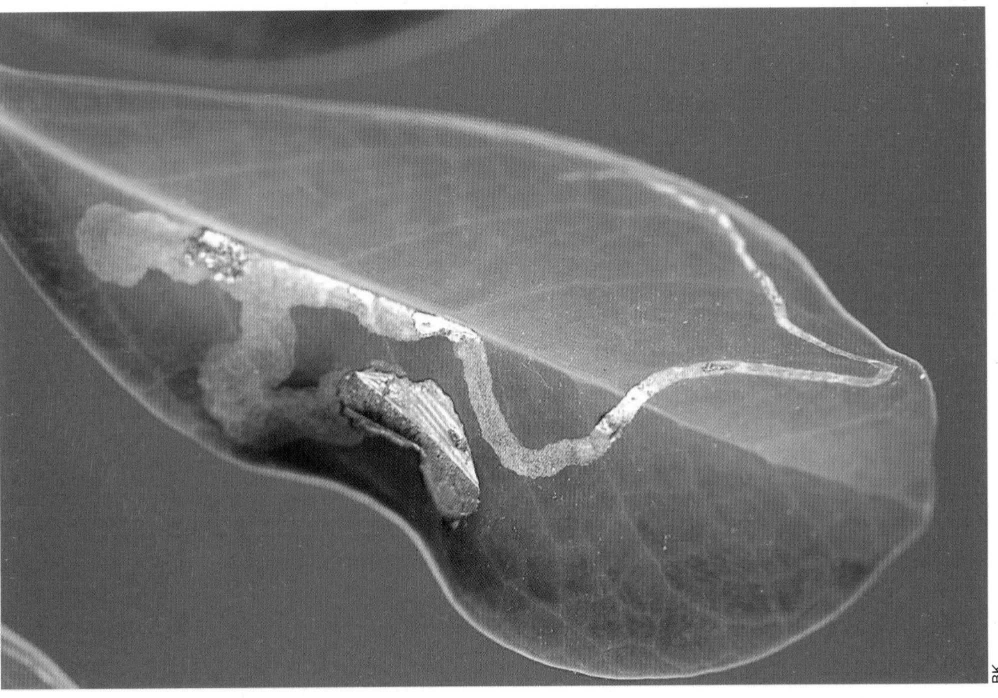

BK

ORDER ANOPLURA

The lice are a peculiar group of wingless parasites found on a wide variety of mammals, including some unlikely ones, such as seals and walruses. Lice, like fleas, never have wings. Two species of lice are found only on humans, an exclusive relationship that has been recognized for hundreds of years. A few hundred years ago, there was actually a lively little debate among scholarly biologists over whether Adam and Eve were created complete with lice, since there would be no place for these lice to live until humans were provided for them. This fussiness and extreme dependence on humans is a great advantage in the perennial efforts to rid humans of lice, because there are no alternate hosts among wild animals, and no hidden animal dens or burrows where lice can persist until the eradication effort is over.

In Florida, human lice are steadily becoming rarer, partly because people today bathe and wash their clothes frequently, and partly because it is socially unacceptable to harbor lice. These are recent developments, and it is sobering to realize that all the notable people of history, from two or three centuries ago on back, were carrying around lice while they were carrying out their great deeds. Human lice undoubtedly made the perilous voyage to the New World with Christopher Columbus and his crew. Here these lice might have met their long lost cousins, as lice were already present, as can be determined by examining the scalps of ancient Peruvian mummies. The book on proper manners copied out as an exercise by the young George Washington says, "Kill no vermin, as fleas, lice, tics, etc. in the presence of others...."

An extreme case of lousiness was the English martyr, Thomas Becket, who wore under his splendid ecclesiastical robes a fur shirt with the hair on the inside against the skin. This was to provide accommodations for hordes of irritating lice, which he encouraged thus to mortify his flesh and purify his soul. As his murdered body began to cool before the eyes of his grieving followers, the lice and fleas began to abandon his clothes in such numbers that, "The vermin boiled over like water in a simmering cauldron." All who were present wept hysterically at this evidence of how holy a man had been taken from them. As this story indicates, lice are very temperature sensitive. They readily leave a dead body that is cooling or even a live body that has become feverish.

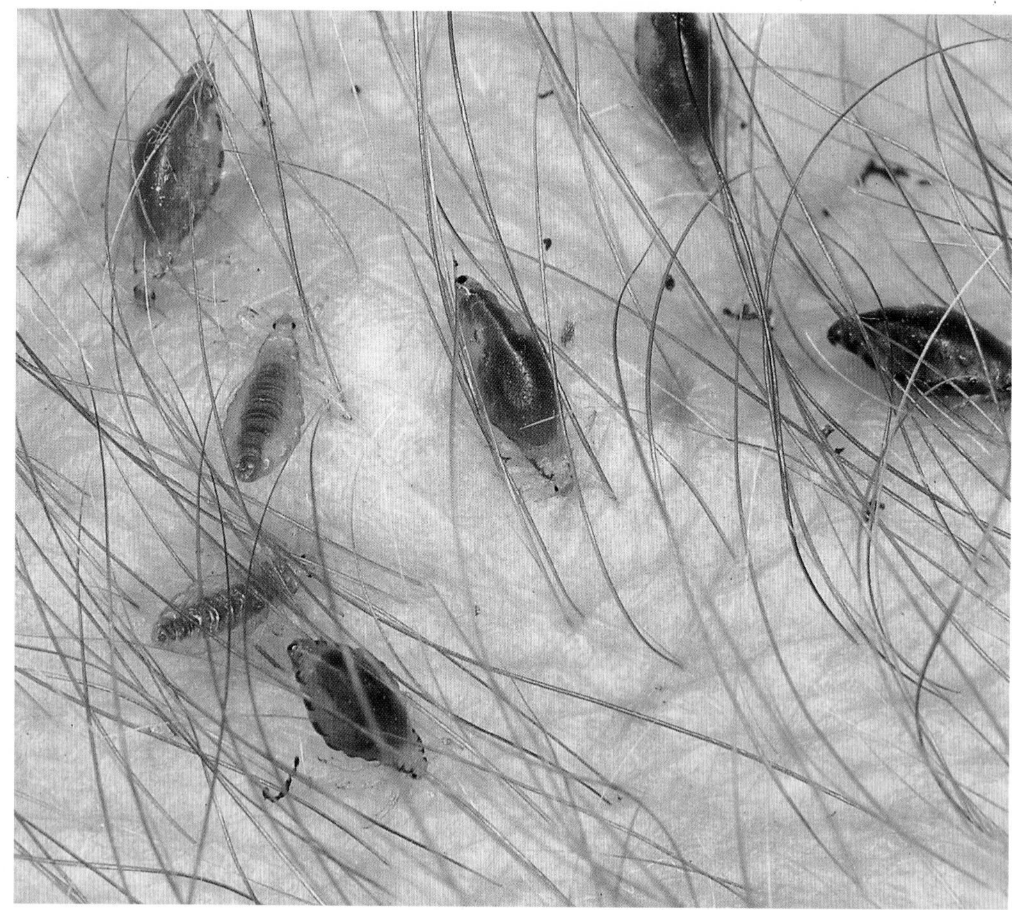
JLC

***Above:* human lice. This species is found in the hair of the head (including eyebrows), and less frequently in armpits. A second species, the crab louse, is specialized for life among the hairs of the groin. Differences in coarseness and spacing of the hairs, and contrasts in temperature and humidity, divide the human body into separate habitats as far as lice are concerned. Some other species of mammals can also boast more than one species of louse, found on separate parts of the body. The eggs of lice are securely fastened one by one to the host's hairs by means of a waterproof glue. These eggs, called "nits," are naturally extremely small. The eggshells remain attached to the hair after hatching, and may grow outward along with the hair to a point where they become visible as little white dots on the hairs.**

Human lice were not seen as a public health risk until about a hundred years ago, when it was recognized that epidemic typhus was transmitted by human lice. Instantly, lice became public enemy # 1, and with good reason. Epidemic typhus is such a serious disease that it has repeatedly changed the course of history, especially during wars and other situations of crowding and deprivation. The avoidance of lice was a strong incentive in those days for a man to shave his head and wear a wig.

Epidemic typhus is high on the list of European diseases that killed many natives of the New World shortly after the conquest of Mexico and Peru. Likewise, many thousands of would-be immigrants to the New World died of typhus while packed into ships during the long trip from Europe. Now and then there is a little outbreak of head lice in Florida, usually detected first among school children (among children, lice are often called "cooties," a relic of World War I soldier slang). This does not mean that there is a threat of epidemic typhus. Like most other diseases with insect vectors, epidemic typhus depends on large numbers of infected people and regular, large-scale movement of the insects from one individual to another. Since lice can only crawl slowly about, this means that there must be large numbers of typhus-infected people who are sick, or even dying, lying right next to healthy people. This does not happen in Florida, or elsewhere in the US.

ORDER NEUROPTERA

The order Neuroptera is an odd group of rather dissimilar insects that look left over from an earlier age. To the fascinated entomologist, the Neuroptera seem like a popular stereotype of the British aristocracy, holding onto the old order by a kind of canny eccentricity.

Most adult Neuroptera have large, intricately veined wings, like fine tatting from the old hope chest of a Victorian spinster. They flutter sedately in the moonlight, although they can dodge quickly and erratically when overtaken by a zooming moth or buzzed by a burly beetle. The larvae, on the other hand, are scary-looking creatures, usually bearing large, curved, channeled jaws that can impale a victim, inject toxins, and suck the body dry.

Neuroptera are most diverse in Australia, which is a bastion of ancient lineages, but the order is well represented even in Florida, with about 90 species.

Owlfly

Family Ascalaphidae

Owlflies are quite common in Florida and their outlandish appearance always causes comment when they land on the screen door beneath the porch light.

The larvae are flattened, with a row of fleshy and hairy projections along each side. The long curved jaws seize passing insects.

The female owlfly has the unique habit of surrounding each of her eggs with a circle or stockade of smaller, infertile eggs containing repellant chemicals.

Owlflies are rapid and agile in flight.

BK

JLC

BK

Top: adult owlflies look like a weird hybrid between a butterfly and a dragonfly, but are actually more closely related to antlions.

Above: owlflies often spend the day in this characteristic pose. It may help camouflage the insect as a bit of twig. Some species have eyes divided into two sections, with larger eye facets in the upper half.

Left: owlflies usually fly at dusk. In Florida, they are usually noticed around outdoor lights or on windows.

BK

Green Lacewings

Family Chrysopidae

Green lacewings are common insects in Florida, where they can be admired not only for their delicate green wings and golden eyes, but also for their habits, as the larvae often feed on aphids and scale insects.

A curious feature of the larvae of lacewings and other Neuroptera, one which might arouse envy in human parents, is that the gut remains incomplete through the larval and pupal periods, and the insect defecates for the first time when it emerges as an adult. The cocoon of a green lacewing is about the size of a BB shot, and it is difficult to imagine how the mature lacewing could have been contained within.

Top: the exceptionally beautiful eye of the lacewing.

Below, right: when a female lacewing lays an egg on a leaf or a bit of bark, she touches the tip of her abdomen to the surface and draws out a long, instantly hardening filament, culminating in the egg, which stands above the surface like a microscopic balloon. The filament is too slender to be climbed by egg-eating insects, such as ants or lady beetles, and may be further defended by a surface layer of repellent chemicals. The stalked eggs are laid in groups, often in a circle or spiral.

Below, left: a lacewing larvae, also known as a trashbug, attaches a a tiny dried flower to its back as camouflage.

PC

BBB

RFS

Top: the larva of a lacewing eating an aphid. The larvae of several common Florida lacewings cover themselves with bits of lichen or debris for camouflage. They are very difficult to spot unless they are moving. Because of this habit, they are sometimes called trashbugs. Another common name is aphid lion. The tip of the abdomen has a pad that can be annointed with a sticky secretion to anchor the larva to a leaf, or smeared on the face of an instrusive ant.

Below: although dainty in appearance, the adult lacewing can emit a foul smell when molested. Another unexpected ability is "singing." Each species has its own characteristic songs. They are played by vibrating the tip of the abdomen on a leaf or grass blade. The pattern of vibrations is received through the feet of an individual on the same plant.

JHR

JLC

Mantisflies

Family Mantispidae

The mantisfly is neither a fly nor a mantis. The mantisfly looks like the prank of an unusually deft student, who has attached the front end of a miniature mantis to a lacewing. The front legs of a mantisfly function like those of a mantis, darting out to snag a nearby insect, and holding it while the mantisfly feeds daintily on its immobilized prey. The mantisfly and the praying mantis are not at all related, and their similarities are a good example of convergent evolution (unrelated species that have independently evolved similar structures or behaviors).

The larvae of mantisflies develop inside the egg sacs of spiders, where they feed on the eggs. The tiny larva of some species rides around on a female spider until she has laid her eggs, then creeps in among the eggs and is sealed into the egg sac by the unwitting spider. There are four or five species of mantisflies in Florida, where they are not particularly common. They are sometimes seen when they are attracted to lighted windows.

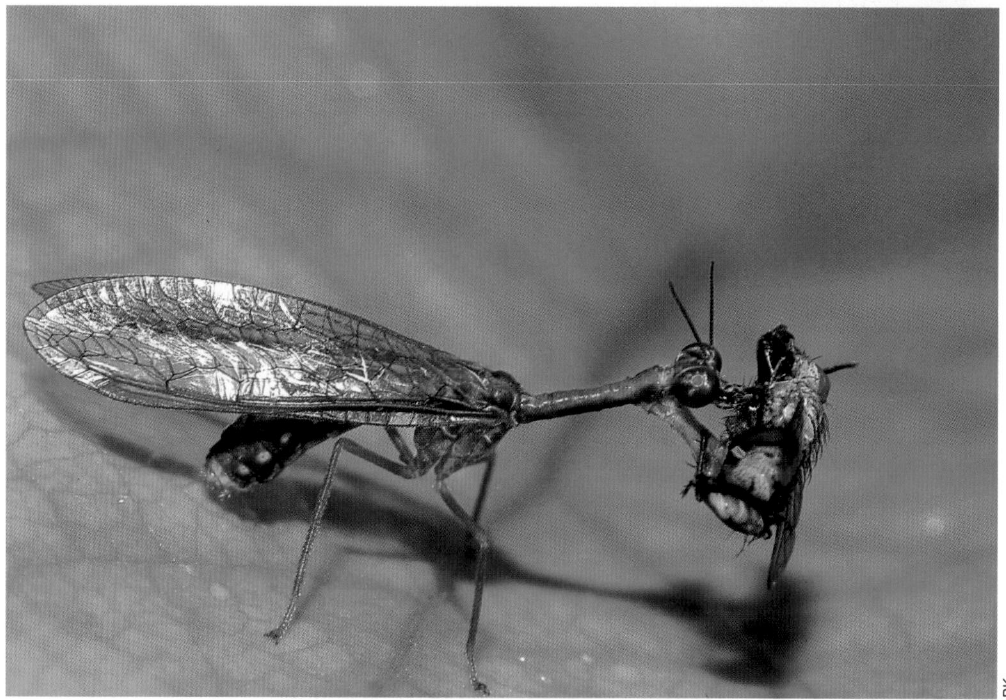

BK

Top: **a brown mantisfly waiting for dinner on lantana. The young larva of this species usually rides on a spider until the spider lays its eggs. It feeds on spider blood while waiting.**

Above: **this species of mantisfly has an unusually long thorax, which enables it to carefully consume a struggling insect without the flailing legs of the prey becoming tangled in the legs or wings of the mantisfly.**

Opposite page, top: **a green mantisfly. The larva can develop in the egg sacs of many different kinds of spiders. The larva does not ride on spiders, but hunts for a spider egg sac and makes a small hole in the tough silk of the egg sac. Once inside the egg sac, the larval mantispid transforms into a plump grub that is no longer capable of crawling.**

JLC

THE BIG CHANGE: COMPLETE METAMORPHOSIS

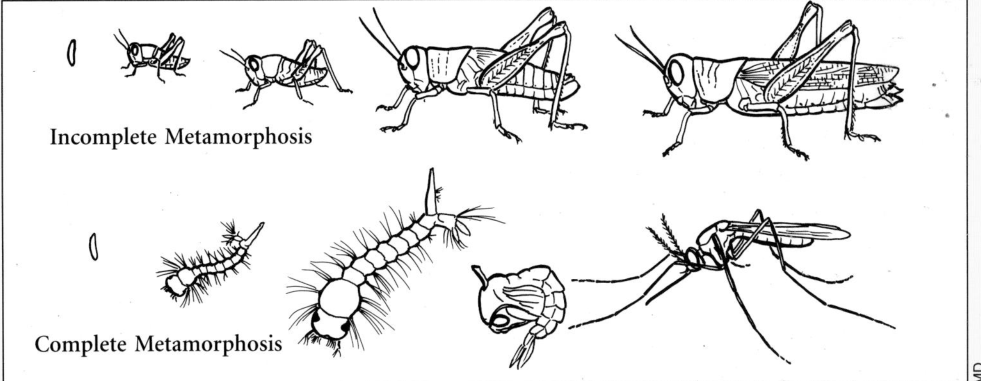

Neuroptera is an order in which there is such a radical difference between the young and the adult that there is no way to make a smooth transition between the two stages. The great majority of insect species in Florida and elsewhere have "complete metamorphosis." This means that between the larval stage and the adult stage there is an inactive period, the "pupal stage." During this remarkable time in the insect's life, the larval organs are largely broken down and new structures are built, so that the adult bears no resemblance to its former self. This total reconstruction of the body allows the insect to have a completely different diet and lifestyle as an adult than it had as a larva.

Complete metamorphosis is especially useful for rapid exploitation of some rich but temporary resource, such as rapidly regrowing plants following a summer fire in Florida, or the wood of recently killed trees, or a mushroom that only persists for a few days. The female insect, with excellent dispersal abilities and specialized senses for homing in on a particular resource, finds the goodies, and her larvae, which are really specialized eating machines, gobble it up as quickly as possible.

For many years, there was a theory that larval insects such as caterpillars and beetle grubs were really "walking embryos." However, the pupal stage is not the resumption of embryonic development, but a new developmental stage. The evolution of this stage was a major evolutionary breakthrough for the insects. But, there is a price to pay. The pupal stage, though often capable of some movement, is not able to actively defend itself against predators or make a rapid escape. Moreover, there are always some ecological roles best filled by generalists, or situations in which there is no big advantage to be derived from superb dispersal abilities.

There remain, therefore, many species with "incomplete metamorphosis," such as grasshoppers and cockroaches. These insects do not transform so radically as they go from immature to adult, when their reproductive systems become functional and their wings become large enough to allow flight. Their behavior, however, is likely to change dramatically, as in other animals when sexual maturity arrives.

Many adult humans, remembering their own adolescence and contemplating that of their children, might long for a pupal stage, in which all the physical changes and professional training needed for adult life would take place in quiet seclusion.

BK

Antlions

Family Myrmeleontidae

With 22 species, Florida is the premier antlion state of the East. Larvae of several of Florida's antlion species make pits in sand or dust to capture ants and other small prey, and are a perennial source of fun and experimentation for naturalists of all ages. It is easy to get antlion larvae to build their pits in a box of dry sand, where one can observe both the art of pit-making and the efficiency of prey capture.

When an insect, such as an ant, tumbles into the pit, it falls into the open jaws of the antlion, which attempts to pierce the prey and immobilize it by dragging it down into the sand. The antlion has sets of forward-pointing bristles which resist any attempt by the prey to pull itself back out of the sand. Digestive fluids are pumped through the ducts in the antlion jaws and into the prey, and the soup that was once prey tissue, neatly contained by the external skeleton of the corpse, is sucked into the antlion. The husk of the prey is tossed up out of the pit, and the jaws at the bottom again open for business.

Antlion larvae are often called "doodlebugs," probably because they make little curving furrows in the sand when they are choosing a place to build a pit. Children have also noticed that when they lean close over a pit and say "doodle-doodle-doodle," the antlion may interpret the little cascades of sand caused by exhalations as resulting from an insect attempting to climb the pit, and start tossing sand up the sides of the pit, as it often does to speed the descent of a victim.

Not all Florida antlions make pits. Some species lie in wait just under the surface of the sand, and may come charging out after prey.

Antlion adults look a bit like damselflies, but have short, curved antennae and are nocturnal in habits. Many people who are familiar with antlion larvae have no idea what the adults look like, and there is no way to make the association between the larva and adult without being told, or raising a larva to maturity. This last was done long ago, as recounted in a book published in 1800, describing the escape of an antlion from its cocoon:

It tears its lodging, and breaks through its wall..... Its body, which is turned like a screw, takes up no more than the space of a quarter of an inch; but when it is unfolded, it becomes half an inch in length; then its fore wings likewise unfold, and in two minutes time become longer than the body. In short, it becomes a large and beautiful Flie, laying aside its barbarity, and rapacious disposition: it has then a long slender body, of a brown color, a small head, with large bright eyes, and long, slender, pale brown legs, with four large reticulated wings.

BK

Top: an adult antlion, one of several Florida species whose larve do not make pits.

Above: seen up close, the bristly legs add to the similarity between antlions and the completely unrelated damselflies. Like damselflies, adult antlions pick small insects off vegetation, but this activity is seldom seen because it happens at night.

Opposite page, top: this unusual Florida antlion has a larva found in gopher tortoise burrows and in dry sawdust in hollow trees.

LS

JLC

BK

BK

ANTLION AND PREY

In the dry sand sheltered by the eaves of a house, a pedestrian insect must pick its way through a deadly maze of little pits. Each pit is a trap made by an antlion larva, which waits at the bottom with jaws cocked, ready to impale an ant or beetle. In creating the pit, the antlion removes all bits of leaves or twigs, and tosses out the sand in such a way that the pit is lined with the smaller grains which make a more slippery slope. If a prey is struggling up the side of the pit, the antlion flings up sand at it to make little avalanches that carry the prey to the bottom.

The big larva at upper right is a giant species that does not make pits.

JHR

DL

ORDER COLEOPTERA

Beetles have been called "armored insects" and "insects with shells" because of the hard shield which is actually their front pair of wings. Their scientific name, Coleoptera, means "sheath wings" in Greek.

Florida is full of beetles of all shapes and sizes. There is the massive ox beetle, whose flight bores through the hot, heavy summer twilight in great droning loops. At the other extreme there is the tiny saw-toothed grain beetle, which may be seen desperately dog-paddling through the milk in a bowl of cornflakes taken from an old box in the back of the cupboard. Almost 5,000 species of beetles have been identified in Florida, but nobody pretends that this list is nearly complete.

One reason for the success of beetles is the wide range of food they can eat. Among the beetles there are predators, scavengers, and an enormous number of species that feed on plants. Not only do beetles eat just about everything, but many species have found specialized and highly efficient ways of making a living, so it sometimes seems as if there is a special beetle species for every possible situation. There is, for example, a beetle in Florida that feeds only on the larvae of flies that live on the dung that occurs in the bottom of the burrows of gopher tortoises. There is a beetle in Florida that feeds only on the inner bark of dying stems of mistletoe up in the tops of trees. This degree of specialization helps to explain why there are so many different kinds of beetles: the general professions, such as scavenging dung or eating the inner bark of plants, have been divided into hundreds of microprofessions.

The second key to the success of beetles is the adaptation of the forewings as a pair of shields that can close tightly, their edges (in most beetles) snapping together in a tongue-and-groove seam, to protect the hind wings. When a beetle wants to take flight, it opens and raises the front wings to reveal the precisely packaged hind wings, which expand outward. Certain support struts snap into place. A set of joints make contact. The powerful flight muscles are engaged, and yank each wing base down on a fulcrum. Suddenly the trundling ground vehicle darts off into the sky, like the fantasy vehicle of a super-spy.

The value of this triumph of aeronautical engineering cannot be overestimated. It has allowed beetles to diversify and specialize. They can dig through the rich mucky depths of composting vegetation, or burrow in abrasive sandy soil, or bore in the resin-oozing bark of dying trees, or even plunge to the bottom of a pond. Their weapon-proof vests securely buckled, they can confidently tread the dark, predator-filled alleyways down in the leaf litter. All

***Top:* this photo of a green June beetle shows how the front wings come together in a perfectly straight line down the back. This makes it quite easy for the naturalist to identify a member of this order.**

***Below:* the tough wing covers of this blister beetle are open for flight and the delicate lower wings are almost unfolded.**

PC

this they can do, while still maintaining the option of fleeing or dispersing through the air on thin, easily damaged, membranous wings.

This talent for survival in nasty but rewarding habitats also explains why it is not very obvious that Florida has a huge number of beetles. Most species remain hidden most of their lives, and spend no time casually flitting about, like flies, butterflies, or wasps, whose adults are specialized as flying machines. The larvae and pupae of beetles (Coleoptera have complete metamorphosis) are even more likely to live hidden from our view, with some exceptions, such as the ladybeetles.

Tiger Beetles

Family Cicindelidae

These voracious beetles run rapidly over open ground, seizing and devouring small insects. They might better have been named for the cheetah than the skulking tiger. Unlike most beetles, tiger beetles can take instant flight when alarmed.

Larval tiger beetles, in contrast to the adults, are sedentary creatures, but they are equally fierce. The larvae live in open burrows in the sand or soil, waiting for pedestrians. Their head and thorax are flattened, like a man-hole cover with jaws.

For all their verve, some species of tiger beetles are vulnerable, because they tend to be restricted to very specific types of habitat. Several of Florida's two dozen species of tiger beetles are rare, and their natural habitats are dwindling.

BK

BK

PC

Top, right: **The long legs of this tiger beetle keep it above the hot sands.**

Above: **a tiger beetle with cricket prey.**

Right: **the face of a green tiger beetle.**

CONSERVATION OF FLORIDA'S VERY SMALL WILDLIFE

The plight of rare Florida tiger beetles is not about to make headlines. Tiger beetles may be handsome when seen close up, but they are small, and they are insects. Most people would consider that an insect conservationist must be deranged. Insects occur everywhere, often in excess. Next to members of our own species, they are our most formidable competitors.

Nonetheless, there is reason to get serious about insect conservation. We are constantly fighting weeds, but this does not mean that there are no legitimately endangered plants. Likewise, there are endangered insects, even though the struggle against insect pests never ends. Habitat destruction and invasive exotics which endanger certain plants, birds, and mammals, also endanger many species of insects.

There are rational reasons to worry about the extinction of these very small wildlife species. Even rare species may have ecological importance. A rare insect might be the pollinator of a rare plant. A cave crayfish that lives in only one cave system in Alachua County might be the lynchpin of that entire cave ecosystem. There is a whole set of species found only in Florida scrub habitat that appear to have major roles as herbivores, predators, and decomposers in that rare community.

Some rare insects may even have commercially valuable qualities. The exploration of the chemicals that occur in nature is just beginning, but it is already obvious that arthropods are leaders in innovative chemistry, with all kinds of original compounds used for defense, and the ability to detoxify the strongest poisons. Insects such as fungus-growing ants and ambrosia beetles produce chemicals that promote the growth of fungi, while other species have fungicidal compounds. Even bloodsucking species manufacture anesthetics and anticoagulants.

Florida wildlife conservation should not depend entirely on the useful qualities that we see in wildlife. Conservation should also be an altruistic act for the benefit of future generations. It is hard to predict how future generations will view the fantastic diversity of native invertebrates, but there seems to be a trend of increasing sophistication and awareness in appreciation of native species. Not long ago, hawks and owls were considered vermin, and wood warblers were of interest to only a small number of specialists. In the future, the freckled face of a rare Florida scrub grasshopper, or the flashing passage of a Florida purple skimmer dragonfly may seem just as exciting as the Florida scrub-jay or the Cape Sable seaside sparrow. Extinction of small creatures is just as irrevocable as extinction of large creatures. A species of grasshopper or dragonfly may represent as many hundred millennia of evolution as a species of mammal or bird.

Fortunately, it is not usually necessary to set up special preserves specifically dedicated to a species of grasshopper, tiger beetle, or some other little critter. Rare species tend to be concentrated in rare habitats, which can be preserved and managed as a whole, not species by species. The recognition that Florida has many species of very small, rare wildlife does not complicate conservation efforts, rather, it validates and adds more urgency to conservation programs already in progress.

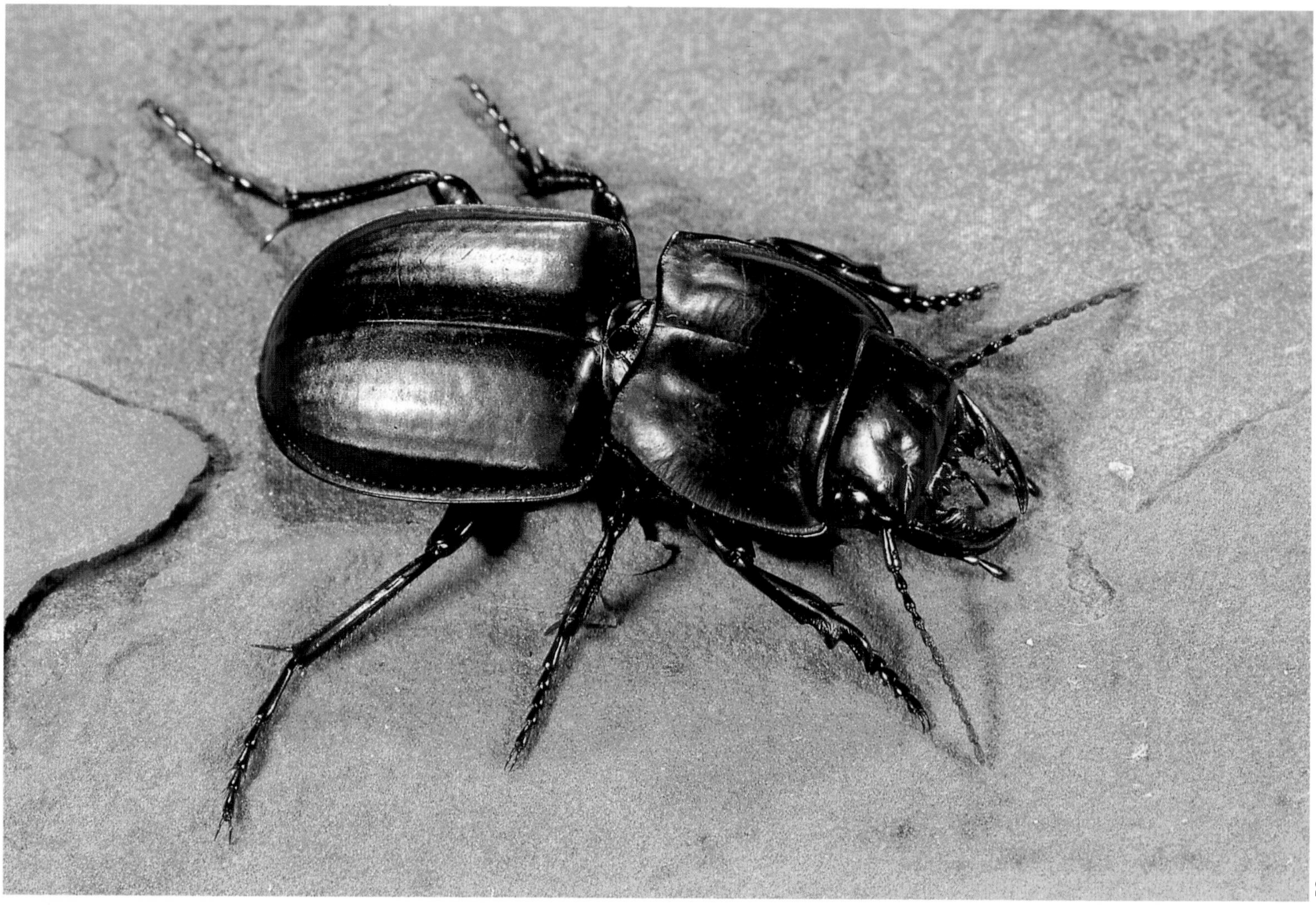

PC

Ground Beetles

Family Carabidae

Ground beetles are a huge, diverse group, with about 370 species found in Florida. Several of these live only in Florida. Most ground beetles are predators both as adults and larvae, and as their name implies, they tend to live in the litter on the ground, making that habitat terribly dangerous for the small and unwary. With their speed and agility, and their great, curved, slashing jaws, the ground beetles fill the role of Velociraptors in the Jurassic Parks of the soil. They occur in all terrestrial habitats, and range in size from puny but fierce species an eighth of an inch long, to the mighty caterpillar hunter, more than an inch long, whose handsome green uniform somehow remains unsullied during remarkably gory dinners of chopped caterpillar.

Top: **this large ground beetle can run and burrow rapidly, but cannot fly, as the front wings are fused together into a rigid shell.**

Below, left: **like some kitchen gadget sold on TV, the multi-purpose jaws of this ground beetle can pierce, chop, slice, and grind. Between and below the jaws can be seen feeler-like structures used for tasting and handling food.**

Below, right: **the caterpillar hunter beetle, also known as the fiery searcher.**

PC

DL

VU/EISNER

Top: **big jaws are not enough. For a ground beetle there is always an enemy with even bigger jaws, perhaps another beetle, a bird, or a mouse. Ground beetles have a second line of defense, repellent chemicals. Only a fraction of these weapons produced by beetle chemists have been studied. The most remarkable defense found to date among Florida ground beetles is that of the bombardier beetle. Within the abdomen of this beetle is a thick-walled reaction chamber, into which can be poured from separate ducts a set of chemicals which combine in a small explosion. From the rear of the bombardier beetle shoots a spray of corrosive chemicals, heated to the boiling point. Compared to the bombardier beetle, the skunk is an amateur. The reaction shown above was triggered in a lab by touching the insect's leg with a pair of forceps.**

Right: **a photo of an exceptionally beautiful caterpillar hunter beetle.**

PC

A FONDNESS FOR BEETLES...

It is widely believed that there are far more kinds of life on earth than have been discovered and named. There are approximately 1.4 million named species of plants and animals at present. Of these, nearly one quarter are beetles. Estimates of the actual number of species on earth, including those known and those not yet discovered, range from four to ten million. It is expected that only small increases will occur in the number of birds (9,000) or mammals (4,000), both of which are highly visible. Most of the increases will come from the insects. Of the undiscovered insect species, the proportion of beetles might be even higher than one quarter because beetles are not so obvious.

In the previous several centuries, it was considered appropriate for scientists to draw conclusions about the nature of God and the superior ranking of mankind from new discoveries showing the awesome diversity of the natural world. This type of thinking was called "natural theology." A well-publicized quote on this topic comes from British biologist, J.B.S. Haldane. When asked, supposedly by a stuffy theologian, what he would conclude about the nature of the Creator from studying his creation, he is said to have replied, "An inordinate fondness for beetles."

Above: some species of scarab beetles, known as dung beetles, gather manure and roll it into a ball to be buried elsewhere. Females and males work as a team in some species. Eggs are deposited inside this ball. When the beetle larvae hatch from the eggs, the soft inner part of the ball will supply their food needs. The flies, however, are also an enterprising group, and there are tiny flies that hitch a ride on scarabs and lay their eggs on the ball of dung after it has been buried in the ground as food for the scarab larva.

Below: the larva of a Florida scarab beetle.

Scarab Beetles (Dung Beetles)

Family Scarabaeidae

This is a large group of beetles (about 250 species in Florida) that have made it big in the scavenging business. These beetles can find filth while you are still looking up "Sanitation Engineers" in the yellow pages. Scarabs that live in dung, carrion, or decomposing plants need large, sensitive antennae to find these substances, especially since many species are rather particular about the kind of material they consume. There are, for example, three species of scarabs that feed only on the dung of the gopher tortoise.

Large, sensitive antennae could get in the way or be damaged while the beetle is burrowing through its favorite substance. Early in the evolution of the scarab group an adaptation appeared that solved this problem: each antenna has a terminal knob composed of a series of plates that can spread like the pages of a book to expose their large sensory surfaces to the air, or close into a compact ovoid when the scarab is digging. The front legs are usually flattened, with teeth and blades for excavating.

There are plenty of nutrients remaining in the dung and other substances upon which these beetles feed, and various insects scramble for these goodies. Flies are particularly strong competitors because their larvae feed and grow with phenomenal speed. Many scarabs, therefore, have evolved ways of removing and storing the resources they need. Most notable is the dung-rolling behavior described in the caption above.

A big contingent of the scarab beetles are not scavengers, but feed on roots as larvae, and the adults of most of these species feed on leaves or flowers. The June beetles (also known as May beetles) are good examples. Some scarab beetle larvae live in rotten wood, or in fungi. As with any other big group of beetles, there are a large number of species whose habits are still a mystery. So many beetles, so few beetle-watchers!

BK

BK

Above: **this male green dung beetle sports a huge horn on his head and sharp points on his thorax. These weapons may make him king of the dung-pile in contests with other males. The fights are less for food than for access to females (which are unarmed). The horns of beetles do not stab or tear like deer antlers; they punch and pry, or they can clamp onto a rival and hurl it away. In this species and some others, some males have much bigger horns than others. It may be that in some species, smaller, more agile beetles can sometimes run away with a female, while the more heavily armed, but cumbersome giants, duke it out.**

Left: **burrowing insects such as this scarab often have hard, shiny bodies that resist abrasion and shed dirt easily. The legs of burrowers usually have strong, tooth-shaped spines for digging.**

THE SACRED EGYPTIAN BEETLE

To the ancient Egyptians, the scarab beetle represented the sun god, Khopri, and was a symbol of eternal life. Carved images of scarabs were placed on the bodies of the deceased in the belief that this would exempt the deceased from punishment for sins committed on earth when the mortal stood for judgment before Osiris, the Egyptian god of the underworld. Sometimes the heart of the corpse was removed and replaced with a scarab carving, along with the words "Oh my heart, rise not up against me as witness." Even today, scarab carvings are popular with tourists visiting Egypt and are kept as good luck charms. Historically, they have been carved from a variety of stones such as jade, malachite, obsidian, and black steatite, but when precious stones are used, it is usually the green emerald that is chosen. To the Egyptians, the projections from the beetle's head represented the rays of the sun. There are five terminal segments on each of six legs, a total of thirty, which matched the Egyptian 30-day calendar. The ball of dung which the beetle rolls represented the earth.

BK

Top: June bugs, also known as May beetles, spend their adult lives feeding on leaves and flowers. The green June beetle, shown here, buzzes about in the evening, looking for flowers and soft fruits. The larva lives underground, feeding on roots. Larvae of this scarab, and some other Florida scarabs, when forced up by flooding, crawl about quickly on their backs without using their legs, a strange sight.

PC

Left: a male Hercules beetle, Florida's largest beetle. Larvae are found in rotting wood, often in cavities in oaks. Males fight over such breeding places, attempting to seize and evict each other using their clamp-like horns.

Right: one of the most noticeable of the Florida scavenging scarabs is the huge, handsome, ox beetle. This beetle digs a vertical shaft about eight inches deep. At the bottom of this shaft is a large chamber packed with dead oak leaves. A single egg is laid on the mass of composting leaves. The male and female often work together on this project. The great amount of effort that goes into providing for each offspring is typical of the scavenging scarabs. These scarabs lay a relatively small number of eggs, but each offspring has a good chance of success because it is tucked away with a private store of all the food it will need to grow to adulthood.

PC

This page shows several Florida flower scarabs. They visit flowers to feed on nectar and pollen, and gnaw on the inner parts of the flower. These beetles are hairy underneath, and thus transfer pollen from one flower to another. A few Florida plants, such as pawpaw, depend on beetles as pollinators.

Above: **an iridescent green flower scarab beetle feeding on saw palmetto flowers.**

Left: **this flower scarab beetle is called the "D" beetle because of the delta-shaped mark on its back. Here it is resting on a zinnia.**

Below: a red-brown flower scarab.

PC

ONLY IN FLORIDA

There are many scarab beetles and other insects that are found only in Florida and nowhere else in the world. About 500 such insects have been listed to date. This number will probably double when more exploratory naturalists turn their attention to Florida.

One reason for this is that much of the land of Florida has remained relatively unchanged for a very long time. Since the state is southern, and its climate is moderated by the sea on both sides, it was less severely affected by the huge climatic shifts from warm to cold and back during the successive ice ages of the last few hundred thousand years. Some species have been able to hang on in Florida that have been eradicated elsewhere.

A second reason why Florida has so many of its own species is that it is an isolated area of warm climate with many unusual habitats, such as scrub and subtropical pine flatwoods. These special habitats have some of their own animals and plants. Some of Florida's swamps, forests, and isolated upland ridges are so old that they have some of their own species, found nowhere else, not even in other parts of Florida.

There is a persistent tendency to think of Florida as a young state, partly because it is growing and changing at such a staggering rate. Moreover, Florida is flat, and there is a subtle temptation to equate age with a high degree of topography: the everlasting hills, the eternal mountains. Groups of insects, however, may be older than any topographic feature. The scarabs and most other families of insects were old at the up-folding of the Rocky Mountains. Life is an ancient tapestry cast over the earth, a tapestry whose form and color shifts as the earth moves restlessly underneath over many millions of years. In this sense, neither Florida nor its native plants and animals are young. Only the landscape of cultivation and concrete is new.

PC

Above: **this large, horned scarab is one of the many handsome species of beetles that live in rotten logs. A rotten log in the forest, or even in the back yard, is a dynamic community, including many kinds of insects and fungi. Different species of trees can have distinctive communities, so a decaying pine has different insects than a decaying oak. The community in a dead tree changes over time, beginning with aggressive scavengers, such as bark beetles and longhorn beetles, and proceeding to rotten wood species such as some scarabs. As the wood softens, it becomes home to small vertebrates, such as lizards, toads, and mice. In much of Florida, rotten wood has always been in short suppy because of frequent fires, so most rotten wood is found in wet areas that do not burn frequently.**

USELESS ZAPPERS

Nothing is as useless as a useful thing misplaced. Insect zappers electrocute flying insects that are attracted to an ultraviolet light, and are useful in an enclosed space where there is a low tolerance for insects, such as a closed milking barn. Placed in a Florida yard, these contrivances are useful only for separating rich and gullible consumers from their money. From the day these traps were invented, unscrupulous advertisers have used them to attract and zap dollars, especially those of people pestered by biting flies.

In the North, where blackflies are a serious problem, there have been claims that these traps kill blackflies (which do not even fly at night), a perfectly valid promise if the blackflies are seized between the forefinger and thumb and tossed against the screen.

In Florida, where mosquitos are the main problem, insect zappers are sold to kill mosquitos in the yard, but the only way to produce the desired effect is to have the customer sit with the trap in his lap, since mosquitos are far more attracted to the carbon dioxide and other compounds exhaled by humans than they are to ultraviolet light. Most of the worst mosquito outbreaks in Florida are the result of heavy rains that fill depressions and ditches that were previously dry and therefore lack the fish and insect predators that feed on mosquito larvae. These seasonally wet places are quickly colonized by aquatic beetles that fly in and lay eggs that turn into ferocious predatory larvae. Although these larvae may not develop in time to affect the first generation of mosquitos after a rain, they control subsequent generations, which is why these mosquito outbreaks are not very persistent. These beetles are powerfully attracted to ultraviolet lights, and killed in huge numbers. It is unlikely that a homeowner would notice an actual increase in mosquito numbers after installing an insect zapper, but the fact remains that these lights benefit mosquitos, even though this benefit would be hard to measure.

The promises with respect to reducing the number of agricultural pests are similar. The claim is seldom made that these light traps actually reduce the damage caused by lawn and garden pests; the claim is that these pests are attracted, often from some distance away, and killed. Studies of the insects killed by zappers in suburban Delaware show a gigantic majority of harmless or beneficial insects are killed, and a tiny number of pests. It is like reducing the number of shoplifters by shooting everybody exiting a mall: one would, in fact, get a few shoplifters, but probably just as many security guards leaving work, and everybody else would be the merchants, workers, and shoppers who keep the mall system going. It is significant that a nighttime drive through the Florida countryside does not show a landscape of groves and fields lit by the glow of zappers. Farmers, who struggle constantly with insect pests, approach insect control with a business sense and common sense foreign to many suburbanites.

Click Beetles

Family Elateridae

These beetles are easy to recognize. Their remarkable clicking behavior make them a favorite with children and adults whose delight in natural oddities has not been replaced by other preoccupations. The clicking behavior is best demonstrated by placing a click beetle on its back, whereupon it usually produces a snap that flips it into the air. The principle advantage to this behavior is not in flipping the beetle over if it is on its back, but in startling predators, or even snapping the beetle right out of the clutches of an enemy.

The front section of the thorax is attached to the rest of the body with a kind of hinge, below which is a projection from the front section of the thorax which fits into a corresponding cavity on the rest of the body. The projection is kept from sliding into this cavity by a catch mechanism. After building up muscular pressure, the beetle releases the catch, and the projection slams back into the cavity with a powerful (and audible) snap whose force is transmitted to the rest of the body in such a way that the whole body jumps. In this ingenious way, the click beetle is able to jump while still keeping all the legs and antennae folded tightly against the body where they cannot be seized by an enemy.

The eyed click beetles are very large species that are not particularly common, but they always attract attention when they appear, because of their size and the big eye-spots outlined on the thorax with white hairs. These are supposed to startle or deter predators. Far more abundant in Florida are the green-eyed click beetles, which also have a pair of eye-spots on the thorax, but these can be lit up at night. Perhaps they use these lights to find each other, or perhaps they signal that these beetles are inedible, or both. The pupae of these beetles also glow, a highly unusual characteristic that is usually associated with chemically-protected insects. It is surprising that the light display of such abundant and conspicuous insects remains so poorly understood.

The larvae of click beetles, called wireworms, are yellowish-brown and cylindrical, looking rather like the mealworms sold in pet stores. The larvae of some species, such as the eyed click beetle, are predatory. Others, including some agricultural pests, feed on roots. Little is known about the feeding habits of adult click beetles.

Top: an eyed click beetle. The larva lives under bark of dead broad-leaf trees, such as oaks. The "eyes" do not glow at night.

Center: most click beetles are dark-colored and only active at night.

Above: this photo shows the hinging on the body at the clicking joint. In addition to making the click, the hinge can nip the toes or antennae of a spider or predatory insect.

Metallic Woodborer Beetles

Family Buprestidae

Adult metallic wood-borers often sport green or coppery metallic colors, perhaps as a warning that they contain unpalatable chemicals. This is another group of beetles whose larvae feed on dead wood. They seem fussy about the condition of the wood, feeding only in very recently killed trees, twigs, or branches, avoiding wood that has begun to rot. Some species are like overeager vegetarian vultures, finding and attacking weakened twigs and branches that are not quite dead. A couple of Florida species have a special technique for finding recently killed trees: they are attracted to the heat of forest fires, and begin laying eggs on fire-killed trees while the trees are still smoldering. About 20 of the roughly 100 metallic woodborers that live in Florida are leaf miners; these are small beetles whose flat larvae live sandwiched between the upper and lower layers of a leaf. The larvae of one species that lives in turkey oak leaves often make, for reasons known only to themselves, loud ticking sounds.

Right: **this species is well camouflaged on bark, but if disturbed, displays a bright, metallic-green abdomen as it flies away.**

PC

MIMICRY IN FLORIDA INSECTS

A quick survey of Florida insects would lead one to suspect the existence of an obscure piece of legislation called the "Florida Pure Food and Bug Act," requiring that poisonous or stinging insects be provided with brightly-colored warning labels. The beneficiaries of this regulation would be all the beautiful, little, insect-eating birds or, from an insect point of view, all the vicious and greedy little feathered dinosaurs. In actuality, both insects and birds benefit from the warning labels. The birds avoid stomach aches and stung tongues, and the insects avoid the trauma of being gulped down and thrown up, an experience that is likely to be injurious, if not fatal. Since both parties benefit strongly, no regulation was actually required to establish the warning system, it developed on its own. The most distinctively marked and conspicuous individuals of noxious insect species were most easily recognized and avoided by birds.

Birds find it easier to learn a few warning label patterns rather than many. For this reason, unrelated groups of insects often ended up with the same warning pattern, black with yellow bands, for example. In this form of mimicry, a whole set of nasty insects have come to resemble each other. Unfortunately for the birds, there is no truth in advertizing legislation, and many species of wimpy, tasty insects have evolved strong resemblances to well-defended insects. This is also a form of mimicry. A batch of insects that have a similar warning appearance is called a "mimetic complex." Such a complex can be all legitimate advertisers, or it can be legitimate species with some phonies thrown in. All of the really large mimetic complexes in Florida include some phonies, although it is not always clear which are which.

Mimetic complexes in Florida have not received much study. They have not been named or cataloged, the defenses of their members have not been verified or proven false. Nobody has really analyzed which warning displays work best, or which birds are wise to which phonies. Nobody has looked at the way some insect species belong to one mimetic complex in Florida, and another complex to the north. All this is worth mentioning because many people, especially young people, seem to have the impression that all the coolest projects have already been done, or are being done. The fact is, biologists are always ready to talk about the fascinating work they are doing or have done, but they are naturally less inclined to showcase their ignorance of areas where there is even more fascinating work to be done. Mimetic complexes have it all. Poisoned daggers, deadly potions, lies and half-lies, outrageous costumes, pursuit and escape, death in a thousand forms—why bother with the feeble imitations sold as video games when the real thing lurks in the nearest patch of brush?

A few of the large mimetic complexes are familiar to most Florida naturalists. The black and yellow species that have yellow bands on a black abdomen are stinging insects, or pretending to be stinging insects. The stinging species, which are bees and wasps, tend to spend time on flowers, where they feed, or gather pollen and nectar for their young, in the case of bees. Many other insects that feed on flowers have evolved color patterns resembling those of bees and wasps. In some cases these are general warning color patterns, in others they are close replicas of the warning coloration of a local species of bee or wasp.

Soldier Beetles

Family Cantharidae

The soldier beetles are soft-bodied beetles and usually patterned in black and orange, indicating that they are probably toxic. They are somewhat similar to fireflies, but the head sticks out more from under the thorax. Several species feed and mate on flowers. The soldier beetles derive their family name from a red British species, which reminded people of the old Redcoat uniform. A bluish-black species was called the sailor beetle, again for the uniform, but this name did not manage to cross the Atlantic. About 30 species of soldier beetles are found in Florida.

***Right:* many soldier beetles feed on nectar and pollen. This common Florida species has a long face and an extendible tongue for reaching into flowers. The sexes frequently meet on flowers. This species often mates for an hour or so at a time: this might be a way for a male to prevent other males from having a chance with his mate. Members of this genus produce a powerful chemical defense, acetylenic acid, from nine pairs of glands on the back, visible as pale brown spots just below the wing covers in this photo.**

Net-Winged Beetles

Family Lycidae

These slow-flying, soft-winged beetles have orange and black patterns to warn that they are inedible, due to poisonous alkaloid chemicals.

It is not only birds that avoid these beetles. A net-winged beetle that gets trapped in a spider web does not struggle, but waits passively as the spider rushes to attack. Upon touching the beetle, the spider instanly recognizes it as toxic, and carefully cuts the strands holding the beetle. The beetle falls to the ground, wipes off any encumbering spider silk, and takes off again.

Adults of some Florida species congregate on flowers, especially saw palmetto. About 30 species are found in Florida.

***Left:* this species is the largest net-winged beetle in the eastern US. Compare its color pattern with that of the completely unrelated milkweed bug on page 52. Both species are protected by toxic chemicals, but while the milkweed bug stores poisons from its host plant, the net-winged beetle probably makes its own.**

LL

Top: **a short time exposure reveals the flashing patterns of *Photuris* fireflies over a grassy field at dusk.**

Opposite page, top: **a *Lucidota* firefly. This is a day-flying species with a flightless female.**

Fireflies

Family Lampyridae

Fireflies, also called lightning bugs, are neither bugs nor flies, but are actually beetles. They are well known for their ability to emit light, a process called bioluminescence. Florida has 57 species, of which 17 are found only in Florida. Some species are rare and others are difficult to find because they do not light up the night like some of their relatives.

Where to Find. Adult fireflies are commonly seen flying along forest edges at ground and treetop levels, depending upon the species and the time of night. They are also common at creek bridges and over marshes, meadows, lawns, and vacant lots. The most dense firefly concentrations in the US are found along a line from Florida's Big Bend to Georgia's Okefenokee Swamp.

The Light in the Night. Fireflies, flashing their sharp messages through the soft spring twilight, must have seemed like supernatural creatures to our forefathers, as they stood in a cabin doorway, cupping a smoking candle against the evening breeze. Unlike most other light sources, the light of fireflies is truly without heat. No heat can be detected, even with sensitive instruments, and even when the chemicals are concentrated a thousand times. Although the process is called "cold light," it is not cold; it just does not produce heat.

Unveiling the secret of the cold light of fireflies was an early goal of biochemists in the 1800s, and it was a disappointment that they could not find a cheap way to reproduce this luminescence.

It was discovered that the light-producing compound of fireflies emits its glow only in the presence a certain crucial, energy-storing chemical. This chemical is also needed for the movement of muscles. The firefly compound can be used to test for the presence of this chemical, making it valuable to medical researchers.

Flashing Codes. Light flashes allow fireflies to find mates and for this reason have been called "love lights." The females come out of their burrows at dusk and remain near the ground in grassy areas. For most species, the males fly overhead, flashing their lights. When a female answers with her own flash, the male lands nearby and mates with her. The color, pattern, and timing of the flashes all have meaning. A number of new species of fireflies have been discovered on the bases of their own recognition codes, including species in Florida, a state that is fortunate enough to have its own firefly expert, Dr. James Lloyd of the University of Florida.

The light-born messages of fireflies have an advantage over the perfume-wafting calling-systems of most insects because it is easy to pinpoint the sender, and the messages go out at the speed of light. The disadvantage is that it works only over a short distance in line of sight, and makes the flashing insect very noticeable to predators. Fireflies can risk their conspicuous displays because most species have toxic chemicals that make them inedible to most predators; indeed, the flash serves double duty as a warning signal to bats or nocturnal birds that eat night-flying beetles.

Firefly flashing patterns vary considerably with the species with respect to color and timing. There are two general patterns common to North Amercian fireflies. In the first, glowing females attract males who have no lights, and then mate with them. In the second system, the one used by most fireflies, females identify males of their own species by the male's flashing pattern and then answer with their own unique flashes.

WHERE HAVE ALL THE FIREFLIES GONE?

Many people recall that fireflies seemed more plentiful in their youth. So, have firefly populations really declined? This is the widespread belief, although it is not yet documented by long-term ecological studies. There are several possible reasons. First, fireflies are particularly vulnerable to loss of habitat because many species require very specific habitats such as wetlands, forests, and old fields. Development of these areas leaves these species with no place to go. Second, many species are site-specific in their breeding. This means that local populations return to the exact same spot each year to search for mates. When such a spot is developed, they are unable to move their reproductive activities elsewhere. Third, in suburbs, soils are often structurally disturbed in the effort to create lawns (monocultures of grass). This makes these areas less suitable for earthworms and other prey of firefly larvae. Fourth, pesticides, herbicides, and other contaminants in the water, air, and soil no doubt kill many fireflies. Fifth, light pollution from street and yard lights make it more difficult for fireflies to find each other in the dark and thus reproduce.

Finally, the extraction of water from deep wells has lowered ground water in parts of Florida, drying up the moist areas that many fireflies need.

ABS

THE COMMERCIAL HARVESTING OF FIREFLIES

About 30 years ago, Sigma Chemical Company of St.Louis, Missouri began harvesting live fireflies as a source of luciferase (the enzyme produced by fireflies and other luminescent creatures). Amateur collectors were paid a penny for each firefly captured and delivered. After processing, the luciferase powder is sold for more than $40 per milligram. Millions of fireflies were collected. This probably did nothing to harm the common species, but since collectors netted anything that was flashing, many rare species may have been pushed closer to extinction. Fortunately, luciferase can now be produced in the laboratory in an even purer form, so it is no longer necessary to collect fireflies from the wild to satisfy the needs of scientific research. However, the live harvest has not yet stopped.

FIREFLY POETRY

Fireflies have inspired more than their share of poetry, mostly the doggerel of romantics. Still, it is an indication of the great interest in these small creatures when humans take the time to compose works like the following:

The firefly appears so brilliant,
But, in fact, has lost his mind,
He stumbles through existence,
With his headlight on behind.
Anonymous

JOIN THE FIREFLYERS

An interesting newsletter about fireflies, edited by Dr. J. E. Lloyd, is available for free. To subscribe, simply write to Fireflies, Department of Entomology, Bldg. 970, Hull Road, Univeristy of Florida, Gainesville, FL 32611.

IDENTIFYING FIREFLIES BY THEIR FLASH PATTERNS

Male fireflies can be identified at a distance by the flash patterns they emit, however, it takes some practice and errors are easily made for several reasons. Flash colors can be deceiving depending on the other lights in the area, such as sunset glow and street lights. The flash cues that fireflies use make use of signals which are quite subtle for human eyes, so they are easily confused. Humans are subject to optical illusions. To us, a short flash by a fast firefly may seem the same as a long flash by a slow flyer. Also, males of some species mimic the males of other species. Sometimes the color of a flash is the only clue, and the color of a firefly flash may be very difficult to judge accurately.

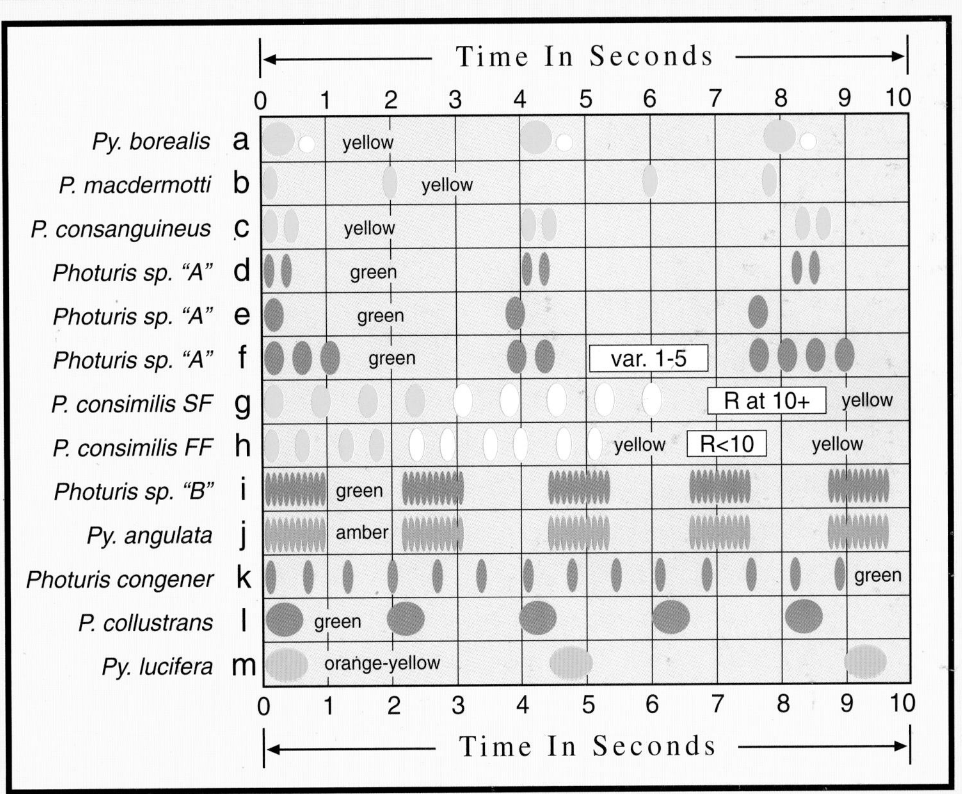

Horizontal axis=time, vertical axis= "intensity"; R=repeat time for flash pattern shown; open flashes indicate optional flashes in male patterns.

DANGER TO COURTING MALES

The insect world is full of strange intrigues. The females of some fireflies mimic the flashes of other species, pretending to be propective mates for the amorous males. The females then answer the flashes of these males by simulating the appropriate "love lights" and then devour them when they approach, all but their toes, eyes, wings, and a few other hard parts. These females, of course, will only mate with males of their own species.

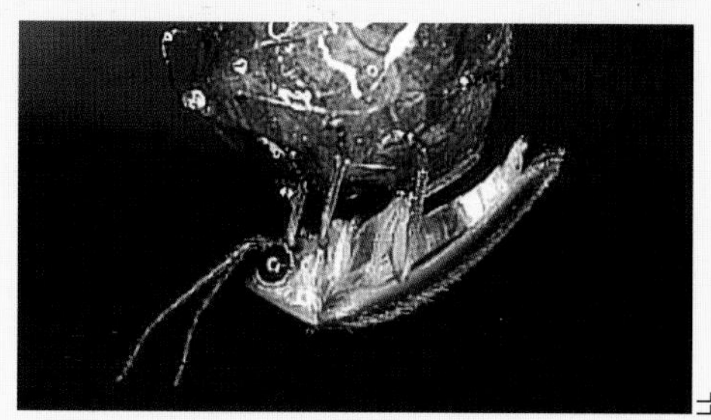

THE MALE FIREFLY MUST BE THE CORRECT SPECIES

A female Photuris *firefly hangs on a sticky ball with a light inside. This ball was an aerial target in an experiment to show that females will attack any lights in the air which do not flash the proper codes showing that they are suitable mates of the same species.*

Opposite page: **a *Photuris* firefly with a trio of pseudoscorpions hitching a ride. These distant relatives of spiders and scorpions sometimes clamp their powerful claws onto a winged insect for free aerial transport to new habitats.**

OTHER GLOWING INSECTS

There are other insects that emit light, such as a few fungus gnats, springtails, click beetles, and giant glowworms, but these are relatively uncommon and seldom seen. One luminescent springtail, three luminescent click beetles, and some giant glowworms are found in Florida.

FLORIDA'S FIREFLY SPECIES

Florida is rich in fireflies, with over 50 species. The hardwood forests and associated habitats of northern Florida have the most species, drawn mostly from Appalachia. In South Florida, there are some interesting West Indian species. On the dry upland ridges of Florida, there are fewer fireflies, but at least a couple of these live only in Florida. When it comes to fireflies, Florida has many more species than the Western states. Even California, which has the greatest variety of natural habitats of any state, has relatively few species of fireflies.

FIREFLIES AND SNOW

This is a famous Japanese expression for hard work and diligent study. In the old days, supposedly, hard-working students continued their studies even after the sun had set, using light reflected on the snow and also the light of fireflies collected in bottles.

FIREFLY LARVAE

The larvae of fireflies are predatory, and move about looking for small insects and molluscs. These larvae are easily recognized: they are hard-bodied and flat, looking a bit like a caterpillar that had lost a confrontation with a small steamroller. While adult fireflies use their flashes to find mates, the reason that firefly larvae glow is still a mystery.

The glowing larva looks like a tiny alligator with a pair of lights under its tail. Some species crawl along damp roadsides, and especially along wooded lakeshore drives, and around creeks where they search for snails, worms, and other prey.

FLORIDA INSECTS AND FIRE

Florida has a very high rate of lightning strikes. The result of this has been the development of natural habitats maintained in an open condition by fires that sweep through at various intervals. Flatwoods, prairies, and sandhills used to burn every few years, scrub and seasonal wetlands less frequently. The plants and the animals, including insects that live in these habitats are dependent on fires to maintain their world. Without fire, habitats change. They still have plants and animals, but those that are characteristic of fire-dependent habitats mostly disappear. Some of the fire-dependent animals and plants are famous: scrub-jays, red cockaded woodpeckers, gopher tortoises, sand skinks, longleaf pines, and pitcher plants. Others are less widely recognized as fire-dependent species: the Florida population of the hairy woodpecker, the gopher frog, the scrub rock-rose. There are at least a couple of hundred species of plants in Florida that are dependent on fire. Missing from the lists are the species of insects that depend on fire-maintained habitats in Florida. Nobody could guess at this point how many such species of insects may exist. A thousand? Three thousand? A whole bunch.

Now that Florida has been carved up by cities, roads, housing developments, and crop lands, fire no longer moves easily across the landscape, and when fires occur they must often be suppressed before they threaten human interests. People who are in charge of natural areas, whose duty is to preserve and maintain the flora and fauna of those areas, have realized that many of Florida's native species will disappear unless fire is introduced back into the habitats. There is now a concerted attempt to restore natural habitats with fire. This may be disconcerting to the visitor to Florida, and even local news announcers have not quite made the transition from "a hundred acres of pine forest were destroyed by fire today..." to "a hundred acres of pine forest were maintained by fire today...."

The fire restoration effort is one of those programs where people are doing a lot more good than they actually know. Nobody is documenting all the grasshoppers and spiders that are making a comeback. Nobody has noticed that a tiny beetle that feeds on orange shelf fungi that decompose fire-killed twigs has undergone a magnificent population explosion. There is no fanfare for the triumphant return of the elegant cone ant from its little refuges along the open edges of the fire lanes back into the newly restored sandhills. Unheard, except by their own species, the scrub pygmy mole crickets sing with redoubled strength in the open scrub. Nobody needs to be noticing these things. If one takes care of the habitat, most of the species take care of themselves. Future generations will blame us for all the species around the world that disappeared under our watch, but here is a case where the naturalists of the future can count up all the species we saved, species that we did not have time to enumerate ourselves.

Even while anticiating the renewal that follows a burn, it is difficult to avoid a pang of guilt when one strikes the match. Many of the species of small animals that inhabit the fire-dependent habitats have ways of fleeing from the fire, or burrowing beyond the reach of the heat. Nevertheless, the little caterpillars living in a cluster of blueberry leaves, the gall wasps in their galls on oak twigs–these kinds of small animals are burned up and their populations temporarily reduced. It is, perhaps, most comforting and reasonable to think of fire in Florida as analogous to winter in the northern states. When winter first bites down hard in the North, astronomical numbers of insects die. All these species, however, have winter built into their long-term strategies. Both the insects and the plants of the North are dependent on winter. If the season were eliminated, a host of species would disappear. If winter was removed as a season, and biologists were somehow able to easily restore winter in local natural areas such as state parks, they would not hesitate to do so.

Viewed in this light, fire management of natural habitats in Florida is a positive action. It is important to use some common sense, reproducing as closely as possible the natural season of fires and the natural intervals between fires. Natural fires were often patchy, leaving refuges from which insects and other animals could move back into the burned area. Restoration of fire in the appropriate Florida habitats is one of those rare examples in which humans are able to quickly and rather easily repair a damaged system.

RFS

JHR

Top: a ladybird beetle that has just landed, with its upper wings still slightly open. _Above:_ a ladybird beetle feeding on aphids, which seem disinterested in the fate of their neighbors. Some species of aphids throw themselves from the plant when a predator attacks, but others do not.

Ladybird Beetles

Family Coccinellidae

The ladybird beetles have definitely crashed through the "yuck barrier" often associated with insects, to colonize the Land of Loveable Creatures. As the most acceptable of insects, ladybird beetles look cute on greeting cards, gift wrap, and in all sorts of crafts. This favorable attitude toward ladybird beetles goes way back to the Middle Ages, when ladybugs were associated with the Virgin Mary (Our Lady's Beetles), perhaps because the black-spotted red species symbolize drops of blood or stigmata (marks resembling the crucifixion wounds of Jesus).

There are many traditional rhymes about ladybeetles. Here is the one that most Floridians know:

Ladybird, ladybird, fly away home,
Your house is on fire, your children alone.

There are many variations of this rhyme, which was first published in the 1600s, but must be much older. It has been suggested that the lines originate from the European practice of burning hop vines after harvest to get rid of aphids. The "children" might be the young of ladybeetles, since young ladybeetles cannot fly and would be destroyed along with the aphid pests. The association with aphids may explain some of the very old names for ladybeetles such as lord's herdsman (Italy), and Indra's herdsman (India).

It has also been known for a long time that both adults and larvae of many species feed on sap-sucking aphids and scale insects, and deserve our kind regard for that reason. Special species of ladybird beetles have been imported for control of certain scale insects. There are also some exotic species accidentally imported into Florida, including a strange hairy black species that appears to have two circular bare patches shaved on its back. There is a group of leaf-eating ladybird beetles, including two Florida species: the Mexican bean beetle and the squash beetle.

The bright colors of most ladybird beetles appear to be warning coloration, signaling to predators (primarily birds) that these beetles have toxic blood. Many ladybird beetles have an easily ruptured membrane in their leg joints, allowing them to spontaneously release drops of poisonous, alkaloid-containing blood when molested. This is surely the only case where the animal with the weakest knees presents the strongest defense.

Florida has about 100 species of ladybird beetles, but many are very small and seldom noticed.

TR

BK

Top: a salmon-colored ladybird beetle found throughout Florida. Adults of this species feed on pollen as well as aphids and mealy bugs.

Left: a spotless ladybird beetle feeding on milkweed aphids. These aphids are protected from birds by poisons that affect the avian heart, but do not affect several insect predators. Colonies of aphids not only attract ladybird beetles, but many other predators, so the aphid colonies usually last only a few weeks. This explains the greedy behavior of ladybird larvae; they must eat and grow fast, because the banquet does not last.

RFS

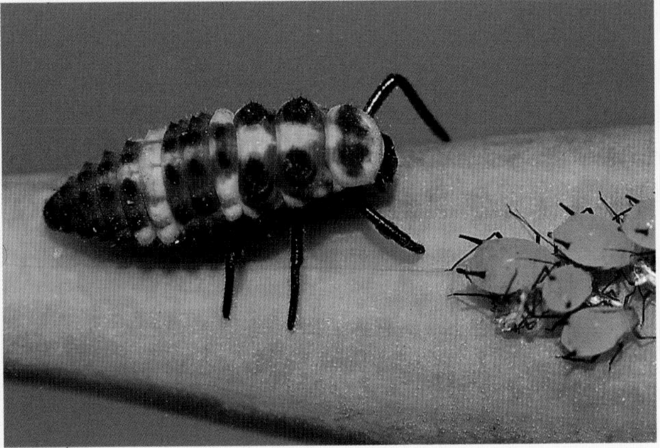

BK

JLC

THE LADYBIRD LIFE CYCLE

The photos above show the eggs, larva, and pupa of the ladybird beetle. Like their parents, ladybird larva feed on aphids, often side by side with the adults.

Although the pupae of most insects are passive and helpless, the pupae of ladybird beetles have an active defense; when the pupa is touched, it rapidly arches and straightens, and the grooves between the abdominal segments spread and close. The edges of these grooves are lined with small, pointed teeth, which can sharply nip the antenna or leg of an investigating insect.

Blister Beetles

Family Meloidae

Blister beetles are soft-bodied, rather clumsy beetles that often occur on flowers, where they feed and wait for mates. They cannot defend themselves by biting effectively, and they are slow in flight. These apparent weaklings, however, have a potent defense in the form of blood mixed with a deadly poison, cantharadin. Even large animals can be affected. Alfalfa hay, especially that grown in the Midwest, occasionally has the dried remains of clusters of blister beetles that were caught up in the haying. The residual poisons can make livestock sick, horses being especially susceptible. Several valuable Florida horses have died from blister beetle poisoning. Even applied to the skin, the blood of blister beetles can be highly irritating, hence the name. Many blister beetles have bright warning coloration, but some common Florida species are surprisingly drab.

The chemical defense of blister beetles is so effective that there is a demand for it among certain poison-resistant insects, which incorporate the poison into their own defenses. It is unclear where most of these cantharadin eaters get their supply normally, although a few species have been seen attacking blister beetles. There is even a record of a bird, a white-breasted nuthatch, wiping the entrance to its nest in a hollow tree with blister beetles, probably to keep out unwanted insects or flying squirrels.

The larvae of most blister beetles feed on the egg clusters of grasshoppers, or on the larvae of solitary bees. About 30 species are found in Florida.

PC

SPANISH FLY

A dried preparation of a European blister beetle was once sold as an aphrodisiac under the famous name Spanish Fly, but its use is now prohibited because of its extreme toxicity. It causes a swelling of the genital tissues which some users equate with sexual arousal. It also causes other ghastly symptoms, including vomiting of blood and kidney failure.

Predaceous Diving Beetles

Family Dytiscidae

Predaceous diving beetles–the name says it all. About 100 species of these streamlined beetles prowl Florida's freshwater habitats, hunting for small insects and crustaceans. Some of the larger species are big enough to eat little fish, but most seek smaller game, such as mosquito larvae. The larvae of predaceous diving beetles are even more voracious than the adults, but do not chew their food with open mouths under water, like their parents. The larvae have sharp, sickle-shaped jaws with internal channels that allow digestive enzymes to be injected and the dissolved tissues to be sucked up,.

Adult diving beetles, like some other beetles, seem to have a long adult life span. Some of the bigger species have been kept in insect zoos for several years. There is no reason to believe that smaller species have shorter lives, but they are seldom kept in captivity, so there are few records.

In Florida, predaceous diving beetles are often older than the bodies of water they inhabit, because many ponds, marshes and ditches have water for only part of the year. Many diving beetles are therefore nomadic, and take to the air the night after a rain to find new aquatic worlds to conquer, rich with newly hatched larvae of mosquitos and other flies. As these beetles fly overhead, they often seem to interpret the roof of a car shining in the moonlight (or streetlight) as a small pond, and they dive down and bounce off. If there is dew on the car, some of the smaller beetles end up trapped in the surface tension of the droplets, where they can be found the next morning. The ability of these migrating beetles to find the smallest pools is shown by the appearance of small diving beetles in birdbaths and the dog's water bowl the day after a rain. These beetles soon recognize their mistake, and take off again.

BK

BK

Above: **a giant diving beetle. These beetles are so smooth and slippery that males of some species have front feet developed into suckers for climbing onto females during mating.**

Left: **the larvae of the predacious diving beetle, sometimes called the water tiger.**

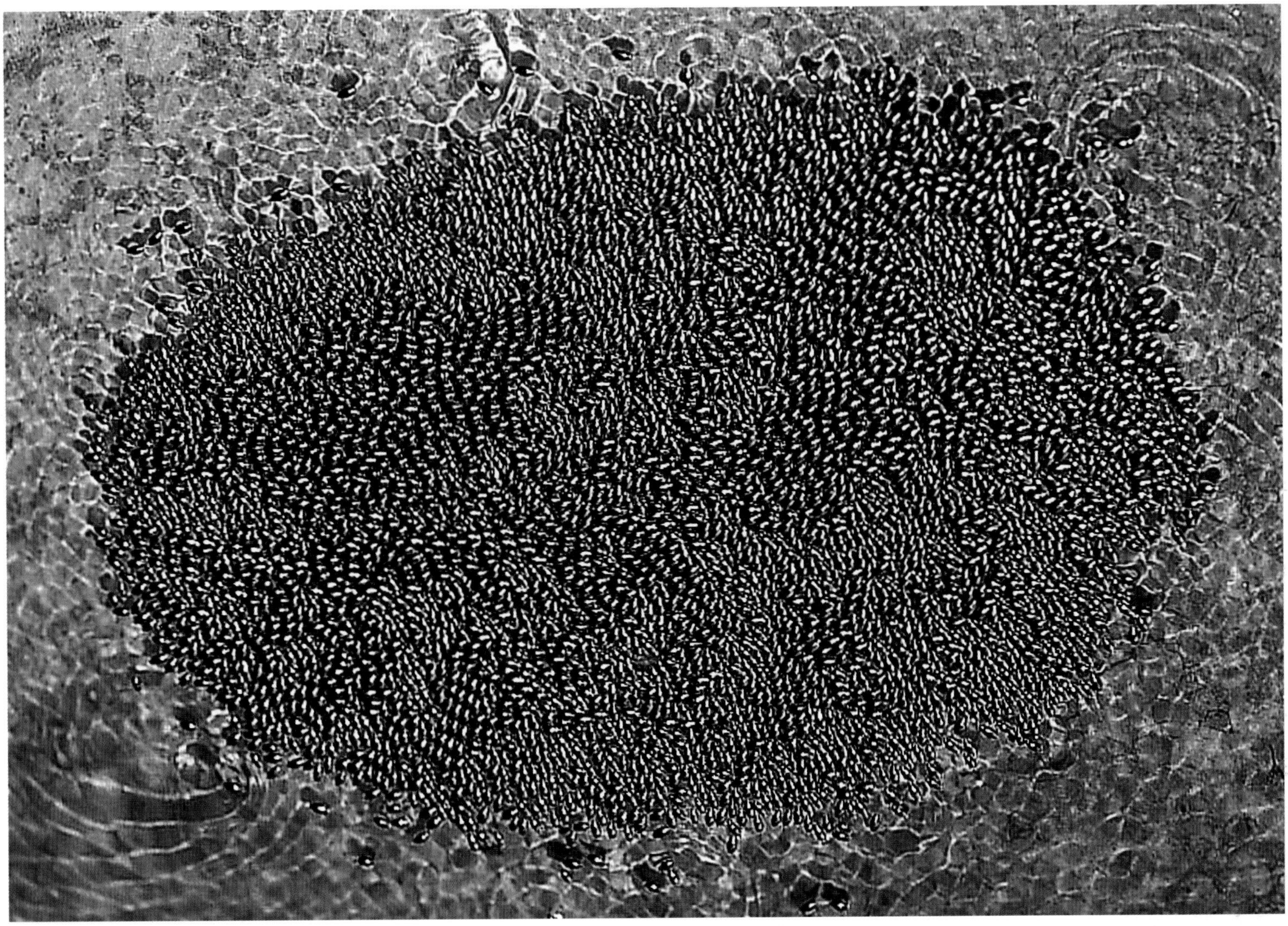

JHR

Whirligig Beetles

Family Gyrinidae

Whirligig beetles, even more than other insects, are delightful to children. Countless children have proven their dexterity by managing to scoop up in their small palms one of the whirligig beetles that gyrate so speedily over the surface of Florida ponds. Held close to the child's eye, the tiny beetle-boat seems to have the metallic sheen of molded tin, and from the beetle there even comes a curious metallic fragrance. All that is lacking is a microscopic wind-up key to power the frantic movements of the paddle-like middle and hind legs. Released into the pond, the surface-swimming beetle turns submarine, and dives to the bottom.

The whirligig beetle is one of the most amphibious of all animals, able to fly through the air and swim underwater equally well, and spending most of its time exactly between air and water, with half its body above, half below the surface. Each eye is divided, with one half looking up into the air, the other half looking down into the water. The antennae are highly developed as ripple and vibration detectors, helping the beetles to locate dead and dying insects caught on the surface of the water. The antennal detectors also help prevent collisions when the whirligigs are zipping about in a dense swarm on the surface. The amphibious nature of whirligig beetles was celebrated by the poet and historian Hillaire Belloc (1870-1953) in one of his nonsense rhymes for children:

The water beetle here shall teach
A sermon far beyond your reach:
He flabbergasts the human race
By gliding on the water's face
With ease, celerity, and grace.
But if he ever stopped to think
Of how he does it, he would sink.
Moral: Don't ask questions

Most Floridians see whirligigs in big groups, because this is how most species spend the day. At night the beetles move out to patrol the water surface for food. The habit of spending the day in groups, which sometimes include more than one species, is probably a defense against predatory fish. More beetles have more eyes to watch for predators, and the hyperactive movements of the mass of beetles when disturbed ought to be confusing to any enemy. In addition, these beetles have defensive chemicals, and a group of a few hundred beetles must pack quite a wallop when they simultaneously release their repellents into the water. Even the components of the chemicals that volatilize into the air are noticeable to canoeists who pass through a swarm of whirligigs.

JHR

Top: **a daytime defensive gathering of whirligig beetles on the water surface. Clustered like iron filings over a magnet, hundreds of whirligigs here form a group that pools repellent chemicals. These groups may form in the same place, day after day. In Florida, aggregations of whirligigs tend to occur in patches of shade.**

Above: **a whirligig beetle underwater.**

During the rainy season in Florida, whirligigs quickly colonize seasonal ponds. Their predatory larvae grow up in the larger, less temporary ponds. Seventeen species of whirligigs are found in Florida.

TR

BK

Leaf Beetles

Family Chrysomelidae

Leaf beetles are very cute, and occur in many different shapes and color patterns. If the people who make refrigerator magnets ever discover these little beetles, the present community of colorful frogs, butterflies, and lady beetles will certainly have competition for decorating the surfaces of kitchen appliances throughout the land. Florida has huge numbers of species, with about 375 leaf beetles listed. The diversity of this group is related to the tendency for each species to be highly specialized, attacking only a few species of closely related plants.

A number of species are pests of Florida crops such as potatoes, tomatoes, peppers, and eggplants. On the other hand, many species help check the populations of Florida weeds (they generally get no credit for this service), and leaf beetles, because of their specialized feeding habits, are often promising prospects for biological control of imported plant pests.

For all their cuteness, leaf beetles are tough little animals. Their bodies are generally well armored, and many species are also protected by toxic chemicals, which explains the bright warning coloration found on such species. There are also behavioral defenses. Many species tuck, drop, and roll from their perch on a plant when disturbed. Others have powerful jumping legs. The blue tortoise beetle, common on palmettos in Florida, is able to grip the palmetto leaf so strongly that an attacking insect is unable to pry it off.

Well-defended animals tend to live longer. Animals that are always in great danger of being devoured by their enemies must grow fast and produce as many young as possible as soon as possible. Animals with a relatively longer life expectancy can spread both their feeding and reproduction over a longer time, and invest more time in raising a smaller number of offspring. There are good examples of this among familiar mammals. The field mouse, which is a favorite snack for many predators, is quick to breed, prolific, and short-lived. The little bat, no bigger than a field mouse, produces one offspring at a time, which it raises until it is full grown. The bat has relatively few enemies, and lives for years.

On a smaller scale, the same principles apply to insects. The blue tortoise beetle, for example, continues to feed through a long adult life. Now and then the female lays a single large egg, that she protects by constructing a heavy shield from her secretions and excretions. Twining through the palmetto stems may be a grape vine, on whose tender shoots a whole colony of rapidly reproducing aphids appears, flourishes through ten generations, and disappears. Meanwhile, the tortoise beetle slowly produces a couple of dozen eggs and larvae. Who wins, the tortoise or the aphid? Both must win on their own terms, or their species would not continue to exist.

PC

Top: **this leaf beetle is found on an unusually large number of plants, including oak and ragweed. The amount of black on the back is highly variable.**

Above: **the camphor-weed beetle. Florida leaf beetles are often difficult to identify because there are so many, and also because many species have several different color patterns.**

Tortoise Beetles

Subfamily Cassidinae

Tortoise beetles are so named because they are oval shaped and their wing covers are flattened at the edges so that the beetle resembles a miniature tortoise. Many have brilliant, irridescent colors including gold and green. These colors sometimes fade and disappear when the beetle dies. Tortoise beetles are part of the family of leaf-eating beetles and feed on plants, chewing many little holes in the leaves. Many species feed on members of the morning glory family.

Tortoise beetle larvae have a very interesting defensive tactic. They create a collection of skin and fecal droppings which they hold above their back. When a predator, such as ant approaches, the larva swings this shield around to block its advancement. Sometimes, if the intruder soils its antenna by touching the fresh droppings, it will simply go away to clean itself. It is possible to observe this behavior by touching one of the spines of the larva with a blade of grass to simulate the approach of a natural enemy. With a little luck, the beetle will respond by presenting its fecal shield.

PC

BM

Above and below: the blue tortoise beetle feeds on palms and palmettos. The yellow feet are covered with hairs, each tipped with a micro-droplet of oil. This allows the beetle to cling to the waxy surface of palm leaves.

Left: the golden tortoise beetle.

PC

FLORIDA AS THE INSECT CAPITAL

It isn't, actually. When more accurate counts are complete, most of the large states will probably have roughly similar numbers of insect species, perhaps around 25,000 to 35,000 species. Florida will probably be somewhere in the middle of the pack, well behind California or Arizona. The US insect fauna, while large, is dwarfed by that of large tropical countries such as Brazil and Indonesia.

So how did Florida, an also-ran state in an also-ran country get such a big reputation as a place for insects? Part of the reason is that Florida has many impressive tropical and subtropical species found together nowhere else in the eastern US. To a traveler coming from the North, Florida insects seem more notable, and this is easily transformed into an impression that there are more insects. A visitor from Maine will likely remark on the abundance of butterflies in South Florida, but is very unlikely to notice a scarcity of caddisflies. A New Yorker may complain about the Everglades mosquitos without ever thinking of the abundant blackflies that infest his own state.

The bottom line is that 25,000 to 35,000 insects is still a huge number. Florida may not be the insect captial of the universe, but it has enough insects to keep naturalists busy for a very long time.

BK

Longhorn Beetles

Family Cerambycidae

This group of beetles is named for their long, graceful antennae, which may be used for catching the scent of a mate or a host plant. It is easy to imagine that a longhorn beetle flying with its antennae extended may even be receiving "stereo smells." The males of some species duel with their antennae.

This is a big group of beetles, with about 225 species found in Florida, and the secret of their abundance and diversity is the ability of the larvae to live off one of the largest resources in nature, dead wood, especially the dead wood of twigs and branches up in living trees. As every carpenter knows, different woods differ in hardness, density, and often in smell; these wood fragrances are usually due to insect repellents and anti-fungal chemicals. All this means that there are many opportunities for specialization among wood-eating beetles, and this leads to a great diversity of species.

A few longhorn beetles do not need to look for dead wood, but create their own. Female twig-girdler longhorns cut a groove around a twig and lay their eggs in the terminal girdled section. The twig often breaks off at the girdle a few months later, and the alert Florida homeowner may wonder why there is a series of twigs with whittled bases on the ground under the oak or hickory tree in front of the house.

BK

Top: an ivory-marked beetle resting on ixora.

Above: this longhorn breeds in recently dead flower stalks of cabbage palms. It appears to be quite rare, even though there are plenty of cabbage palms available.

Right: a striped longhorn beetle on a spurge plant. This common species breeds in stalks of ragweed and tickseed sunflower.

BK

Weevils

Family Curculionidae

This is a gigantic group of insects, with about 575 species that are known to occur in Florida. There are more species of weevils than of any other beetle. Our knowledge about the number of Florida's weevil species is due largely to the prodigious efforts of a single weevil expert who works out of Tallahassee. The weevils are vegetarians, whose astounding success is due primarily to their absurd-looking elongated snout with a pair of ridiculous little jaws at its tip. The weevils stand as a reminder that one should never sneer at innovators who may look a little peculiar. That long snout allows weevils to bore through the protective outer coverings of plants—the rinds of fruits, the shells of seeds, the bark of twigs and tree trunks, the coverings of roots, the hardened rims of leaves—and feed on the less protected tissue within. Even better, female weevils can drill out an excavation in a plant, then turn and insert eggs into the plant tissue, where the eggs are hidden from predators, protected from the weather, and surrounded by edible tissue.

Not surprisingly, these talents have guaranteed that a number of weevils would become agricultural pests that are difficult to control, such as the cotton boll weevil, the pecan weevil, weevils that attack stored grain, and many others. Most species of plants, in fact, are attacked by one weevil or another. Fortunately, only a tiny minority of Florida's species cause any economic damage, and several species of specialized weevils have been introduced for the control of weeds.

A common and amazing weevil in Florida is the oak leaf roller, a beautiful red species with black legs and antennae. The female rolls up a small oak leaf, starting by cutting the leaf near the base so that only the midrib is left. Then she folds, notches and rolls the leaf, starting at the tip. When finished, the leaf has been folded and rolled up into a cylinder like a tiny green sleeping bag, held together by notches and flaps. The egg is in the middle, and the larva feeds on the moist dead leaf tissue.

Weevils are the biggest family-level group of beetles in Florida, the biggest family of insects, and the biggest family of animals. Is this because Florida is the world hot spot for weevils? Not really. The number of weevil species described for the world is about 40,000, so only about one weevil in 65 calls Florida home. Since many thousands of weevil species undoubtedly remain to be discovered in the tropics, Florida's share of weevils is even smaller. Still, 575 species is a lot of insects.

BK

ESR

BK

BK

Top and center left: **the giant palm weevil lives in dying palms and palmettos.**

Center, right: **sunflower weevils**
Above: **citrus root weevils preparing to mate.**

PC

Top: **a bee fly, one of the many insects that feed on the flowers of St. John's wort. This photo illustrates two features of a fly: the single pair of wings, and the halteres, the tiny, knobbed organs directly behind the wings which help maintain stable flight.**

ORDER DIPTERA

True flies are distinguished by having only one pair of wings. "Diptera" means two wings. In place of the second pair of wings found in other insects, flies have two knobbed organs called halteres. These are thought to function like gyroscopes to provide stability in flight and also serve various sensory functions.

Flies cannot eat solid food, but can only sip liquids. They have a variety of mouthparts, piercing and non-piercing. Some species of flies, such as the house fly, can regurgitate liquids to dissolve solid food, such as a lump of sugar, so that it can be sipped.

Of all the major groups of insects, the flies are the least understood and most detested. There are no apologists for flies, there are no lobbyists or hobbyists for flies, there are no fly-watchers, no fly-gardens, no picture guides to flies. Nobody knows any good flies. Even if one were to ask Florida naturalists what flies they know, one would only get a list of bad guy flies. "Let's see," they would say, "there are house flies, horse flies, fruit flies, sand flies, mosquitos, love bugs, and those gnats that get in your eyes...."

It is admittedly difficult to look past the flies that are darting around one's eyes and humming in one's ears. If one could do so, however, a rich and dynamic world of useful and interesting flies would be revealed. There is a huge group of aquatic species, including species that filter the water of lakes and ponds in Florida. There is another big batch of predatory species, including numerous species that help hold in balance leaf-eating insects such as caterpillars and grasshoppers. Most important of all is the enormous team of scavengers, which recycle everything from berries that fall from a bush to leaves that fall in a swamp, from dead deer to dead beetles, from cow patties to bird droppings.

These useful flies are mostly small insects, or insects that do their business quickly and quietly behind the scenes of nature. Few of these flies are covered in this book on Florida insects, because this book is intended to focus on the insects that most people see and wonder about. This dictates an emphasis on the pesky species. Beyond these flies, however, there are many, many others.

Flies are a group with complete metamorphosis, so the larvae look nothing like the adults. Many flies, such as the mosquitos, have aquatic larvae, while many others, such as the love bug, have larvae that feed in composting leaf litter in moist areas. A large group of flies have larvae that are stripped-down eating machines, called maggots, that scavenge such ephemeral treats as carrion or rotting fruits. Some of this last group of flies carry scavenging to its next logical step, and attack fruits, or other insects, while they are still healthy.

Many flies do not feed at all as adults, and others feed on nectar or fermenting fruit juice and sap, while still others are sharp-beaked aerial predators that seize other insects in flight. The most notorious flies, however, are the bloodsuckers such as mosquitos. Females of these flies draw blood from vertebrates, as a form of prenatal care, since the nutrients in the blood are packed into the eggs. Males of these bloodsuckers feed daintily on nectar or dew-drops—no red blood for them!

Bloodsucking has some interesting variations. Some nocturnal gnats bite humans, others attack birds, others sip from the wing veins of large sleeping insects. A group of flies bite tree frogs, and are attracted to their calls. Many biting flies are fussy about what animal they bite, even about what part of the body is targeted for a blood donation. Most species attack only at certain times of the day or in certain habitats.

Crane Flies

Family Tipulidae

Crane flies are skinny, with extraordinarily long, slender legs. These legs look so awkward and cumbersome that some empathetic naturalist of bygone days came up with the rhyme,

My six long legs, all here and there,
Oppress my bosom with despair!

A few hours in a modern airline seat might have raised the compassion of this commentator to an even higher pitch. Strangely enough, the value of these long, slender appendages is not clear. Crane flies can be supported on water films by their legs, but there are many species that are not aquatic. Some crane flies have a remarkable habit of hanging by their front legs from spider webs. The legs also detach from the fly fairly easily, and crane flies with only four or five legs can sometimes be seen, apparently functioning well. Perhaps one of the long legs can be left as a distraction in the grasp of a predator, like the detachable tail of some lizards. Many species of crane flies raise and lower themselves on their long legs as if doing pushups. The significance of this behavior is unknown.

For all their awkwardness, the crane flies are brilliantly successful, with over 1,500 species in the US. Florida has a relatively small share of these species, because crane flies do best in cool, wet climates. Still, Florida probably has at least a couple of hundred species. The best place to find crane flies in Florida might be Torreya State Park, with its cool, damp ravines and its links to the insects of the Appalachians.

Most Floridians are likely to view crane flies with some suspicion, because there is a certain similarity between crane flies and mosquitos, even though most crane flies are much larger. Crane flies also lack the biting mouthparts of mosquitos and are completely innocent of any blood lust. Some crane flies feed on nectar, but many do not apppear to feed as adults, living off energy stored as fat by the larva. Most larvae feed on roots or decaying vegetation.

Top: **a crane fly on Spanish needles. Note the halter visible in this photo (see caption, page 112).**
Below: **a crane fly on goldenrod. This species has a long beak for extracting nectar.**
Bottom: **a pair of crane flies mating.**

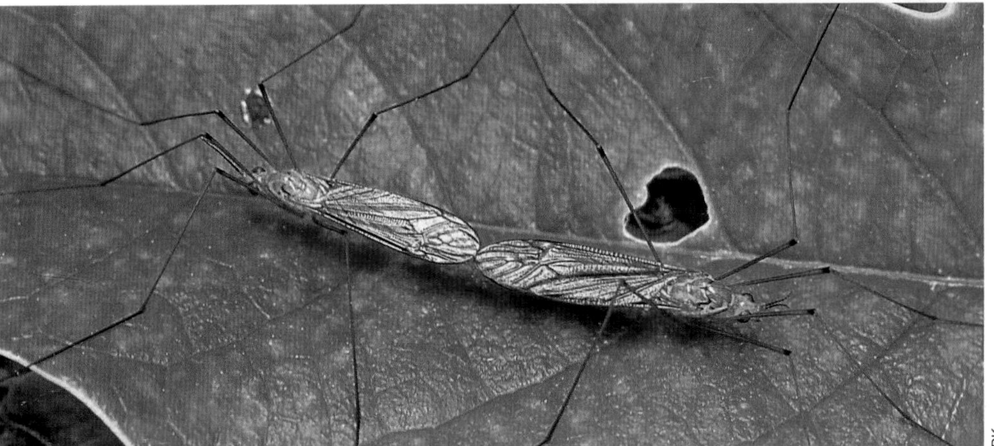

Fruit Flies (including the Medfly)

Family Tephritidae

A few Mediterranean fruit flies found in a set of baited traps set out near a citrus grove can mobilize a small army of agricultural experts, sometimes followed by sorties of airplanes carpet-bombing with insecticides. This may be followed by a sophisticated and expensive program of sexual subversion in the form of millions of specially bred sterile males released into the area, like parachuting in male Mata Hari's in numbers far greater that those of the enemy. This extreme reaction reflects two features of these flies: first, they represent a major threat, both direct and indirect, to Florida agriculture, and second, the aim is not to control the flies, but to eradicate them, a much more ambitious goal requiring more radical measures.

These fruit flies are not closely related to the tiny, red-eyed flies that hover about a rotting tomato in the garden or march up and down an elderly banana in the fruit bowl. Although these little flies (belonging to the family Drosophilidae) are popularly known as fruit flies, there has been an effort to distinguish them with the common name of vinegar flies, or pomace flies, rather than calling them the pygmy or red-eyed fruit flies. The "real" fruit flies, shown here, belong to the family Tephritidae. They are larger insects, usually about house fly size, with spotted or striped wings.

There are about 50 species of fruit flies native to Florida, a couple of species that were accidentally introduced and established, and a couple of species that were introduced and eradicated. Unlike the little red-eyed flies, the pest species of fruit flies generally lay their eggs in fruits that have just ripened, and the larvae can cause the fruit to drop, or, worse yet, the maggots may be revealed when the fruit is cut open in the kitchen. Many countries and states, including Florida, have erected quarantines against fruit imported from areas infested with certain destructive fruit flies, so the immediate result of the discovery of any of these flies in Florida is that a whole series of export markets automatically slam shut.

JLC

DPI

JLC

BK

Top: papaya fruit fly.

Center left: Mediteranean fruit fly or medfly.

Center, right: a Caribbean fruit fly.

Bottom: an insect trap used by the state to monitor insect populations. Such a trap can give warning if the dreaded medfly appears in Florida.

HUGE EYES FOR MALE FLIES

To a connoisseur of flies, this horse fly can instantly be labeled as a male, because the eyes meet in the middle of the face and the top of the head, unlike those of female horse flies (see page 125). The same pattern of oversized male eyes can be seen in a number of unrelated insect groups (flower flies, house flies, plus some bees and wasps). A survey of insects shows that outsize male eyes are not always the rule, but it would be difficult to think of any insects in which the eyes of the female occupy more of the head than those of the male. The biggest eyes are found in those males that have aerial courtship displays, either dancing in a swarm or hovering in place. It seems that insects that must accurately identify other insects while in flight need special equipment, and insects which have statonary targets have fewer problems.

Vinegar Flies

Family Drosophilidae

Many of the vinegar flies are irresistibly drawn to the odors of fermented fruit, whether that odor comes from a rotting orange or a crystal glass of fine wine. It's all one to the vinegar fly looking for a batch of overripe fruit on which to lay her eggs. The vinegar flies are those little red-eyed, yellowish flies that are often called fruit flies. The alternative name of vinegar flies is used to distinguish them from the fruit-eating flies, such as the Mediterranean fruit fly (medfly), that attack fresh fruits and other healthy plant tissues.

The insignificant vinegar fly, often seen carefully surveying an old strawberry to see if it is sufficiently decayed, will be forever famous in the annals of science as the little animal that taught mankind so much about genetics. These flies were valuable for genetic research due to a combination of several features, including giant chromosomes in the salivary glands and a short life cycle (typical of scavenger insects that breed in rapidly decomposing substances).

Not all vinegar flies feed on decaying fruits. Some of the 45 Florida species are found in mushrooms, dying cacti, sap flows on trees, or dead flowers. A few species are predatory.

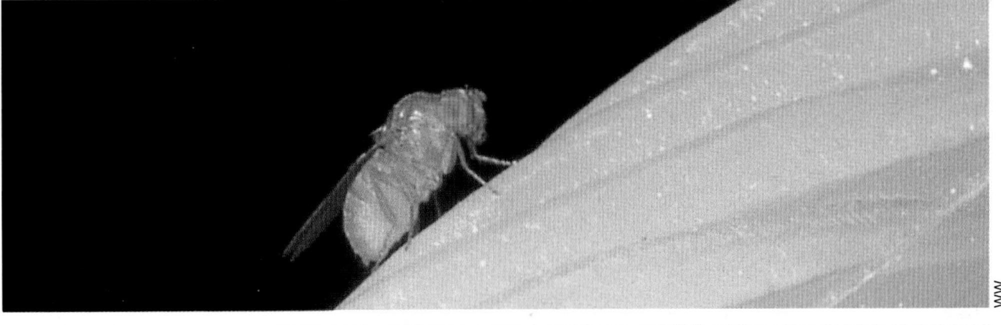

RECIPE FOR VINEGAR FLIES

Many naturalists have a special fondness for vinegar flies because creating colonies of these flies is so quick and easy. Such a colony can provide a rapid demonstration of the life cycle of an insect with complete metamorphosis. In the classroom, vinegar flies can be raised to feed small predators, such as spiders or assassin bugs, that are being kept alive in temporary displays. For school projects a good feature of vinegar flies is that the colony can be established with native flies lured into a jar with fermenting fruit set out in the schoolyard, and when the study is over the entire colony can be released outside without any concern about adding non-native species to the area.

Laboratory colonies of vinegar flies are usually fed on a simple medium, such as corn meal cooked up with a little molasses and sprinkled after cooling with a little bakers' yeast. Such recipes may become more liquid as the larvae feed, so paper toweling is often added to soak up excess moisture. About half an inch of the food is put in a small jar. The top of the jar can be covered with plastic cut from a plastic bag, held in place with a rubber band. A pencil-sized hole is cut in the plastic, and plugged with a little wad of cotton. To remove flies, the cotton is pulled out, and a vial quickly upended over the hole. Flies soon begin to move up into the vial. Vinegar flies can also be raised in a jar in which a small section of banana resting on half an inch of dry sand. However the vinegar flies are to be raised, the colony can be started by setting the jar with the corn meal or fruit outside in a shady place. The flies usually appear within an hour or two, and just a few flies can produce hundreds of larvae.

House Fly and Relatives

Family Muscidae

The house fly is one of a number of insects that love human company. House flies breed in garbage and manure, and the adults are strongly attracted to moist foodstuffs and human bodies. Because of these associations, it has long seemed logical to suspect that house flies transmit diseases, and they have been accused of carrying dozens of infections, from polio to leprosy. Around 50 years ago, the house fly was considered one of the most important disease carriers in the US, and there were popular articles on how many people the house fly might have killed by spreading diseases, and careful enumerations to the number and types of bacteria a house fly can carry on each foot. Actual investigations, however, do not support these accusations. The 1950s mothers who threw out the fried chicken at a picnic because a house fly had landed on it are unlikely to have saved their families from any diseases. Still, the house fly can be an intensely bothersome insect. Even if it is not quite the mobile disease factory that it was once thought to be, it is still a non-native insect with nothing to recommend it.

Florida's problems with annoying house flies pale beside those of many other regions. In Australia, the bush fly, a close relative of the house fly, may settle on the hiker's head and back in a solid carpet. The hand motion of brushing flies from one's face is known, with a cheerful unpretentiousness typical of the only nation with a humorous national anthem, as "the Australian salute."

Some Floridians swear that house flies bite, a belief based on the very similar stable fly, known in North Florida as the dog or beach fly. The stable fly resembles a very fast house fly that, when biting humans, lands and takes off several times before settling to bite, and is extremely difficult to swat. The mouthparts of a stable fly are not blade or needle-like as in deer flies or mosquitos, but resemble a group of sharp, curved thorns on the tip of the tongue, that can rasp the skin until the blood begins to flow. This is why the bite of a stable fly hurts so much, and also why the stable fly is so hard to swat, since there is no beak sunk into the flesh to hamper a fast getaway. The stable fly is also a major irritant for livestock.

In addition to the house and stable fly, Florida has several other non-native species in the house fly group, and many native species that few people notice.

JHR

BK

Top: **a house fly on a plum. Note the tiny, knobbed, yellow halter, a remnant of what probably was a second pair of wings millions of years ago. The halteres now function as sensory organs and help the fly balance during flight. There is a whitish lobe behind each wing and above the halter which is called a calypter. The function of the calypter is unknown. Much of the detailed structure of insect wings is still a mystery and even the general principles of insect flight are just being discovered. House fly feet have claws and adhesive pads which allow them to cling to both smooth and rough surfaces.**

Bottom: **a house fly using its hind legs to clean its wings.**

VERSES TO A HOUSEFLY

The house fly seems an unlikely focus of poetic attention, yet it is the subject of one of the most charming poems ever addressed to an insect, written by the English poet Vincent Bourne (1695-1747). One can clearly see the poet, slightly wistful, slightly mocking, slightly drunk, sharing his cup of English hard cider with his only drinking companion, a fly.

Busy, curious, thirsty fly,
Drink with me, and drink as I,
Freely welcome to my cup,
Couldst thou sip and sip it up.
Make the most of life you may,
Life is short, and wears away.

Both alike are mine and thine,
Hastening fast to their decline;
Thine's a summer, mine no more,
Though repeated to threescore.
Threescore summers, when they're gone,
Will appear as short as one.

Green Bottle Flies and Relatives

Family Calliphoridae

The green bottle fly is a common, conspicuous Florida insect, found in many disturbed habitats, for example, at a boating and fishing access on some Florida lake or river. In such a place one can admire the full breadth of the green bottle's taste, seeing it at one moment sipping nectar from a palmetto flower, the next mopping up the fluid seeping from the sunken eye of a fish head. Green bottles are also called blow flies, because some species lay their eggs in the nostrils of live animals.

Green bottles are one of the most aggressive groups of scavenging flies, arriving speedily at fresh carcases, and laying row upon row of eggs that quickly turn into larvae that feed with desperate haste on the rapidly decomposing body.

BK

***Above:* a green bottle fly. Note the feathery projections from the antennae.**

PC

A*bove:* a green bottle fly feeding on nectar.

Green bottles occasionally come indoors, attracted by some neglected treat, perhaps a lump of cat food that fell underneath a counter, or a forgotten sandwich. The larvae may work undetected, as they are not necessarily associated with any terrible odor of decay. In fact, one of the chemicals that they secrete to help break down organic matter is ammonia, whose smell is more reminiscent of zealous cleaning. When these larvae mature indoors, they wriggle into the darkest place they can find, sometimes ending up in peculiar locations, such as the toe of a shoe lying on its side. A week or so later, a mysterious plague of flies appears.

A few species of these aggressive scavengers may go the next logical step, and attack their meat on the hoof. The eggs are laid in small wounds or abrasions, which are turned into huge sores that can be fatal. The notorious screw-worm fly, the object of a major eradication program in Florida, is one of these flies.

Weirdly enough, a few species have been used medicinally for "maggot therapy." It was observed long ago that wounds from which fly larvae had been removed had a good chance of healing. This led to the practice of temporarily introducing fly larvae into wounds to clean them. We now know that these larvae produce substances that kill or inhibit bacteria, such as the bacteria that cause gangrene. This treatment, used most between 1920 and 1930, was largely replaced by antibiotics, but fly larvae have been used recently to cure unusually stubborn bone infections.

WHO IS COUNTING FLIES IN FLORIDA?

Entomologists have been slow to document the diversity of flies, beyond the biting flies and those that damage crops. There is no list of Florida flies. There is no estimate of the number of species of Florida flies. Are there 3,000 species? 4,000 species? Nobody knows. Understanding this sizeable chunk of Florida's biological diversity has been left for future generations.

The gaps in knowledge of Florida flies reflect gaps at a national level. Many large groups of flies are studied by only one or two people. Some of the smaller families of flies are "orphaned." The only people who knew those groups of flies have died and have not been replaced. This, in turn, is part of a more general phenomenon. The number of experts who can identify species of insects may be shrinking, while the number of insects that need to be identified for ecological studies or agricultural research has been increasing sharply. The problem seems to be that the institutions, including universities and museums, that used to employ people who could recognize thousands of insect species are employing different types of scientists today.

The ability to learn to identify large numbers of organisms is widespread. Only a few thousand years ago this must have been a survival skill, when humans depended on their knowledge of many species in their natural habitats. It is likely that gaps in expertise about insects could be filled by almost anybody who took the trouble to work on a group. Perhaps a few users of this book will be inspired to acquire the specialized knowledge that could make them a world expert on some interesting group of Florida insects.

PC

Parasitic Flies/ Tachinids

Family Tachinidae

The parasitic flies may well turn out to be the largest family of flies in Florida, although at this time only several hundred species have been identified. These are buzzing, bristly flies which always seem to be on the move. The reason for the activity is that the females are constantly searching for places to lay numerous eggs. Some species lay eggs directly on insects, such as stink bugs or caterpillars, and this requires a feverish hunt for as many hosts as possible. Other species lay huge numbers of eggs near places where hosts may occur, and this also involves rushing around. Males tend to congregate in special waiting sites, and dash out after any insect that looks to their eye even slightly like a female. Both sexes must make hurried trips to flowers or honeydew sites to charge up on sugars. The result of all this busyness is a lot of flies that look as if they had drunk an extra cup of coffee.

Top: **tachinid flies mating. Adult flies spend most of their lives in reproductive activities. Males hunt for and court females. Females mate and search for the right place to lay eggs. Larvae of this family are internal parasites of other insects and, along with parasitic wasps, are very important for the population control of many insect species. Eggs are deposited onto the host insect or sometimes onto plant tissue which is eaten by the host. By the time the larvae emerge from the host, ready to pupate, the host is usually dead. The adult flies feed on nectar.**

Below: this tachinid fly with the handsome black fringes on its legs is an internal parasite of squashbugs.

JLC

BK

Small-footed Flies

Family Micropezidae

Only a few species of small-footed flies occur in Florida. They never appear in large numbers, nor do they bite, or act as pests in any way. Nevertheless, curious naturalists are always asking about these flies. Small-footed flies are often found around buildings in rural and suburban Florida, where they promenade with exaggerated care, as if on thin ice. As they walk, they stop frequently to lift their front legs, which are ornamented with white bands. Unlike most flies, they do not seem distressed if they enter an open door and get trapped inside a building. They continue to march delicately across the kitchen table as if it were a palmetto leaf out in the woods. Why do they walk this way? Is the gesturing with the front legs some kind of signal? Where do they breed? Nobody knows the answers to these questions.

WHAT ATTRACTS THE QUESTING FLY?

In the last hundred years, several hundred papers have been written about the possible attractants that flies use to zero in on humans. The drive behind these studies has been the hope that if we knew what attracted biting flies, perhaps we could eliminate or mask the attractant. Failing that, perhaps the attractant could be bottled and used to trap all the biting flies in the neighborhood. So far, the mystery of the questing fly remains unpenetrated. One might have expected that with so many biting flies around, scientists would have come up with an irresistible lure for at least one type of fly, but this has not happened. The Canadian entomologist Brian Hocking once summed it up this way:

"Every imaginable part of the human body and its products must by now have been fractionated in every possible way in the search for a specific chemical attractant. While certain attractive materials have been found...nothing proves to be so attractive as the intact man. This seems to suggest that the blood-sucking arthropods recognize man for what he is, by his complex of effluvia, and not by any specific indicator."

It is not that there are no clear patterns in the attraction of blood-sucking flies to their hosts. There are plenty of patterns, in fact, far too many. It is known, for example, that horseflies are attracted to movement, and that many species are more attracted to dark-colored, moving objects. Mosquitos are attracted by heat and humidity, and can easily become distracted into circling a plate of hot scrambled eggs or a bowl of oatmeal if one is eating breakfast outdoors. Certain biting flies are attracted to sweat. Some flies are more attracted to sweat from below the waistline than from the upper part of the body.

On any walk in a Florida woodland in summer, one can see differential attraction, even if there are only three or four people present. "Oh, yes," says one of them, "Bill always has more deer flies on him than I do, even if he wears repellent." Everywhere one looks there is another pattern. Everywhere one looks there is another attractant chemical: lysine, lactic acid, octonol, human sex pheromones, carbon dioxide. Nowhere is there a simple set of chemical or visual cues that can be masked or eliminated. Nowhere is there a magic cocktail that can be bottled and used to lure all the flies to their doom in a trap.

All this means that biting flies are using multiple cues, the insect equivalent of the odor, atmosphere, and circumstances of a home-cooked Thanksgiving dinner. All these attractants are being produced by the human body all the time, as long as it is breathing, moving, and metabolizing. The processes that keep the human body alive are attractants. There are, of course, repellents that are so distasteful to biting flies at close range that they refuse to bite. In most situations, this is a good solution. Some problems are best dealt with at the personal level, rather than by trying to change the whole system.

BB

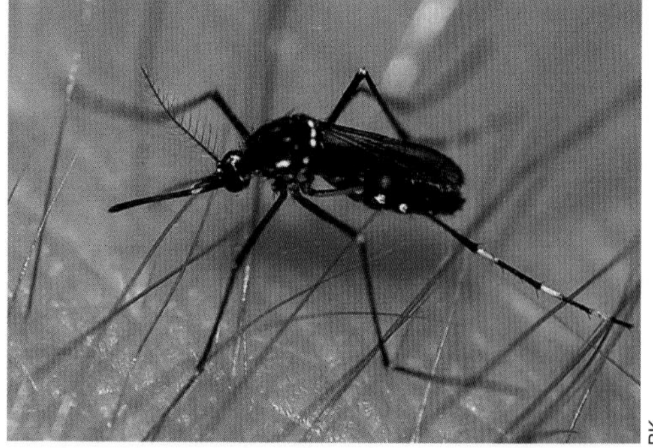

BK

JLC

Left: **the elephant tree-hole mosquito. This mosquito feeds on nectar and does not bite.**

Top: **the Asian tiger biting mosquito.**

Above: **the Gallinipper, a large, biting mosquito.**

Mosquitos

Family Culicidae

Scientists who study mosquitoes are constantly impressed by the amazing abilities and complex behavior of these little flies. Such scientists still swat biting mosquitoes just like everybody else, but with much more respect. This little smear of legs and wings on the mosquito scientist's arm was, a fraction of a second ago, a tiny organism with a much tinier brain. This fly could nonetheless engage in fancy courtship behavior, track down a host over long distances, cautiously stalk the prey at close range, delicately and precisely draw off a drop of blood under the most dangerous working conditions imaginable, find a safe and secluded place for digestion and incorporation of the blood meal into eggs, and carefully choose the perfect site to lay the eggs where the water is rich in the microscopic organisms that the larvae eat, yet relatively free of predators. The mosquito is not a contemptible, bloodthirsty, teasing irritant; it is a worthy opponent, engaged on a perilous mission of life and death.

The scientific interest in mosquitoes derives primarily from the saliva that the mosquito injects rather than from the blood that the insect withdraws. The mouthparts of a female mosquito consist of a long sheath that protects a delicate hypodermic that has two channels. Saliva that contains an anti-clotting agent is injected in, then the blood is withdrawn. The saliva causes an allergic reaction, hence the itching from a mosquito bite. Most people get decreasing reactions from bites as the mosquito season progresses, although a few unfortunate people become increasingly sensitive. In some parts of the world, the saliva may also contain disease organisms, such as those that cause malaria. Malaria and most other diseases carried by mosquitoes do not occur in Florida. These diseases can be conquered by prompt treatment of people carrying the diseases, and by reducing the likelihood that diseased people will be bitten by mosquitoes. Screening, the advent of air conditioning (allowing houses to be closed up on hot nights), and control of disease-bearing mosquito species were all important in breaking the cycle of disease in Florida.

Encephalitis has been more difficult to eradicate, in part because the disease organism has hosts other than people, so it cannot be stopped by changing human behavior, and in part because the disease is so rare that it has been difficult to see the patterns in its occurrence. It is now known that the encephalitis virus takes some time to incubate in the mosquito, and scientists suspect that if a mosquito picks up the disease during a blood meal, lays a batch of eggs, and quickly goes to get another blood meal for a second batch of eggs, there may not be time for the virus to incubate. If the life cycle of the mosquito is put on hold by a drought that keeps the mosquito from finding a good place to lay eggs, the virus may have a long enough time to incubate before the second blood meal. This explains why the prevalence of encephalitis is not well correlated with the abundance of mosquitoes.

Since mosquitoes act as little hypodermic needles, and are known to transmit diseases, it is easy to get an erroneous impression that these needles could be contaminated with all kinds of diseases, such as cold viruses, or the AIDS (HIV) virus. The mouthparts of mosquitoes are too small, too clean, and used too infrequently to carry diseases by simple contamination. Mosquito-borne diseases are those that have evolved special mechanisms to escape from the mosquito digestive system and colonize the salivary glands, without harming the mosquito, so that they can be injected in quantity at the next blood meal. This explains the fortunate fact that there are relatively few diseases carried by mosquitoes, although even one such disease is one too many.

Florida has about 80 species of mosquitoes, but not all of these feed on blood, some prefer hosts other than humans, and not all the species that bite humans can carry diseases. Of the diseases that can be carried by mosquitoes, only encephalitis occurs with any regularity in the US, and this disease is very rare in Florida. Probably more people wrap their cars around a telephone pole while trying to swat a mosquito than are sent to the hospital by a mosquito-borne disease. Still, mosquitoes can be a major nuisance in Florida, and there are times and places where the mosquito is queen, and one can only keep one's sanity within her realm when armored with protective clothing and repellent.

***Right:* a female mosquito gorged with human blood. Only the females feed on blood.**

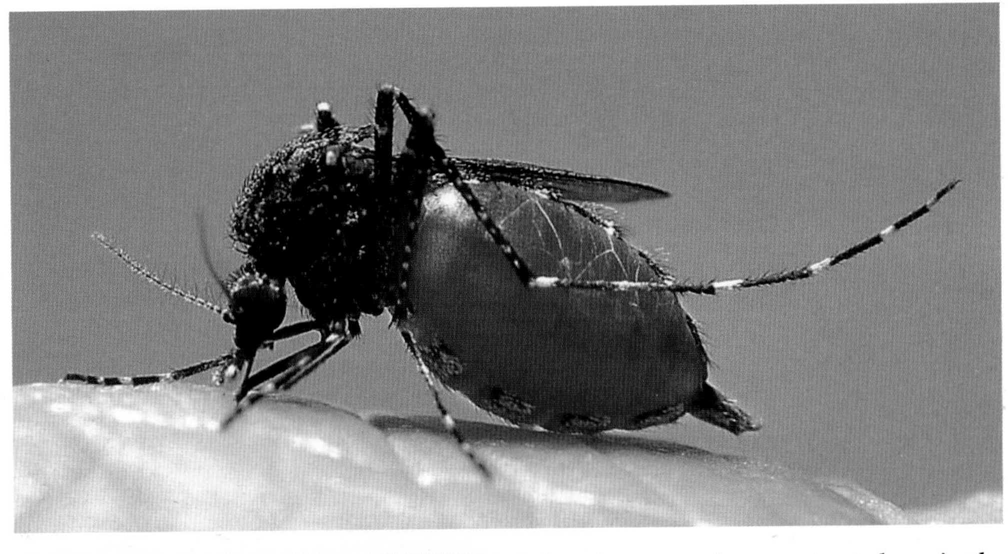

NT

GM

***Left:* a dew-covered mosquito at dawn in the Florida Everglades is transformed into a work of art.**

Below: The nectar-drinking males do not even have the sharp mouthparts necessary to pierce flesh. Note the feathery antennae that are typical of male mosquitos.

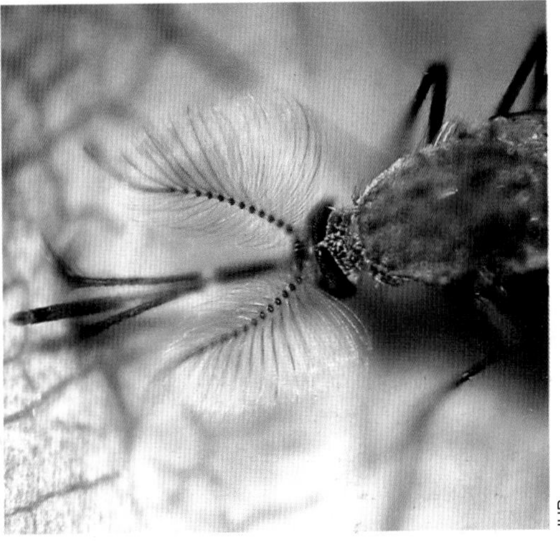

JHR

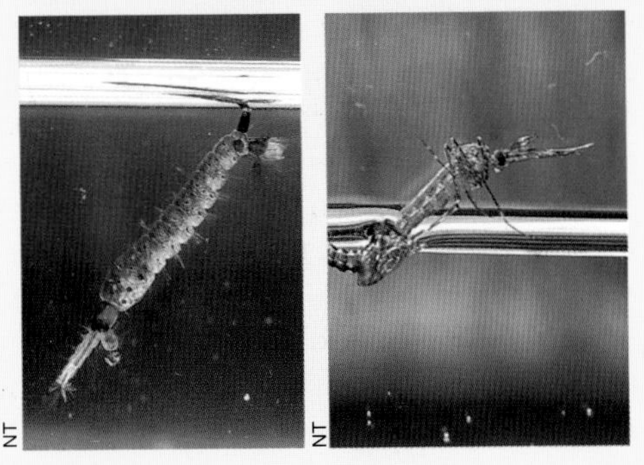

NT NT

MOSQUITO LIFE CYCLE

Mosquitos depend on still water to reproduce. That is why mosquito control programs educate homeowners to turn over all containers such as old pots which may hold rainwater, as these are ideal mosquito breeding ponds. In the wild it could be a cavity in a tree or a temporary puddle. The photo above, left, shows a mosquito larva floating head-down near the surface and breathing through its abdominal tube. The photo above, right, shows the adult emerging from the pupal case which also floats in the water.

THE FAR SIDE by Gary Larson

THE FAR SIDE © FARWORKS, INC. Used by permission. All rights reserved.

Wait a minute.... McCallister, you fool!
This isn't what I said to bring!

BK

Love Bugs/March Flies

Family Bibionidae

Some myths are almost too delightful to examine with the spectacles of accuracy. One of these is the widespread story that the lovebug was developed by entomologists at the University of Florida to attack mosquitoes. All of this is pure fantasy! The only true association between the lovebug and the University of Florida is that most of the research on this species took place there.

The lovebug is a red-blooded American insect (actually, yellow-blooded) whose ancestral home seems to be west Louisiana and South Texas through Central America. Its larvae consume dead plant material in open grasslands and the edges of disturbed woods, and the species was probably traditionally barred from the Southeast by the extensive flood plain forests of the Mississippi. With the development of the interstate highway system, a corridor of open grassy road shoulders was established, and the lovebug began its long trek eastward. It became established in the Florida Panhandle in the late 1940s, and moved east and south in a more or less solid front, hitting the peninsula in the early 1960s, and South Florida in the 1970s. Meanwhile, like a red carpet laid out before the lovebug, forests and natural prairies were being modified into improved pastures, lawns, and disturbed road edges. The lovebug showed its appreciation of these modified habitats by multiplying greatly.

While the lovebug is not an agricultural pest, nor does it bite or sting, its huge swarms along highways, usually during a few weeks in May and September, cause great distress by covering cars and trucks with the corrosive and smelly results of many collisions. Lovebugs, for some unknown reason, are attracted to chemicals in the exhaust of both gas and diesel engines. Perhaps these fumes contain some crucial components of the bouquet that rises from decaying vegetation where the lovebug lays its eggs. It does not seem likely that the exhaust compounds attract lovebugs due to a resemblance between these chemicals and the sex-attractant chemicals of lovebugs, because almost all the lovebugs seen on the highway are already engaged in long-term copulation. All this sex must provoke some interesting questions and answers in the cars of visitors bringing their children to Disney World in May and September. Biologists have some of the same questions, and it is still not clear whether the prolonged mating (12 hours is normal) is a form of mate-guarding, as occurs in some insects, whether the male is passing on some useful compound that requires more time than the transfer of sperm, or whether dispersal ability is improved if two flies fly as one. Adult lovebugs are also attracted to flowers, where they feed on nectar.

Florida entomologists are sometimes told that they should try to "do something about lovebugs," but it is difficult to think of an effective control for a species whose larvae are concealed in the soil and distributed widely over the countryside. It might be difficult to find natural enemies that could control lovebugs, even if one looked in their land of origin. Natural enemies, moreover, do not necessarily reduce their prey to low numbers. Many insects, some midges, for example, can have huge emergences of adults even in natural conditions and in the presence of a host of natural enemies. Pesticides are an even more unlikely solution, since they would need to be applied on a scale that would be too expensive and ecologically risky. Lovebugs share with us a preference for open, disturbed habitats, and highways. In other words, our own ecological niche.

BK

CS

POISON BLOOD?

Lovebugs have a vile taste. Some dedicated entomologists have actually sampled lovebugs, as have many Florida motocyclists. Apparently, nobody has gone so far as to swallow a batch of lovebugs to see if they are lethal. Even without personal experience, one might suspect that an insect whose blood can take the finish right off a car, is probably inedible. Birds, lizards, and dragonflies do not eat lovebugs. A few spiders eat love bugs, but most do not.

Strangely, nobody has analyzed lovebug blood to identify the repellant or toxin. Who knows? This poison, like many other natural poisons, might have useful pharmacological properties.

PC

Opposite page, top: a pair of lovebugs copulating. The "swarms" of lovebugs seen along the highway are different from swarms of lovebugs that are seeking mates. Groups of male lovebugs form swarms of hovering individuals, usually in the morning. Some conspicuous object, such as a large shrub, is used as a swarm marker to keep the swarm compact. Females ready to mate fly up through the swarm of males to pick up a mate. Couples fly off to nearby vegetation to copulate, and remain together while feeding on nectar or congregating around the sites where the eggs will be laid.

Top, left: the front of a van that has been driven through a swarm of lovebugs along the highway. During the swarming season, highway shops do a big business selling nets to protect cars and also scrubbing equipment.

Left: a pitcher plant filled with its lovebug prey.

Above: lovebugs on a thistle bud. Lovebugs fly from flower to flower when feeding, and might pollinate plants, since their bodies are usually covered with pollen.

PC

Horse Flies and Deer Flies

Family Tabanidae

Florida has many more species of horse and deer flies than most people realize, largely because one squashed fly looks rather like another. There are about 100 species in Florida. This large number is not an example of insect diversity running rampant in the subtropics, but is rather due to the great variety of available aquatic habitats, in which the larvae of horse flies and deer flies occur. Northern states are also well endowed with horse flies and deer flies. Idaho, for example, in spite of its bracing climate, has about 80 species.

The bites of horse flies are notoriously painful, and many an ax-toting woodsman has had the experience of almost braining himself by reflexively swatting at a horse fly that has suddenly undertaken an excruciating excavation in his forehead. An examination of the mouthparts of a horse fly under the microscope explains the pain: a frightening bundle of six daggers, both broad and stiletto.

Between the curses elicited by a swarm of satellite horse flies or deer flies, people sometimes wonder aloud, "What do all these flies eat when I'm not around?" One answer is that there are probably many of these flies that never do get a blood meal, but the ones that do lay enough eggs to keep the population strong (as in other biting flies, only the females bite). Moreover, many species are able to lay one batch of eggs without a blood meal, but two or more batches of eggs with the nutritional boost provided by blood. Some mosquitos also have this same ability.

Wildlife, rather than humans, are the natural blood donors for horse and deer flies in Florida, heavily supplemented by livestock in the last few centuries. There are no horse flies or deer flies that seem to be highly dependent on humans, and with our quick-swatting hands, we are a dangerous cafeteria choice. These flies are fast, in the sense that they can fly laps around a human runner, but they are not agile. Although many people are stabbed by horse and deer flies, the meal is seldom completed before it is lethally ended by a slapping hand. Some people are even able to snatch a horse or deer fly out of the air. A deer or a horse has fewer defenses, and makes a much more suitable host. So, when all these flies are not biting humans, they are probably biting wild animals or livestock, or making do without a blood meal.

The perception of the abundance of horse and deer flies on a per acre basis is probably hugely exaggerated. These are often rather rare as insects go, but they are good at finding large mammals, so that the entire supply of flies from a considerable chunk of real estate may be concentrated around the head of a single hiker. The proof of this is that the male flies, which are not attracted to humans, are seldom seen, and are rare in museum collections; this is especially true of deer flies.

Although Florida horse and deer flies do not seem to carry diseases, some people develop an alarming temporary swelling around the bite. This is particularly true of the bite of the "yellow-fly," a sneaky, and persistent, orangish fly of shady places that tends to bite on the legs and hands.

Top: **a crepuscular or green horse fly, which is nocturnal. This individual is male, feeding on nectar. Only female horse flies bite.**

Below: **the remarkable compound eye of the horse fly. The bands of color probably do not indicate some specialized kind of vision as one might think, but are just displays that males and females use in recognition.**

ABS

JLP

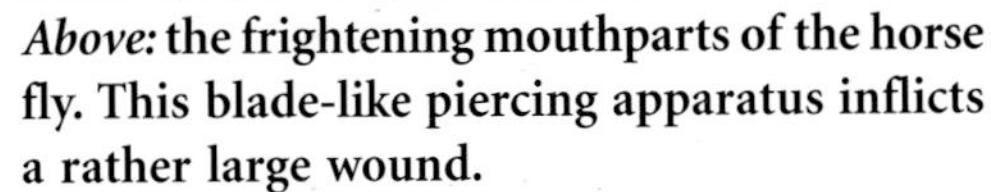

Above: the frightening mouthparts of the horse fly. This blade-like piercing apparatus inflicts a rather large wound.

BK

Right: the horse fly's iridescent eye colors disappear quickly after the death of the fly. This individual is a female. The eyes of males meet on the top of the head (see opposite page, top photo for comparison).

SWD

JLC

PC

Above: the colorful eye of the deer fly is visible in this photo. This is the dreaded "yellow fly." Dark bands or spots on clear wings help distinguish deer flies from horse flies.

Above, left: the giant black horse fly. The abdomen of this species has a bluish sheen in certain light. For this reason, it is sometimes called the blue-tailed fly.

Left: the horse fly's saliva contains an anticoagulent which prevents clotting, so a wound inflicted by a horse fly will continue to bleed for a few minutes. The loss of blood can be significant if large numbers of these flies attack an animal.

Non-biting Midges (Blind Mosquitos)

Family Chironomidae

The "blind mosquitoes" are a group of mosquito-like midges, some species of which emerge from Florida lakes in astronomical numbers, covering the walls of lakeside houses and forming heaps of wispy corpses under outdoor lights. In Florida they are called blind mosquitoes because when their multitudes are disturbed in their resting places on lake shore sedges, they rise up with a mosquito-like whine and fly clumsily away among the vegetation, as if too blind and stupid to recognize a good meal when it walks into their back yard. Actually, these flies do not feed as adults, and live only a day or so, which is time enough for myriads of them to vanish down the gullets of swallows and dragonflies.

JLC

The larvae live in the mud of lakes, where each constructs a small open-ended tube, through which they draw a little stream of water from which they remove algae and microscopic debris. They act, in their millions, as the filter for our lakes. They are also an important food for larger animals, including fish. These are beneficial insects that get little appreciation, but they have, in any case, no place to hang a medal, and neither the time nor the digestive system for a recognition dinner. "Gotta go," they would say, if they could think and talk. "Gotta go, gotta fly, gotta mate, gotta lay eggs, gotta die. Life's so short. So long."

Sand Flies

(No-See-Ums)
Family Ceratopogonidae

For many Floridians, sand flies (also known as punkies, or no-see-ums) are the smallest insects that they will ever see. These flies are felt. It is a beautiful, calm afternoon on the beach. Suddenly, perhaps on the left forearm, there is a tiny but intense pain, as if one of the little armhairs had just gotten red hot. Glancing at the arm, there is nothing there—wait a minute! There is a speck of dust, no, it is a pygmy fly, just barely visible. That is a sand fly.

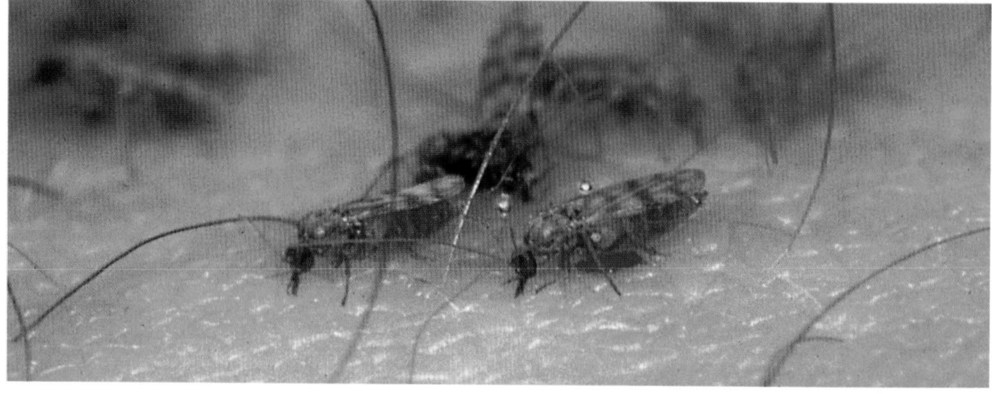

VU

Sand flies are the smallest of the bloodsucking insects, and the amount of blood that they take is totally insignificant. Unfortunately, as they feed, sand flies inject substances to prevent the blood from clotting and gumming up their little beaks. This can cause a reaction out of all proportion to the size of the bite in the form of a large round welt. In some parts of the world sand flies are also carriers of human diseases, but this does not seem to be the case in Florida.

Sand flies are often specialized in their biting habits. There are species that feed only on the blood of certain birds, and others that only suck the blood of insects that are resting during the night. Sand flies also tend to be specialized in their larval habitats. Some species breed in ponds and ditches, others along muddy or sandy shorelines, others in seeps or wet leaf litter. The adults of some species do not fly far from the breeding habitat, so one is sometimes unpleasantly conscious that one has just entered a sand fly zone, perhaps a muddy area of mangroves, or the intertidal area of the beach. Females of other species seem willing to travel at least a couple of hundred yards to visit, for example, a group of cows in the middle of a dry field. Most species are specialized in their flight times, and a number of biting species seem most active at dawn and dusk.

With so much specialization, it is not surprising that sand flies have diversified, and there are many species in Florida. The final count will probably number a few hundred. Only a small number of sand fly species bite humans. Several specialists have studied sand flies, because of their medical importance in the tropics.

Like other biting flies, sand flies earn grudging respect for their remarkable ability to perform complex and dangerous tasks. This is all the more astonishing because of their minute size. How do they squeeze enough cells into their microscopic brains to orchestrate all the behaviors needed for maneuvering around obstacles, avoiding enemies, pursuing and feeding on their hosts, courtship and mating, and finding sites to lay eggs?

The smallest flying insect also faces problems that are unfamiliar to larger species. Since the sand fly weighs so little, it must work hard to maintain a course when there is even the lightest breeze. For sandflies, the problem is compounded by the fact that air itself has viscosity (thickness). While not noticeable to larger insects, this thickness becomes significant for insects as small as a sandfly. All this means that the sand fly hovering around one's head, waiting for a good chance to bite, must beat its wings at the amazing rate of 1000 beats per second.

Long-Legged Flies

Family Dolichopodidae

The legs of long-legged flies are not particularly long by fly standards. The group would have been better served by a more descriptive English name, such as the "minute metallic flies." These flies are best recognized by their small size, metallic colors, bulging and widely separated eyes, and by their habit of running about rapidly on vegetation. They also fly readily, and many species show a characteristic pattern of short dashes alternating with very short flights that allows the experienced naturalist to recognize a long-legged fly when it is just a glistening dot on a leaf two or three yards away.

If one were to pick a group of flies to show the delights of looking at nature close up, most naturalists who study flies would probably unhesitatingly choose the long-legged flies. Under high magnification the little green metallic dot is seen to have patterns whose overlying sheen is copper, blue, or purple. The legs may be canary yellow, with chocolate knees, and along each yellow leg are three rows of precisely spaced short black spines. Between the large eyes with their curving rows of facets sprout a pair of antennal knobs colored in patterns of black, white, or yellow. The front feet may be ornamented with great fans of silver and black hairs. All these patterns vary delightfully among the hundreds of species.

BK

These little flies are among the least known treasures of entomology, and are destined to be discovered one of these decades as the wood warblers of the insect world. At the moment, they are the private enjoyment of a handful of specialists, who are still happily adding new names to the many hundreds of long-legged flies already described. It would be hard to guess how many species occur in Florida, as little survey work has been done; 200 species would not be an excessive estimate, considering that Florida has connections with the fly fauna of three major regions: the West Indies, the southeastern coastal plain, and the southern Appalachians.

The larvae of long-legged flies tend to live in wet areas, but there are some upland species even in the driest Florida scrub and sandhill. It is safe to say that there is no marsh or pond in the state where one could not find a dozen species of long-legged flies along the margin.

BK

Flower Flies

Family Syrphidae

These flies have everything to recommend them: they are colorful, speedy, diverse, large enough to easily observe, with a variety of habits, some of which are beneficial to humans. Most species of flower flies, as their name implies, visit flowers, where they feed on nectar, and in some cases pollen as well. This gives the group an important place as pollinators.

One can glimpse the effect that differences in life styles may have on pollination by looking at two big groups of pollinators in Florida: solitary wild bees and flower flies. Solitary wild bees, which are gathering pollen and nectar for their young and for themselves, are much more intense and dedicated in their flower visiting than flower flies, which are only feeding themselves. Flower flies, on the other hand, are more likely to cross-pollinate plants that live some distance apart, and are especially important for that reason. Solitary bees, busily shopping for pollen as close to their nest as possible, thoroughly pollinate nearby patches of flowers. Flower flies, moving casually through the area, are more likely to bring with them the pollen from distant patches of flowers.

Flower flies appear to have no defenses other than extremely fast, evasive flight. However, many species have evolved a defensive mimicry of the stinging bees and wasps that are often found on flowers. One measure of the effectiveness of this mimicry is that students in introductory entomology classes often include flower flies among the Hymenoptera in their collections.

Flower flies are sometimes called hover flies because they are so proficient in hovering in one spot. They may do this momentarily while checking out a flower, but the males hover for several minutes watching for females, or perhaps showing off for them. With the wings moving so fast as to be invisible, the flies seem to be casually levitating until one makes a sudden movement, disappearing from one spot and immediately reappearing suspended in another.

The larvae of Florida flower flies are remarkably diverse in their habits. Many species are predators of aphids, and their green or pink maggots can often be seen cutting a destructive swath through a heedless crowd of aphids. Other species feed on decaying vegetable matter, such as the decomposing pads of fire-killed cacti, or the bacteria-rich oozes around wounds on trees. Several Florida species have flat, slug-like larvae that live in ant colonies and feed on larval ants. About 90 species of flower flies are listed for Florida.

Top: **a flower fly on lantana.**

Opposite page: **another species of flower fly.**

FORENSIC INSECTS

Insects sometimes provide clues that are important in solving violent crimes. A predictable array of insects are attracted to human remains over time. The particular species varies with geography, but this too may provide valuable clues as to whether a body has been transported. The stage of the life cycle of the insects found on a cadaver, combined with weather reports and known insect development times may lead to accurate estimates of the time of death. Flies are particularly useful because of their predictable habits, ranges, and development times. Beetles and wasps sometimes help. In one case, a paper wasp nest was found inside a skull. Since these wasps only nest in dry weather, the season of death was fixed.

J. L. Castner

Soldier Flies

Family Stratiomyidae

In spite of their militaristic name, soldier flies have mouthparts that are too weak to offer any defense, and the species that are brightly colored do not seem to resemble any uniform. Perhaps the old name of soldier fly is derived from swarms of black soldier flies emerging from the sloppy latrines and worse decaying matter that were left in the wake of military campaigns of a hundred years ago.

There is no list of Florida species, but there might be 30-40 species in the state. A few brightly colored species occasionally turn up on flowers, where they feed on nectar. The larvae have varied habits: some are predatory, some live in composting materials or dung, some live in the nests of mammals.

Above: **this fast-flying soldier fly feeds on nectar as an adult. The larvae are aquatic, air-breathing insects. The larvae capture air bubbles with long hairs attached to their breathing tubes. They hold these bubbles underwater as oxygen-exchange devices.**

The only Florida species frequently noticed is the cosmopolitan black soldier fly. This species normally lives in compost, or in the old days, in poorly maintained latrines. Occasionally this species finds its way into a Florida septic system, and then the larvae may appear in toilets, where they horrify the homeowner. In flight, the adult black soldier fly is remarkably wasp-like. The wings are dark like those of many wasps, the pale legs hang down, the short antennae are elbowed, and the buzz has a wasp-like pitch as the fly circles around the picnic table or explores the kitchen after entering an open window. The body is elongate, and for lack of the characteristic wasp waist, there is a pair of translucent patches at the base of the abdomen, so one can see right through the body. This very common insect of South and Central Florida is almost never recognized as a fly.

PC

Bee Flies

Family Bombyliidae

The long, swept-back wings of the common, large, Florida bee flies are most distinctive, making the group easy to identify, even though the species are diverse in the coloration of their fur and the dark patterning of their wings. The bee flies are among the most elegant insect fliers, able to hover and dart in any direction at great speed, or to land on a flower petal without dislodging the drop of dew trembling on its tip. Some species hover while feeding, the hair-like tongue thrusting precisely into a floral tube smaller than the diameter of a sewing pin. This is a group that Florida naturalists often get to see and enjoy because many species are common in open sandy habitats, such as scrub and sandhill.

The adults of many bee flies feed on nectar and pollen, and are easy to find around flowers. The nectar is sucked up with the long tongue, the pollen raked from the anthers with special hairs and transferred to the tip of the tongue. Bee flies may be important pollinators of some native plants because these flies move around rapidly, and do not comb most of the pollen from their bodies in the manner of bees.

The larvae of bee flies are predatory. Various species feed on the larvae of solitary bees, or the egg pods of grasshoppers. There is a Florida species that attacks antlion larvae. The feeding habits of many Florida species are unknown. The US headquarters for the bee flies is California, where there appear to be hundreds of species. About 25 species are listed for Florida, but the real number must be at least twice that, including many species that nobody has named.

JLC

Top: **a bee fly on St. John's wort. This bee fly species is common in sandy areas. The female lays her eggs in sand, often placing them in the sides of a deep footprint of a deer or human. The larvae dig into sand to hunt prey.**

Above: **in Florida, this species of bee fly visits flowers from February through May. The larvae feed on the eggs of grasshoppers.**

Opposite page, top: **a mist-covered bee fly. It will not become active until the sun is high and the temperature hot.**

GM

THE MEANING OF GREEN

Many hundreds of Florida insects share the metallic green color of long legged flies. This color is not caused by green pigments, but by specialized structures, usually fine layers of transparent materials, that interfere with the passage of light beams so that green wavelengths are in phase with each other, while other wave lengths are weakened or eliminate each other. With small changes in the thickness or orientation of the layers, the color can become bronze or purple.

The brilliance of these structural colors, often called iridescent colors, depends completely on the intensity of the light that shines upon the insect. This last feature is of great importance to iridescent insects, because they can go from inconspicuous to spectacularly conspicuous simply by moving from shadow to sunlight. An iridescent green insect that dives into the shade of leaves seems to suddenly disappear, and the insect that is flying through a pattern of shadows made by grass blades produces a confusing irregular strobe light effect. The danger over, the insect can return to the sunlight to parade before possible mates or rivals.

Among the larger insects, iridescent green may warn birds of defenses. Many species of solitary bees are iridescent green, as are some leaf beetles and metallic wood borer beetles, which have defensive chemicals. The green bees seem to have a series of mimics that are less well defended, such as cuckoo wasps and green bottle flies.

Many of the smallest parasitic wasps are iridescent green or blue, and it seems unlikely that these pin-head sized insects are warning of some potent defense. For small wasps and flies, the synchronized wavelengths of light that shoot out from their tiny bodies may be most useful in making them stand out to others of their species amid the gigantic objects that surround them.

Eye Gnats

Family Chloropidae

The eye gnats are a great example of a large, diverse group that is widely known only through the annoying activities of a few species. These are the tiny black, or black-and-yellow flies that sometimes swarm around one's eyes in spring and summer in Florida. They do not bite, but are on a mission to collect secretory fluids, such as those that bathe the eyes. They are frequently found around the genitals of male dogs. They are attracted to scratches on the skin. In some parts of the world, these eye gnats are important carriers of eye diseases and perhaps other infections, but this does not seem to be a problem in Florida. The medical insignificance of eye gnats in Florida is not due to some more harmless feature of the Florida species, but rather due to the level of medical care in this wealthy country. In the US, it would be most unusual to find large numbers of people with serious eye and skin infections sitting around outdoors surrounded by uninfected people, with flies moving busily back and forth.

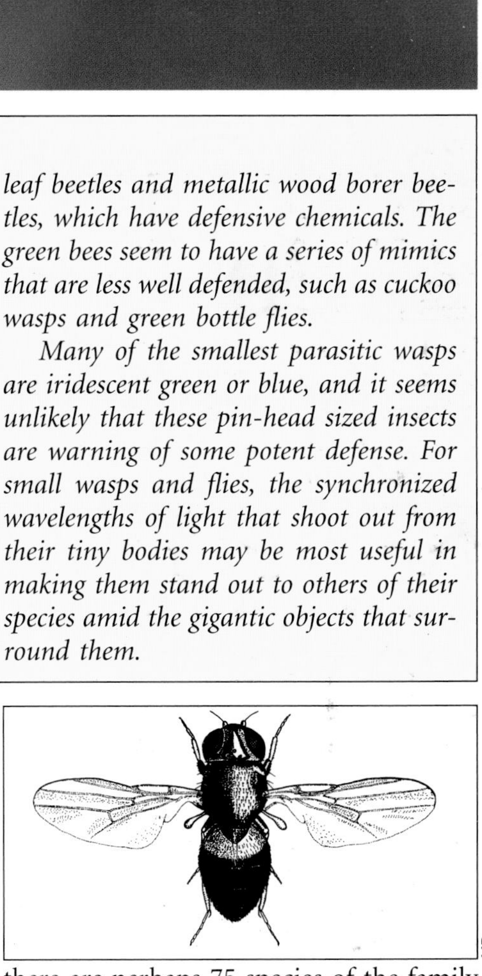

Aside from the species of eye gnats,

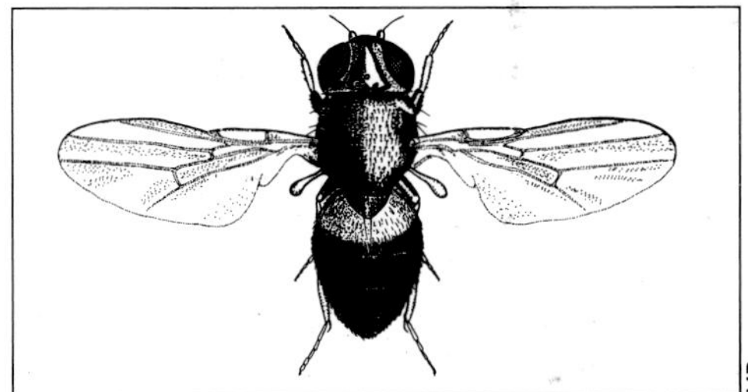

MD

there are perhaps 75 species of the family Chloropidae in Florida. They have the most varied larval habits, with some species that attack aphids, others that breed in mushrooms, others in dead plant material, or in the egg sacs of spiders, or the tissues of live plants.

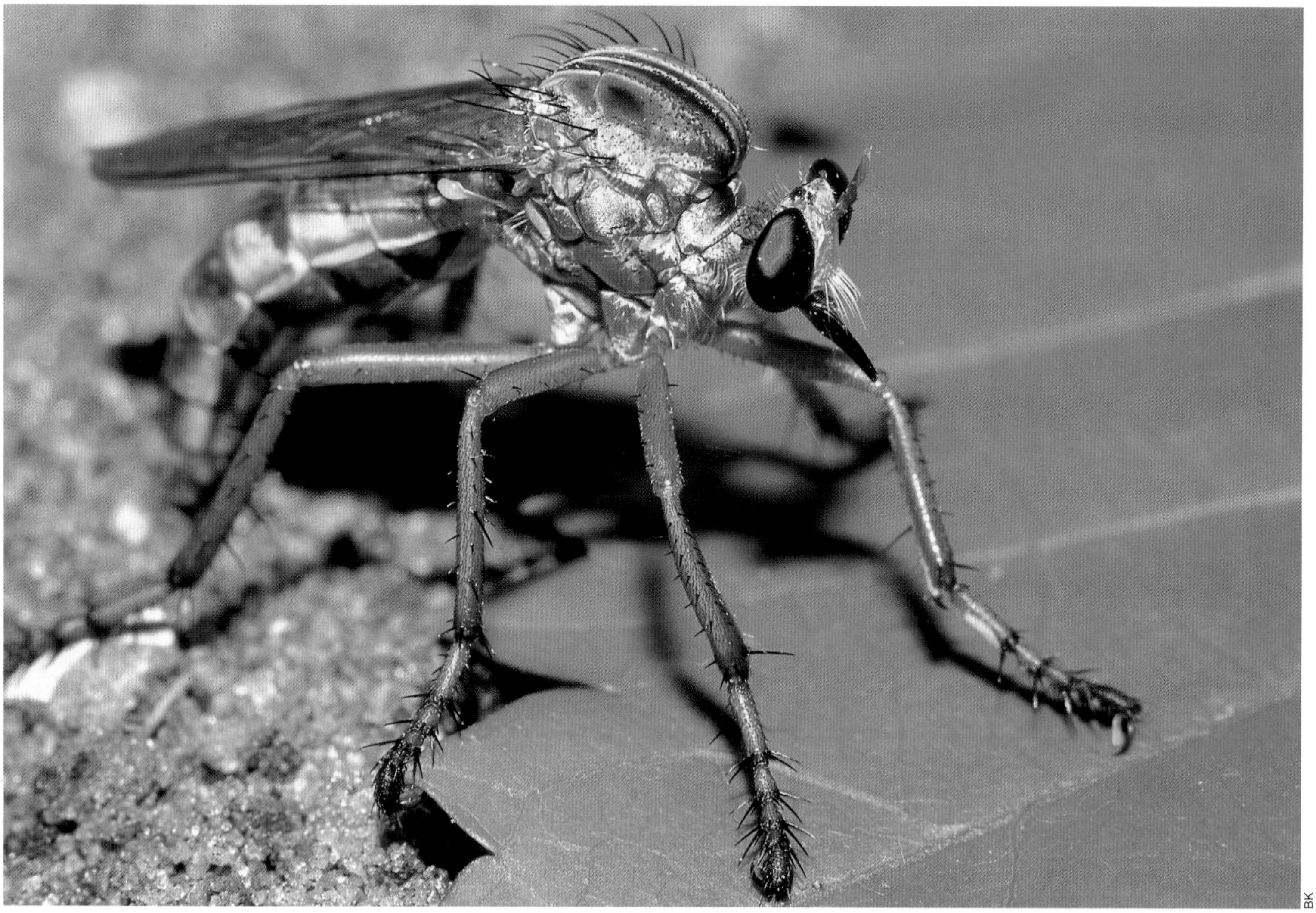

Robber Flies

Family Asilidae

Robber flies are fierce and handsome insects. Many are large enough to admire without a magnifying lens. The name robber fly appropriately conjures up the image of a bearded desperado, but does not reflect the role of the robber fly, which is after the body, not the possessions of its prey. In predatory behavior, robber flies resemble small birds, such as the feisty little flycatchers that dart out from a perch to capture a small insect. Robber flies have big eyes and a sharp beak. The front of the face is usually set with bristles that help keep a struggling prey from damaging the fly's eyes in the few seconds before the injected digestive chemicals take effect.

Many larger species of Florida robber flies are rather rare by fly standards, and naturalists have no clear idea why these flies should be so scarce. Some species are territorial and can be found every day in the same place for a month or more. Observations of these easily watched individuals show that they are not particular in their choice of prey. There is no dependence on a scarce type of prey that can help explain the scarcity of the flies.

Perhaps the larvae have some special requirements that are difficult to find. The larval habits of Florida robber flies are almost completely unknown, but they are probably predatory. Eggs are laid in or on soil, in the cracks of dead wood, or in the tissues of plants. After the eggs hatch, the larvae burrow off to begin their secret lives.

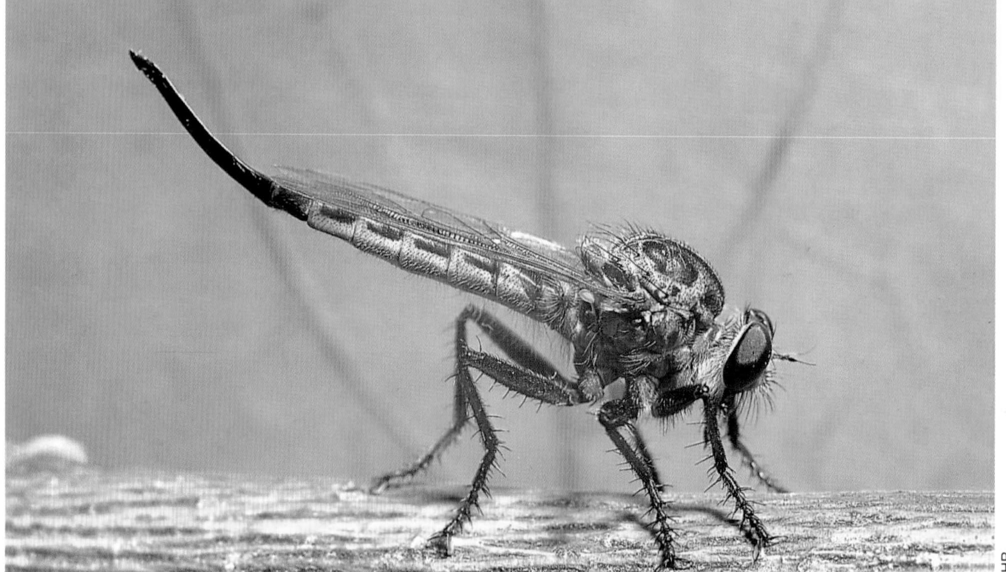

Top: **this robber fly is laying its eggs in sand. Females of this species have stout spines at the tip of the abdomen used for digging.**

Above: **the flattened, egg-laying apparatus of this species might be mistaken for a stinger. It is used to insert eggs into cracks in dead wood.**

HOW ROBBER FLIES HUNT

Robber flies perch on a branch and look about for prey. The robber fly only considers insects that approach within a few yards of its perch. It does not chase its prey from behind, but intercepts the prey by anticipating the path of its flight. After capturing an insect, such as a bee, using its legs for grasping, it then uses its mouthparts to inject a paralysing chemical. The robber fly carries its prey back to its perch where it consumes it by sucking out its insides.

BK

BK

NT

Top: this species, when flying, is a convincing mimic of the bumble bee. The species name of this fly translates as the "wooly one from hell." No one knows why it has such a name.

Center: the large structures on the rear of this species are a set of highly complex, male genitalia.

Left: another bee-like species, whose name means "wooly bee-like one."

Right: the dense hair on the face of robber flies is thought to protect the head against struggling prey.

PC

PC

Mydas Flies

Family Mydidae

There are only eight species of mydas flies in Florida, but some are very conspicuous because of their large size. Although these flies look dangerous, their mouthparts are weak, and they cannot bite, even when handled. Two species can be found regularly on gopher apple flowers. The larval habits of most Florida mydas flies are unknown.

Mydas flies are an ancient and primitive group, geographically widespread, but composed of a relatively small number of species, most of which are large in size, but never abundant. One is tempted to think of them as dinosaurs among the flies. They retain gigantic size and ponderous mobility which seems antique and out of place in the modern world of swooping robber flies and skillfully hovering gnats.

JLC

Top: **a female mydas fly on saw palmetto flowers. The male of this species is black with white bands. The larvae feed on the larvae of June beetles.**

Right: **long antennae that are thickened at the tip are characteristic of mydas flies.**

Opposite page, top: **one of the largest Florida flies, the red-banded mydas fly mimics spider wasps.**

JHR

Black Flies

(Buffalo Gnats)
Family Simuliidae

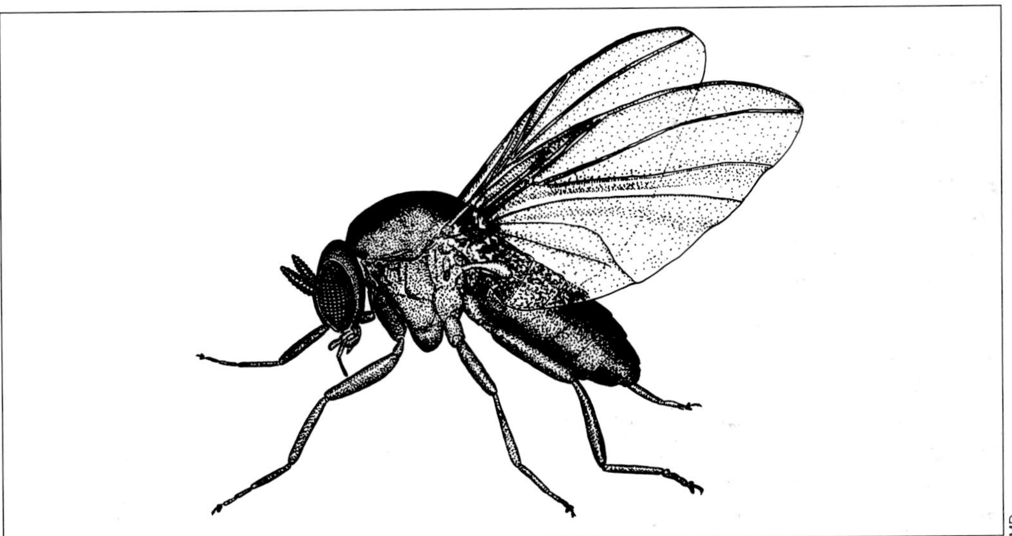

MD

For a black fly, the ideal real estate ad would read, "Mtn. torrent, lg. boulders, lg. flow cold water, commuting distance to moose." Florida offers none of these features, and has a correspondingly small variety of black flies. The scarcity of cool water, which has a high concentration of oxygen, is a particular problem, since most of the rain comes in summer when the temperatures are hot. Nevertheless, Florida does have a few species, mostly in the north, but a couple occur around clean running streams even in the south-central part of the state.

In the El Nino winter of 1997-98, the unusual rainfall brought out little swarms of black flies in most of the state. Even then, a visitor from the banks of the Allagash River in northern Maine would not have been impressed with the Florida version of fly season. "You call this fly season?" he would ask cheerfully. "When you eat with the first breath you draw in the morning enough flies to skip breakfast, then you are in fly season."

Black flies, for those who are not already familiar with them, are about the size of a small mosquito, but much stockier and tougher, with short legs. They do a great deal of rapid flying around before they settle to bite, and even after they have landed they run about prospecting for a good drilling site, the front legs tapping away on the skin like tiny dousing rods. These behaviors make black flies maddening even before they bite. The bite is not particularly painful, but unlike other small flies, it is large enough and the blood anticoagulants are powerful enough that a drop of blood may appear on the skin after the fly has left.

There are some particularly troublesome tropical species of black flies that seem to have adapted well to warm rivers and streams. Unlike tropical mosquitos, none of these species have been accidentally imported into Florida. This is not because people have been especially careful, but because the larvae of black flies, which live attached to objects in flowing water, are not likely to be accidentally picked up, or survive an ocean voyage. In these days of rapid air travel, however, there are new possibilities for the transport of pests. It is not farfetched to imagine some of the durable adult flies following baggage handlers into the cargo hold of an airplane on an airfield near some African river, and getting off in Miami or Tampa the next day.

INTELLIGENCE AND INSTINCT IN INSECTS

Until about 200 years ago, it was erroneously believed that the complex behaviors of insects, such as the hunting raids of ants, were demonstrations of intelligence. This is an understandable error, since among humans the mastery of complex skills requires huge learning ability. But, the complex behaviors of insects are not the result of rational thought. They are genetically programmed responses, often occurring in a series.

The degree of rigidity necessary for this programming can lead to vulnerability. Once a wasp has stocked an underground chamber with beetles and laid her egg, she does not show any intelligent concern for it. If a parasitic fly has succeeded in getting its own larvae into the chamber with the beetles, the fly larvae can eat all the beetles and the wasp larva starves. The mother wasp does not pause while stocking more chambers to open the first one and see if it had been invaded by flies. The entomologist J. Henri Fabre (1823-1915) watched a spider spinning her egg sac. In one experiment, he interrupted the spider when the egg sac was partially completed and removed all the eggs. The spider inspected the empty egg sac, and then completed the process of construction, even though all the eggs were gone. This is not the behavior of an intelligent animal, but neither is it dysfunctional behavior. It would be unlikely for the eggs to suddenly disappear from a partially completed egg sac, and spiders have evolved no behavioral sequence to deal with such an unlikely event.

All this does not mean that insects are unable to observe and learn. Hunter wasps, for example, are very good at learning locations such as the location of their nest hole and the places where they can regularly find prey. Bees memorize the location of certain plants that are in bloom day after day. Once it is understood that insects are not intelligent beings, there is a temptation to consider them as mechanical devices. This view is equally wrong.

A practical difference between instinctive behavior and intelligent behavior can be seen in the ability to change, and to deal with change. A thousand years ago the hunter wasp that collects metallic wood boring beetles in Florida hunted the same beetles, in the same way, in the same kinds of oaks and pines as it does today. Over that same thousand years, human ways of making a living are likely to have changed remarkably. These days, important changes occur in even smaller time spans. One may worry whether the right to bear arms, bestowed in a time of flintlocks, applies to heat-seeking missiles. The paper wasp, sharpening her sting as she guards her nest under the eaves, can make no such decisions, nor does she need to.

While intelligence seems better able to deal with change than instinct, extreme intelligence is a new experiment for animals, and its success is not certain. The faster things change, the easier it is to become confused. Bees and butterflies don't have to think too much, but they have no way of avoiding the tornado of changes roaring up out of the human brain.

MORE INFORMATION ABOUT FLORIDA INSECTS

What would be the next step after this book for those who do not want the story to end? Presently, there is no other general book about Florida insects that could be considered the next step. However, there are other valuable books. The Peterson Field Guides to insects, beetles, and moths are all extremely useful in Florida. The Pictured Key Nature Series guides to the true bugs and to the grashoppers, cockroaches and their allies are both models of their kind. Some groups of insects have their own guides, including butterflies (Florida's Fabulous Butterflies). There is an even more specialized book called Florida Butterfly Gardening by the U. of Florida Press. There are guides to Florida dragonflies and damselflies from Scientific Publishers in Gainesville. The Florida Department of Agriculture issues a series of pamphlets on various Florida insects. And finally, the U.F. Dept. of Entomology maintains an informative insect website.

THE VALUE OF FLY DIVERSITY

Considering the huge group of parasitic flies, one can get a feeling for the diversity of ways insects prey upon each other, and even perhaps derive a slight understanding of what such diversity means. Take, for example, the forest tent caterpillar that sometimes occurs in large numbers in spring in Florida wherever there are large oak trees. There are 26 species of parasitic flies that are known to attack the forest tent caterpillar. Included are species that glue their eggs on the caterpillar, species that attach already developed larvae (still in the egg shell) to the caterpillar, and species that deposit many tiny eggs on the leaves where the caterpillars live. The caterpillars are likely to gulp them down with a mouthful of leaf. Some of these flies occur in different areas or habitats than others. In addition to all these flies, there is a larger number of parasitic wasps that are known to attack forest tent caterpillars. Then there are all the birds that eat caterpillars, the spiders that trap the adult forest tent caterpillar moths, and so on.

HOW FLIES ESCAPE FROM THEIR PRISONS

The pupal stage of flies often occurs underground, where the transforming larva is less accessible to all the predators and parasites that move about on the surface. However, the adult fly that hatches from the pupal stage seems to have no devices for digging its way to freedom. The legs of flies are long and slender, without the thick teeth or trowel-like plates seen in digging insects. The mouthparts of flies are modified for sucking, stabbing, or lapping, but not for digging. Even many knowledgeable naturalists would be stumped if asked how adult flies can free themselves from the prison of their pupal cell and burrow up to the surface of soil or through the outer layers of a rotten log.

In some groups of flies, such as the robber and bee flies, the pupa itself digs. The pupa has rasping teeth on the front of the body, and bands of short, backward-pointing spines on the posterior part of the body. By wriggling, the pupa can loosen the soil above it, and the backward-pointing spines give enough traction to allow the fly to move upward. Once the front half of the pupa reaches the surface, it splits open to allow the adult fly to emerge and expand its wings.

The big group of families of flies that include the fruit flies, house flies and their relatives, and the parasitic tachinid flies, have a different, even stranger mechanism. In these flies, the pupa forms inside a tough case that is the hardened larval skin. This case has the shape of an elongated egg, and has a line of weakness circling its front end. When the adult fly is ready to emerge, it forces blood into a big balloon-like hernia that pops out of the head of the fly between the eyes. This forces open the front end of the pupal case. If the fly has pupated under ground, the balloon begins to inflate and deflate, pushing aside the soil particles. At the same time, the legs thrust the fly upward into the space that opens in front every time the balloon deflates. After reaching the surface, the fly carefully cleans any dirt off the digging balloon, then pulls it back into the head for the last time. Finally, the wings begin to expand, and a little later the fly buzzes away.

FLEAS

ORDER SIPHONAPTERA

Members of this order have biting-sucking mouthparts and lack wings at any stage of their development. Both male and female fleas must feed on blood. Fleas are known for their jumping ability which allows them to escape danger and also to move easily from one host animal to another. A human flea can leap 13 inches.

When the Conquistadors and the earliest European settlers came to Florida they would have brought with them in their ships and on their bodies the human flea, *Pulex irritans.* This insect, fortunately, is now rather scarce, thanks to advances in housing construction and much higher standards of cleanliness of clothes, bedding, and bodies.

In its time, however, the human flea had an interesting place in human culture. When magnifying glasses first became widely available, the most familiar, truly remarkable thing to look at was the nearest flea, and small magnifying glasses were even sometimes called "flea glasses." The initial wow-reaction might be followed by a profound discussion on the mystifying nature of Creation, in which such elegance of detail was lavished even upon a lowly parasite. At a different level of human preoccupation, a well-timed twitch of the body might elicit a friendly and not-so-innocent offer to assist in the pursuit of a wayward flea, which might lead to other pursuits. So, an evening with fleas might be at least as instructional and entertaining as an evening with sitcoms.

Fleas also had a darker side. The Black Death (bubonic plague) that periodically decimated much of Europe and Asia was carried by fleas, primarily rodent fleas. Fleas are still a health problem in some parts of the world, where they transmit plague, tularemia, and murine typhus.

Most native Florida mammals have fleas. These fleas are often specialized to live their lives on a single species of host, or a few closely related species. The specializations of fleas are usually related to fur density, grooming behavior, blood chemistry, and nesting habits of the host. Larval fleas live in the nests or dens of the host, where they feed on organic matter, including dried droplets of semi-digested blood produced by adult fleas. Animals that have no nests or dens, such as deer, do not have fleas. Horses are also flea-free. In the old days, stable boys, whose clothes, workplace and living quarters were saturated with the odor of horses, were known to be ignored by fleas.

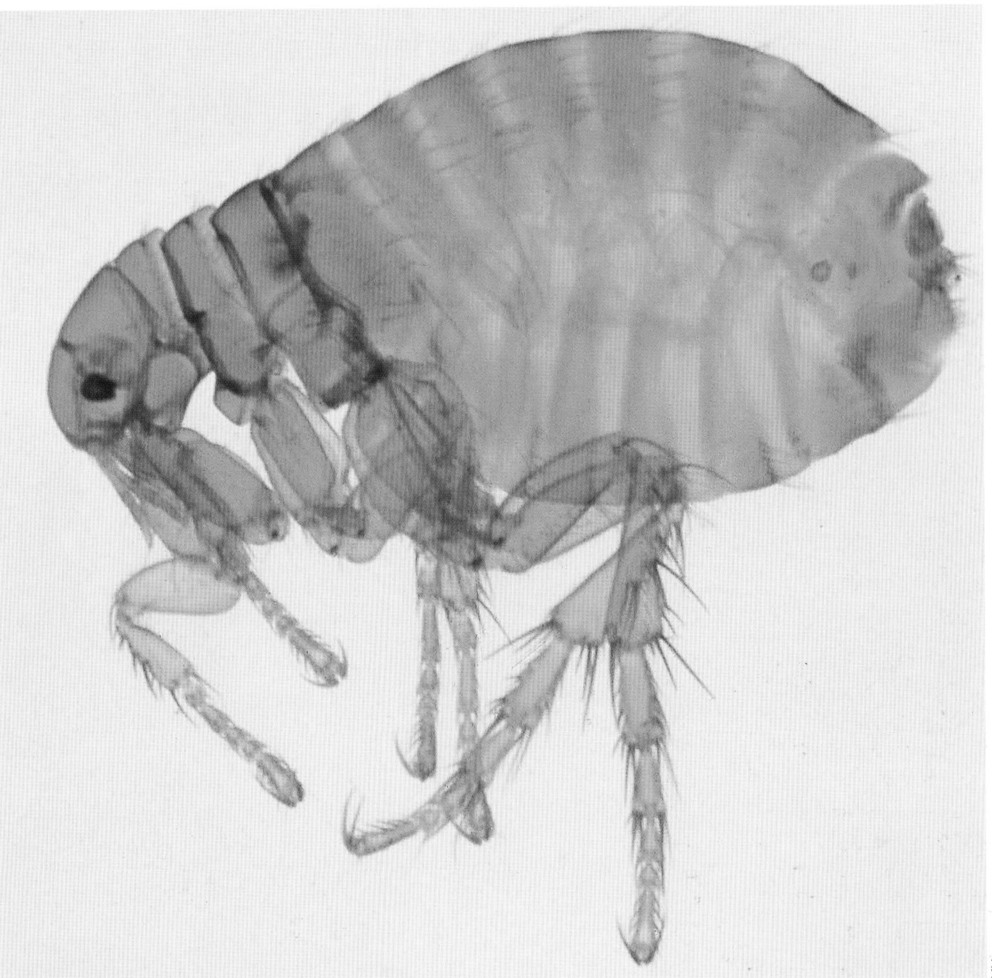

VU

FLEAS CAN REALLY JUMP!

The legendary leaping ability of fleas allows them to make a quick getaway from the claws, teeth or tongue of a grooming host, or to make a flying leap onto a new host. Some observers have fantisized that a flea scaled up to the size of a human could leap tall buildings. This comparison may be misleading, but jump of a flea is still impressive. The hind leg of a flea contains an elastic protein that can be compressed to store energy far more efficiently than rubber, plus a quick-release mechanism. As it hurtles through the air, a flea does somersaults with its claws outstretched.

A FLEA STATE?

Until recently, Florida was notorious among pet owners as a land fiercely infested with fleas, but newly discovered chemical controls that can be applied directly to pets have changed this completely. Ask any Florida veterinarian, and avoid the fate of some who have become desperate.

A fussy young man from the Keys,
Thought his house was infested
With fleas,
So he used gasoline,
And his form was last seen,
Sailing over the tops of the trees.

Top: some peculiar adaptations for the life of a parasite can be seen in this photo. Fleas are compressed to allow them to dash through dense hair. They are covered with backward pointing bristles that allow them to easily move forward, but not be dragged backward. The head can be tucked down and the antennae are set in protective grooves. The animals which host fleas have their own adaptations. For example, the rough tongue of the domestic cat is covered with sharp papillae that are effective in grabbing and mangling fleas, which are then swallowed.

BIG AND SMALL ITS ALL RELATIVE

The following rhyme illustrates the popular belief that no matter how small an animal is, there is usually another, smaller animal which feeds upon it.

Great fleas have little fleas on their backs to bite 'em.
And little fleas have lesser fleas, and so on ad infinitum.
And the great fleas themselves, in turn, have greater fleas to go on;
While these again have greater still, and greater still, and so on.

In reality, the chain of parasites is usually not that long. For instance, there is a flea-mite feeding on fleas which probably has bacteria and viruses on it, but that is the end of the line.

BK

ORDER HYMENOPTERA

This gigantic order of insects humbles and delights the naturalist with its size and complexity. So varied are the Hymenoptera, that there are no simple features that label its members at a glance, except perhaps the possession of two pairs of transparent wings, the forewings much larger than the hind wings. This is one of those classroom distinctions that is wonderfully obvious in diagrams, but not at all obvious out in the garden. Living Hymenoptera have their hind wings linked to their forewings by a row of small hooks, and both sets of wings beat at the same time, so they look and function like one set of wings.

Studies of Florida Hymenoptera are still in a pioneering stage, and even guesses about the number of species in the state have a wild and wooly quality: probably more than 3,000; probably less than 6,000. More than 1,000 species have been found on the Archbold Biological Station in south-central Florida, so there can be masses of species even at a single site. All specialists working on groups of Hymenoptera find species unknown to science when they begin working in Florida. Beyond the simple enumeration of species, there are the more interesting questions about the different ways these species make a living. It is commonplace to find a dozen very similar, closely-related species all living in one area. One often sees, for example, ten or more species of leaf-cutter bees living in a natural area in Florida. Do they differ in the kinds of flowers they visit and the places they make their nests? Nobody has worked out answers to these kinds of questions.

A huge number of species of Hymenoptera are very tiny, around 1/8 inch in length or smaller, and this makes them more difficult to find and study. People who come to Florida from the North often comment that insects in Florida are extra large. It is true that there are some impressively large and conspicuous species, such as the lubber grasshopper, and the various exotic, tropical cockroaches that have invaded Florida. The resident naturalist, however, is even more impressed with the numbers of extremely small insects. This can be clearly seen in a few of the better known groups of Hymenoptera. Among the ants, for example, the proportion of very tiny species is much higher in Florida than in New England or New York. Throughout the East there are large numbers of tiny parasitic wasps, but one gets the impression that the proportion of tiny wasps to bigger wasps is much higher in Florida than in northern states. This pattern, which remains poorly documented and understood, is a reminder that even the overall, large-scale characteristics of Florida's insects remain to be studied.

***Top:* a southern yellowjacket with gaping jaws. These jaws have many uses including killing and dismembering prey, shaving off wood fibers for the construction of a nest, constructing the nest, and carrying objects, including larvae.**

LL

Sawflies

Suborder Symphyta, Several Families

The sawflies are a distinctive group of thick-waisted, non-stinging wasps whose larvae are vegetarians that look and act like caterpillars. Sawfly larvae have more pairs of fleshy feet (usually eight) than butterfly or moth larvae (five pairs or less). Many sawfly larvae, including the pine sawflies that are relatively common in Florida, have the interesting behavior of curling up the rear of the body into the air, while holding on with their front feet. Sawflies are named for the saw-like egg-laying structure of the female, which she uses to slit plant tissues and insert eggs where they will be moist and protected.

This is a group that is most common far north of Florida. A survey site in south-central Florida produced 20 species; one in Nova Scotia produced about 200 species; a specialist in the Washington, D.C. area found about 80 species in his back yard. Even within Florida, the northern tier of counties probably have the largest number of sawfly species. There is no list of Florida sawflies, but there are probably more than 50 species that occur here.

Top: **this sawfly, like a fairy-tale princess, is as good as it is beautiful: its larva feeds on poison ivy. The bright colors probably advertise toxins, or at least a bad flavor. A similar species feeds on sumac.**

BK

Wood Wasps

Family Siricidae

The female wood wasp has an egg-laying device like a hollow needle that she uses to bore into the wood of recently killed trees. The egg is then injected into the wood, along with a solution of fungus that spreads through the wood and makes the wood more edible for the larva. This is only one of many examples of insects and fungi working together. Only a few species of wood wasps occur in Florida, and the group as a whole is small.

Left: **a female wood wasp. This species was introduced from the Orient.**

PC

Hunter Wasps

Family Sphecidae

The hunter wasps are a large and highly diverse group of solitary wasps that is not easy to define in any convenient way. Included in the hunter wasps are the mud daubers and some other species that have a very long, slender "waist." There are also compact species, with the general form of yellow jackets, but unlike yellow jackets, the hunter wasps cannot pleat their wings lengthwise to get them out of the way. Hunter wasps may be large or small, brightly-colored, or inconspicuous. All are very active wasps, with large, bulging eyes for spotting prey, and large jaws used in carrying prey or constructing a nest.

About a dozen species of Florida hunter wasps collect flies. The mother wasp digs a burrow in the sand, using the front legs, which have small rakes on them. When the wasp is moving sand at the entrance, she digs like a dog, head down, tail up, the sand shooting out from under the body. One of the larger Florida species prefers to catch horse flies, and in the old days was known to Floridians as the horse guard (see photo on opposite page). This is an impressive yellow and black species, and when it buzzes around looking for horse flies near the legs of a person brought up in the city, it is more likely to provoke terror than gratitude.

Strongly rooted in the human psyche is a respect for the noble hunter. The hunter wasps have been the subject of studies by admiring scientists for over 250 years. There are hundreds of scientific papers, even whole books, devoted to the behavior of the hunter wasps. Humans easily understand the problems of the solitary hunter wasp trying to make its way in a huge world, forced to wander long distances in search of prey, but also needing to know the way home. We may not wish to be big game hunters, but we still understand the challenge of stalking and overcoming a large, well-defended prey. The moment of vulnerability when one fumbles for the door keys while laden with heavy bags of groceries is also experienced by hunter wasps, whose predators wait by the burrow entrance as the wasp appears, dragging home a large grasshopper or stink bug.

Because it is easy to understand the problems of hunter wasps, they have long provided good models of the ways that insects can do complicated tasks without being able to think things out as a human hunter might. Insects generally use a combination of instinct and learning. Instinct is inborn behaviors, many of which occur in series. Sometimes instinctive behavior is triggered by a stimulus, so if a horse guard is out looking for horse flies, she will approach any large animal she happens to see, and fly rapidly around its legs. If she sees a horse fly, a whole series of fly-catching maneuvers will be triggered. Horse flies, in turn, often respond to the stimulus provided by a buzzing horse guard by zipping off to the nearest shelter.

Top: **the cicada killer wasp, Florida's biggest wasp. This gorgeous wasp catches cicadas and laboriously carries them to her burrow. This wasp is not aggressive toward humans.**

Opposite page, top: **this horse guard wasp is working in her burrow, and sand can be seen flying out beneath her body. This species prefers to collect horse flies, sometimes gathering a dozen or more for each larva. Horses and cows seem to recognize this helpful wasp and are not alarmed by it. People usually lack this "horse sense," and may be terrified.**

Below: **a digger wasp.**

BK

There is considerable flexibility in these behaviors. If the horse guard leaves her nest to hunt for flies, and encounters a patch of flowers from which she can get nectar, she appears to be able to put her fly-hunting behavior on hold, and stop for a drink. If she is in pursuit of a horse fly, and the horse's tail starts to swing her way, her evasive behavior can take over momentarily. If she catches and subdues the horse fly, she uses navigation techniques that involve memory to take the most direct route back to her burrow.

BK

THE STINGING INSECTS

The sting of the ants, bees and wasps is derived from a tubular, egg-laying device, the ovipositor, found only in female Hymenoptera. This egg-laying tube eventually evolved to become a dagger with a channel for venom, with the egg shunted out of an opening near the base of the sting.

The stinging ability of solitary bees and wasps, of which there are several hundred Florida species, tends to greatly overshadow all their other attributes. However, very few people ever get stung by a solitary bee or wasp. The primary function of the sting in solitary wasps is to disable or paralyze prey, including even active animals such as jumping spiders and crickets.

In contrast, the types of venom that have a powerful effect on mammals have evolved primarily in the social insects, such as the honey and bumble bees, yellow jackets, and paper wasps. The large colonies of these species, with many larvae and adults present in one place, make them attractive targets for insect-eating mammals, such as racoons and bears. Humans can be the unfortunate incidental recipients of the strong venom and suspicious attitude of social bees and wasps. Social bees and wasps are normally only aggressive around the nest, a fact which Aristotle (534-522 BC) noticed in honey bees: "Away from the hive they attack neither their own species nor any other creature, but in close proximity of the hive they kill whatever they can get hold of."

Solitary bees and wasps, in contrast, do not even defend their nests in the face of danger. A solitary bee or wasp is the sole provider for any offspring she will produce, so perhaps it is too risky to challenge any animal large enough to destroy her nest. Mud daubers, for example, which often build on walls in Florida, do not even sting the hand that is removing the nest. Even a queen paper wasp that has just started a nest and has no workers to assist her is quite likely to simply fly away when her nest is destroyed. However, a paper wasp nest that is defended by workers does not go down without a fight.

THE GOLDEN AGE OF DISCOVERY OF FLORIDA INSECTS

Species new to science are being described in Florida all the time. These are often called "new species," but they are not new in the sense that they just evolved, but rather they are new to scientists, who never saw them before. The person who first writes a formal description of a species gets to choose the scientific name, and can pick any name, appropriate or not, as long as it has not been used previously, and as long as it is not lewd or excessively frivolous. The author of this book once named a cute Florida grasshopper in honor of his wife, Nancy, who helped find the species: Melanoplus nanciae. *Any natural area in Florida, such as a state park, has its share of undescribed species. The difficult part is to figure out which ones they are: the recognition of an unknown species in a group implies a knowledge of the species that are already known.*

For the naturalist who loves bugs, the golden age of discovery in Florida is right now. In many parts of our country the process of cataloging species and studying their biology occurred in the 19th Century and the first decades of the 20th. Most of Florida was then a trackless wilderness, and not very accessible to biologists. At this time, biologists began to retreat to the laboratory, where the processes of genetics, physiology, and behavior could be studied isolated from the natural world. Consequently, although Florida is now easily accessed in our air-conditioned vehicles, its insect species are still largely unexplored.

One could take up the study of almost any large group of insects (with the possible exception of butterflies) and soon begin to discover species previously unknown to science. One could start cataloging the species in any Florida suburban yard and quickly begin to find new county records, and even new records for the state of Florida. One could study the diet, defenses, courtship and foraging behavior of almost any Florida insect taken at random, and immediately add to our knowledge of that species. Almost everything remains to be done.

PC

CB

Mud Daubers

A common Florida hunter wasp is the handsome black-and-yellow mud dauber, which often makes messy, but interesting nests on the walls of buildings. These nests are built with great speed and skill, the female dauber making many trips to the nearest source of mud and plastering each dab in a distinct crescent-shaped pattern. If her source of mud gives out and she is forced to collect a different type, this will be evident from the pattern on the nest. If one enjoys a little innocent interference in the lives of insects, one can sometimes find the source of mud and change its color with food dyes, which later appear as bands of colored mud on the nest.

The nest is constructed with several chambers, and usually plastered over with a final layer of mud. Each chamber is packed with spiders and sealed. When the mud dauber is working on her nest, she "sings," with a high-pitched buzzing. The mud dauber is a harmless insect, that never stings humans unless the wasp is grabbed by hand. Its collecting of spiders is not particularly useful, but it is not harmful either. It is sad that it is so ruthlessly attacked for the crime of messiness. Perhaps one could post an attractive "mud dauber habitat" sign on the house to deflect the criticisms of neighbors.

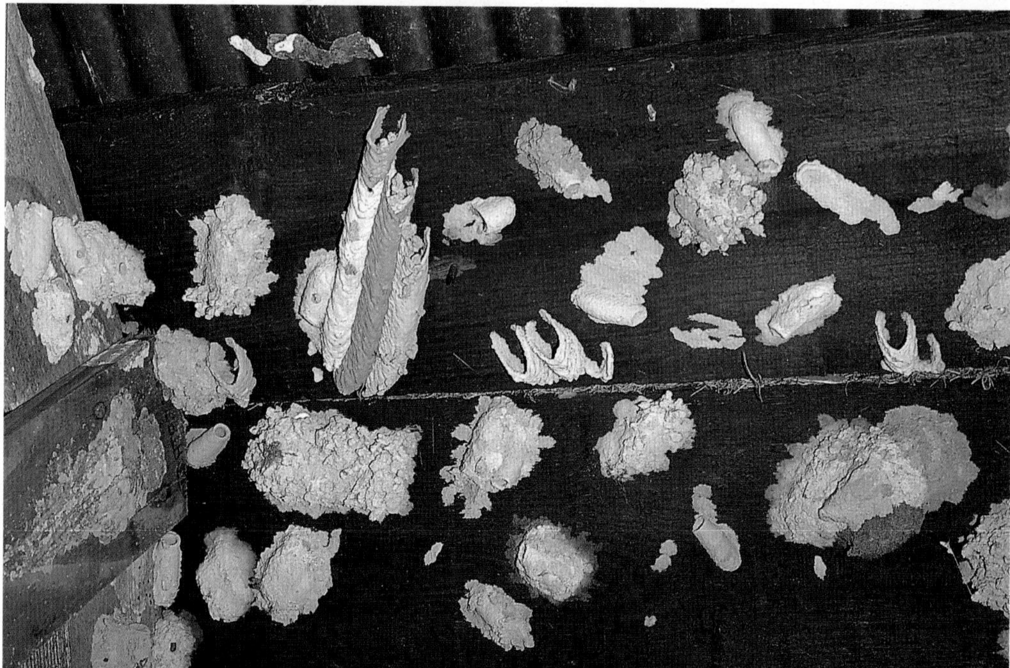

TR

JHR

BK

Top, left: a thread-waisted wasp. The female of this species collects caterpillars for her young.

Top, right: organ pipe mud daubers at their nest entrance.

Left: a black-and-yellow mud dauber gathering a mud ball for nest-building.

Center: a variety of mud dauber nests constructed under the roof of a boat shelter.

Above: a closer look at the contents of a mud dauber nest when opened. All these paralyzed small spiders were collected as food for the larvae.

Potter Wasp

Some species of folded-wing hunter wasps, called potter wasps, build a mud nest in the form of a narrow-mouthed pot. A single egg is placed in each pot, along with several caterpillars for food. The pot is then neatly sealed.

Left: **a folded-wing hunter wasp on flowers.**

Below, left: **a potter wasp transports a ball of mud to construct its nest.**

Below, right: **the potter wasp prepares to close the top of the pot after laying an egg inside along with paralyzed caterpillars for food.**

BBB

BK

BK

Folded-Wing Hunter Wasps

Family Eumenidae

The folded-wing hunter wasps include about 40 Florida species, most of which are black with yellow markings, or black with spots and bands of dark red. These are solitary wasps, although quite closely related to the social wasps like the paper wasps and yellowjackets. They are commonly seen on flowers, where they are drinking nectar. The females hunt for caterpillars, which they paralyze and store away in a nest for their larvae.

Many folded-wing hunter wasps grow up in hollow twigs or in abandoned beetle burrows in dead trees. The nest consists of a series of cells in the tubular space, such as a hollow twig, with a little partition of mud or plant material between each cell. Like airplane passengers, the caterpillars and egg at the back of the tube are packed in first, and naturally the adult wasps that have developed in the cells at the back must emerge last, because their younger brothers and sisters are blocking the way to the exit. It is normal for the wasps at the back to wait for days until the individuals at the front are ready to leave. The wasps must get some kind of signal, perhaps the sound of the wasp in front gnawing through the partition toward the outside. Male wasps mature more quickly than female wasps, and since female wasps can determine the sex of their young, they often lay female eggs at the back, and male eggs at the front. This reduces the time that the oldest offspring need to wait after they become mature.

The young wasps also need to know which way is out. The exit sign is provided by the partitions between the cells. When the mother wasp builds the partition, she carefully smooths the outside face of it, but the inside of the plug is rough. The wasp larva, in a cell that is plugged at both ends, is programmed to face toward the rough wall only, so it will emerge in the right direction after it has become an adult.

Many eumenid wasps are infested with mites which move into the nest and feed on the blood of mature larvae without injuring them.

THE RED SHIFT

A strange feature of folded-wing hunter wasps in Florida is that a number of species that are yellow-and-black in other parts of their ranges to the north are dark red-and-black in Florida. The same pattern of special Florida red-and-black subspecies is found in some other groups of wasps, and in some flies that mimic stinging wasps. Nobody knows the origin of this "red shift" in color patterns in Florida. What is seen today must be the result of a very long process in which a few dark red-and-black species were so well-defended that this color pattern became recognized by birds as a strong warning signal. The yellow, orange, and red pigments are quite variable in many species of insects, and if the redder individuals were seen by birds as likely to be particularly awful tasting, there might be a slow selection for the red and black pattern. A strange thing is that this selection must have happened despite the fact that yellow-and-black was already well established as a warning coloration throughout North America.

BK

Ichneumon Wasps

Family Ichneumonidae

The hyperactive and elegantly marked ichneumon wasps occur in such a dizzying profusion of species that most Florida naturalists are happy to be able to recognize a tiny fraction of them. This is not one of those groups that is difficult because so many species look almost exactly alike. Nor is it a group that is difficult because there are a batch of species the size of a pinhead. It is the sheer number of species that is daunting, with about 375 known so far, and the number expected to reach 500 or 600. Even recognizing the group is not so easy, because they vary so much, but most species are slender and elongate, with transparent (or sometimes brown) wings, and the body often marked with white, black, orange, and yellow. Many species have orange legs, and many have a white band on the antennae.

The female ichneumonid has a probe for egg laying, called an ovipositor, that may stick out behind her. She can jab with this structure if molested, but it is not a true stinger. The ovipositor of some species can drill through tough substances, even wood, to get at a larval insect, such as a beetle grub or caterpillar, that is concealed from view. Once she has drilled down to her prey, she stings it and lays her egg on its body.

Everything about this process is slightly improbable. It seems unlikely that the wasp could so precisely determine the location of her prey without seeing it, but she does so, possibly by picking up the vibrations it makes while moving and eating. It seems unlikely that a flexible ovipositor finer than a hair could pierce a hard substance, such as the bark of a tree. The ovipositor, which is covered with a protective sheath when not in use, is tubular and composed of an upper and lower section that fit together to make the tube. During operation, the two sections slide against each other, with the sharp tip of each section advancing alternately. Microscopic backward-pointing ridges on the tips help anchor the ovipositor as it goes in. It seems unlikely that the wasp could actually lay an egg, since the egg, as it is seen attached to the host larva, is much too swollen to fit in the ovipositor. When it is laid, however, it is compressed into a tiny thread, which is forced down the tube, popping back into an egg shape as it escapes from the tip of the ovipositor.

Many species of ichneumon wasps lay eggs in exposed larvae, such as leaf-eating caterpillars. Their main challenge is finding hosts. They appear to do this in a series of steps, going first to the right habitat, then the right kind of foliage, then to damaged leaves, and finally tracking down their prey.

Ichneumon wasps that attack leaf-eating caterpillars may be assisted in their search by the chemicals whose odor streams out from plant tissues when they are cut by a caterpillar's jaws. There may be more going on here than the simple release of chemicals, such as the smell one gets by cutting a mint leaf with a knife. It is now known that many plants have special defensive chemicals that they manufacture only when they are being attacked by leaf-eating caterpillars, chemicals that appear to be induced by caterpillar saliva. Perhaps ichneumon wasps are zeroing in on these chemicals. The name ichneumon comes from Greek, and means "a tracker." The name was first bestowed on one of these wasps by Linnaeus in 1758. Today we are only just beginning to understand the perfection of Linnaeus' choice of a name, and the sophistication of these tracker wasps.

The ichneumon wasps are generally considered highly beneficial because it is difficult to find a crop-eating grub or caterpillar that is not attacked by one or more ichneumon. They are also vital in Florida's natural habitats, because they help keep the plant-eating insects in check. Populations of caterpillars and other grubs help maintain diversity and balance in natural systems, but they themselves could easily have population explosions that would wipe out whole species. Many plants, for example, can only take complete defoliation in rapid succession a few times before they die. In a natural area, such as a Florida state park, there are hundreds of species of plants, attacked by several hundred species of plant-eating insects, which are controlled in turn by hundreds of species of predatory insects, including the ichneumon wasps.

***Top:* this ichneumon wasp is known to attack the larvae of wood-boring beetles and moths. It shows the white antennal bands found on many species.**

BK

PC

JHR

Top, left: **an ichneumon that drills through bark and wood to lay its egg on a beetle larva. In flight, this species resembles a paper wasp.**

Top, right: **this species belongs to a genus with several species in Florida. This is the largest genus of ichneumons, with an estimated 1,000 species wordldwide. This species attacks the caterpillars of moths.**

Left: **an eastern giant ichneumon wasp inserts her long oviposter into a tree limb to deposit an egg on a wood wasp larva. The thicker filaments are the sheaths of the ovipositor.**

CONSEQUENCES OF BEING A GOOD MOTHER

Most Hymenopteran mothers provide everything for their offspring. They arrange things so that their larvae will not need to forage for food, move, or defend themselves, from the moment that the larvae hatch from the egg until the moment that they emerge as an adult.

The Hymenoptera is an order of super-moms. Compare the mother midge (a fly) and the mother digger wasp. The mother midge flies around, mates, and deposits her eggs in or near the water. The mother digger wasp flies around, mates, finds a good home site, digs a burrow, makes a separate chamber to hold each of her offspring, comes out, closes the burrow, hunts for a particular type of prey (a cricket, for example), paralyzes the prey by stinging it in just the right place, hauls it back to the burrow, opens the burrow, drags the prey down to a chamber, lays an egg on it, seals the chamber, and leaves to hunt again. All these operations require special tools, so, compared to the midge, the digger wasp has a lot of complex equipment. Not least among the digger wasp's tools are those needed for her own survival. It may take her weeks to take care of the needs of a small number of offspring, and during that time she must feed and defend herself.

Not surprisingly, male Hymenoptera tend to be pale copies of the females. The males are usually notably different from the females, because they lack all the special structures associated with hunting, digging, gnawing holes, gathering pollen, or whatever the female of their species may do in the course of her maternal duties. In fact, it is often difficult to decide which female goes with which male unless the two are seen together. It is as if the males were courtiers and dandies in the court of Louis XV, while the females were the mechanics, tradesmen, and farmers who did all the work. In this kind of peculiar society, both sexes might show comparable levels of elaboration and sophistication, but meaningful professional differences and major advances in ways of doing things would all be carried by the female line. In the Hymenoptera, the professional differences and major advances in ways of doing things, all in the area of maternal care, explain most of the diversity of the order.

BK

JHR

Braconid Wasps

Family Braconidae

Braconid wasps are parasitic insects (whose young eat other insects or larvae of other insects) like the ichneumon wasps, but are smaller and generally more compact. Most species are brownish or blackish, but there is a big batch of Florida species that are beautifully marked in bright red and black, with black wings. These scarlet tanagers of the wasp world are probably flaunting their nasty flavor, although nobody seems to have tested this in the obvious way. Some species also emit an obnoxious odor when handled.

The braconid wasps include a huge number of very specialized species, most of which are small and easily escape notice. The females spend their lives diligently hunting for particular kinds of insects, perhaps the larvae of leaf-mining moths, beetle grubs that live in seeds, aphids found on shoots of plants, or even tiny bark lice. The group as a whole seems less frenzied than the larger parasites, such as the ichneumon wasps and tachinid flies. The females may be seen flying slowly, or walking carefully around the possible site of hidden prey. Perhaps this slower searching behavior reflects the tendency of the group to attack prey that occur in numbers in one place, so it is better to search methodically for all of these prey than to dash off to a different site. Another feature of some braconid wasps is that they may breed in large numbers in a single host, such as a big caterpillar, a habit that also reduces the need to race about.

Many of the braconid wasps that attack caterpillars lay their eggs in the eggs of the host. The wasp larva hatches, but then remains like a little time bomb in the caterpillar as it feeds and grows. It is not until the caterpillar is half grown, or even larger, that the wasp larva begins to consume it from within, like some parasitic alien in a science fiction film. As one learns more of the lives of insects, one becomes increasingly aware of the multitude of terrible fates that can overtake them, of the many kinds of dangers that do not affect huge mammals such as ourselves.

The number of braconid wasp species that live in Florida cannot be estimated at present, but the number could even exceed that of the ichneumon wasps. The ichneumons achieve their greatest diversity in the Appalachians, and rapidly decline as one moves south in the peninsula. The braconid wasps, on the other hand, occur in great numbers throughout Florida. A good proportion of the smaller braconid wasps are undescribed, and therefore have no names. One study in south-central Florida found eleven species of braconid wasps that were parasites of mushroom flies. Nine of these species were undescribed.

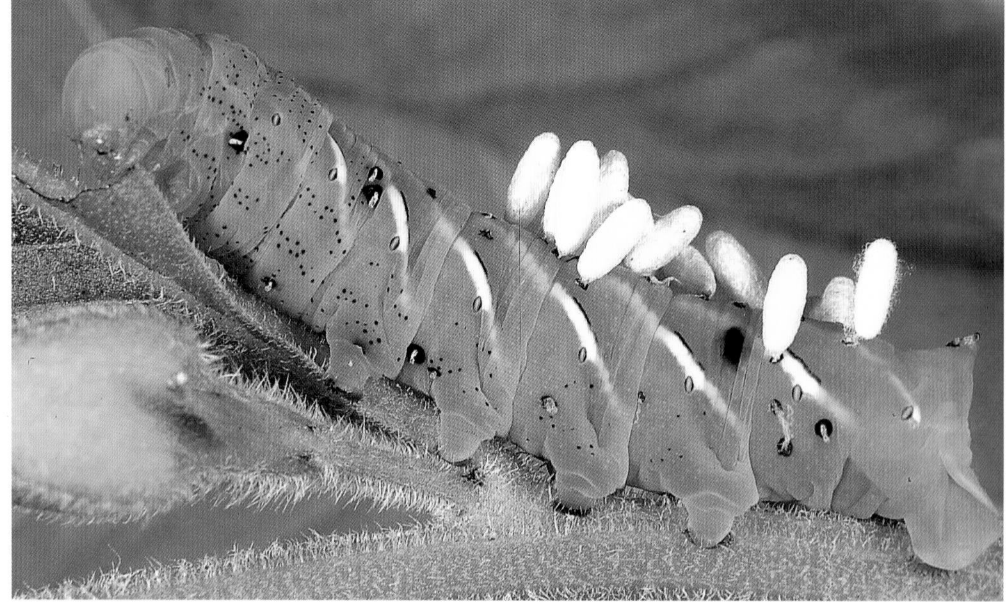
ABS/EISNER

Top, left: **one of the supposedly inedible species of braconid wasps.**

Top, right, and above: **moth caterpillars with cocoons of braconid wasps. The wasp larvae feed inside the caterpillar, then make small holes through which they emerge. The caterpillar seems undistressed until its body has been almost completely consumed.**

WHEN IS A PARASITE NOT A PARASITE?

A parasitic wasp has a very close relationship with a single host insect, such as an individual caterpillar. The wasp, or maybe several of them, completes its development on or in this host. A braconid wasp, for example, may get enough nourishment for its entire growth by eating a single weevil larva living in a stem gall in a scrub wildflower. In this intimacy with a single host individual, the parasitic wasps resemble typical parasites, such as fleas and lice.

On the other hand, the parasitic wasp always kills its host, which fleas are unlikely to do. True parasites, in fact, have an interest in becoming as numerous as possible, while causing as little injury as possible. The perfect parasite causes no perceptible difficulty for its host. The hair follicle mites that most people have in the hair follicles of their eyebrows are a good example of a perfect parasite.

Parasitic wasps, therefore, are more like predators in their relationship to their victim. Unlike more familiar predators, such as a bobcat or a spider, these wasps attack only a single prey during an entire lifetime. Ecologists have invented the word "parasitoid" to cover the thousands of kinds of predatory wasps and flies that consume only one insect in a lifetime of growth and development. Except for a few specialists, nobody knows this word, so it seems sensible to use the terms "parasite" and "parasitic" for this book.

BK

Scarab Hunter Wasps

Families Tiphiidae and Scoliidae

The yellow and black tiphiid wasps that buzz around flowers are a familiar sight in natural areas in Florida. The adults feed on nectar, and the male hangs around flowers waiting for females to stop in for a drink. The female spends much of her time burrowing, and her legs are much more muscular than those of the male, and equipped with heavy spines used in digging. She digs through the soil looking for the larva of a scarab beetle, and when she finds one she paralyzes it and lays an egg on it. She then resumes her search for larvae. There is probably some method to her hunting, but this has not been studied. Although one sometimes sees groups of tiphiid wasps together, especially males, which may sleep in groups on grass stems, these are not social wasps, do not live in a colony, and are considered solitary wasps.

Top: **a male, five-banded tiphiid wasp. Males have a curved spine on the abdomen with which they can pretend to sting a predator.**

A BOGGLING OF BUGS

There is a mind-boggling diversity of insects in Florida—many thousands of species. Most people are more interested in the number of species that might occur in their neighborhood. Unfortunately, there are few localities anywhere in the US where there has been a serious attempt to list all the species living in one place. One such place, however, is the Archbold Biological Station in south-central Florida. Its study has already listed over a thousand species of moths and butterflies, over a thousand species of beetles, and impressive lists in several other insect orders.

These lists of species, even if complete for all organisms, would be only a small fraction of the biological diversity on a site. The real diversity is in all the relationships these insects have with each other, other animals, plants, and microbes. A single species of insect might have a host of relationships. The larva of a flower fly feeding on aphids would be a predator to the aphids, an enemy to the many kinds of ants and other insects that feed on the honeydew produced by aphids, a benefactor to the plant and to animals dependent on that plant, a competitor to the other insects that eat aphids, a prey to specialized wasps that feed on flower fly larvae. As adults, this species of flower fly might pollinate many species of flowers, and be eaten by any one of hundreds of species of predators, such as spiders, robber flies, or flycatchers. Multiply the number of species on a site by the number of relationships in which each partakes and it becomes apparent how complex the natural world can be.

Naturalists might occasionally wonder how there can be any stability, order, or meaning in a system in which there are so many possibilities, so many combinations. It turns out, surprisingly, that all complex biological systems, from a single cell, to genetic systems, to whole communities, are similar in their basic structure, and to understand one is to understand all.

The efficiency and precision with which energy and materials move through an ecological system relies on the presence of large numbers of unique species, many of them rather rare, appearing in an endless number of combinations. Species in a community are somewhat like words in a language, appearing over and over again in different contexts. Some words and some species are common and appear frequently, while others are seldom seen, but may fill some special role.

Minute Parasitic Wasps

(About 20 Families of Florida Wasps)

There are numerous families of minute parasitic wasps. These wasps taken together must include 1,000-2,000 species in Florida. They join with all the other parasitic and predatory insects to guarantee that there will be few outbreaks of any one species overrunning the state.

Some of these wasps are among the smallest Florida insects. This is because there are whole families of minute parasitic wasps that attack eggs of insects or spiders. Each wasp completes its entire development within a single egg, so they can be no bigger than the egg itself. There are, for example, species that live in the eggs of stink bugs, the eggs of water striders, the eggs of katydids, and so on. There are many species that attack eggs of insect pests, and some of these are used for biological control, especially in green-houses. There are many others whose effects on biological systems would be hard to guess. For example, if one looks in the web of a large spider, such as the golden orb weaver, one can often find a small silvery spider that lives on little insects that get caught in the web, but are too small to interest the big spider. This silvery spider spins a tiny urn-shaped egg sac, from which may hatch minute spiderlings, or equally tiny adult wasps, a couple of which could easily tango on the head of a sewing pin. This spider egg wasp has no economic importance. It is unlikely to be a mainstay of the larger biological systems they inhabit. It is of no interest whatsoever, except that it is an extremely cool animal.

Floridians are more likely to know what the Chinese giant panda eats for breakfast, than they are to know anything about the biology of the tiny parasitic wasps in their own back yard. We are aware of few contacts with these micro-beasties. Occasionally, while reading out on the patio, we see one of these wasps, like an errant punctuation mark, walking purposefully up the page. We know nothing more about it. There is nothing really wrong with this situation. The little wasps will do their jobs without our knowledge or approval. Still, it is good to know that there are hundreds, probably thousands, of these species out there, helping to preserve the biological balance.

ABS/EISNER

ABS/EISNER

Top: **this minute parasitic wasp is laying eggs on the hairy seed pods of a blue lupine. The larva attach themselves to ants and get carried into ant nests where they eat ant larvae.**

Above: **a parasitic wasp about to lay an egg in the egg of another insect.**

Velvet Ants/Cow Killers

Family Mutillidae

Velvet ants are conspicuous insects, usually clothed in brightly colored fur (hence the name "velvet"). The largest Florida species is sometimes called a "cow killer" because it looks deadly enough to kill a cow. Velvet ants are often seen racing boldly about in open areas. They are not actually ants, which are social insects and live in colonies, but are solitary, ant-like, wingless wasps. Male velvet ants have wings, and spend most of their time flying low over sandy areas in search of females. The female velvet ant, when pursued by a male, usually races for cover in the leaf litter. Perhaps, like many other insects, female velvet ants need to mate only a single time, while the males live in hope of multiple matings.

Male velvet ants often look so completely different from females of their own species that the only way to be sure which kind of male goes with which kind of female is to catch them mating. To make matters worse, mating in velvet ants often lasts less than a minute. For this reason, for many years there were Florida velvet ants that had two scientific names, one for the female and another for the male, but almost all the Florida species (about 50) have now been matched up by sharp-eyed entomological voyeurs.

PC

Velvet ants are parasitic insects. This does not mean they are lazy or careless of their offspring; in fact, they are particularly energetic and enterprising. In most species that have been studied, the female slips into the burrow of a solitary bee or wasp, where she lays her egg on the mature larva of the bee or wasp. This is why velvet ants are often seen running along in open places where the concealed burrows of sand wasps and digger bees are likely to be found.

The female velvet ant is a tough insect. She may be covered with fur, but beneath the fur is a remarkably hard exoskeleton, which the velvet ant needs if she is attacked by a bee or wasp. She also has a long, strong sting, capable of injecting a painful dose of venom if she catches the eye of a bird or lizard while traversing open sandy areas. Among her other defenses are repellent chemicals, warning coloration, warning noises, extremely rapid, evasive, zigzag running, and as a last resort, playing dead.

While notably well defended, velvet ants are not at all aggressive. They sting humans only when picked up or stepped on. The sting hurts a lot for a short time, but the pain does not last.

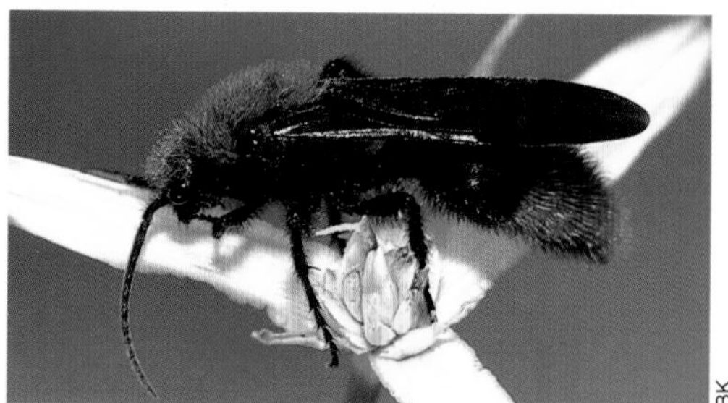

BK

Top: **a female velvet ant.**

Above: **the male velvet ant has wings.**

ABS

BK

Gall Wasps

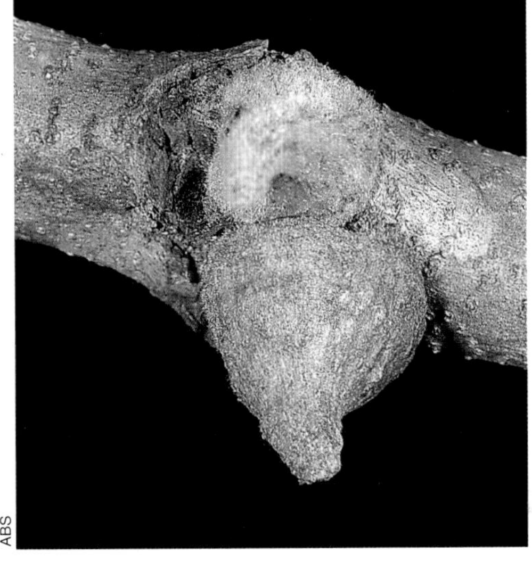

ABS

ABS/DEYRUP

***Photos:* different types of oak galls caused by gall wasps. The gall at top right has been attacked, probably by a bird. Gray squirrels sometimes eat whole galls.**

Family Cynipidae

When insects are in an unfavorable environment, they can relocate with speed and purpose. Plants cannot do this. From this elementary distinction springs another set of opportunities for insects. Because an individual plant cannot flee its problems, it compensates by growing to adjust to the effects of light levels, the availability of water, wind speed, and injury. This is why most plants are so much more plastic and variable than animals, and incidentally, why rows of precisely clipped shrubs always have that spooky, living dead look. A plant is an orchestrated organism, positioning its flowers, shoots, leaves, and roots in appropriate places, constantly adjusting through growth. This complicated orchestration is mediated through plant hormones, that tell the tissues how to differentiate. Growth is therefore controlled through a chemical code.

Certain insects have cracked the chemical code of plants, producing their own chemicals to stimulate grown-to-order structures that both house and feed a larval insect. Since some insect galls on plants appear as irregular, lumpy swellings, or as a mad proliferation of leaflets, there is a tendency to think of galls as plant cancers. If there is an opposite of a plant cancer, an insect gall is it. A gall is a highly controlled, highly structured plant organ that an insect has designed for itself. A gall is like a seed, with all its nourishing and protective layers, and at its heart is a tiny animal.

Several groups of Florida insects have the ability to stimulate plant gall formation. The most familiar galls are those made by little gall wasps on oak trees. These galls appear in various places on the tree: on roots, twigs, leaves, buds, flowers. One species of tree, even one individual tree, may have several kinds of galls. For example, at one site in south-central Florida ten kinds of gall wasps are found on sand live oak, eighteen kinds on Chapman oak. Although the greatest diversity of oak galls is usually found in natural areas, even the oaks in the parking lot of the nearest Florida mall are likely to have galls. Sometimes oaks in urban areas have unusually high concentrations of galls. It is possible that the parasitic wasps that attack gall wasp larvae find it difficult to survive in the city, so some urban gall wasps are able to multiply faster.

One thing that all gall wasps need is actively growing plant tissues. Each year's oak galls are usually formed on the new growth. Different parts of the oak tree grow at different times of year. The flowers appear in early spring, leaves and shoots continue to appear through early summer or beyond, buds may form in fall. Many gall wasps have expanded their period of activity by forming one kind of gall on one part of the tree early in the season, perhaps on the male flowers, and another kind of gall later, perhaps on the leaves. The wasps have two possible lines of development, depending on where and when the larvae are growing, so the spring generation of wasps may not look like the summer generation. Usually, one generation is composed of females only.

Since a species can appear in two forms, the number of Florida gall wasp species is unclear. To make matters worse, there has been relatively little study of gall wasps in the northern part of the state where the greatest number of oaks (25 species) can be found. At the Archbold Biological Station in south-central Florida, one of the few oak gall wasp specialists spent part of the winter and spring raising gall wasps from the local oaks. He found about 80 kinds of gall wasps, even though only eight species of oaks occur on the site. The actual number of species, of course, might be somewhat less, perhaps 60 species. Who knows how many species occur in North Florida? Maybe 200? 250? One thing is certain, any high school student who decided to see how many kinds of gall wasps could be raised from local oak galls would find undescribed species of wasps.

Paper Wasps

Family Vespidae

Without anybody noticing, a paper wasp has begun making her nest in the corner of a garage doorway, out of the way of the raising and lowering of the door, sheltered from the wind and rain. Day after day, the mother wasp works on her paper honeycomb, using a pulp of fibers scraped from the dried stems of nearby tall weeds. Day after day the mother wasp hunts caterpillars, chews them up into nutritious meatballs, and offers them to her hungry larvae. Soon the older larvae are spinning a silk cap over their hexagonal cells. A couple of weeks later, the first adult worker wasps emerge. They take over the duties of enlarging and guarding the nest, and hunting and preparing food for an ever-growing brood of their baby sisters.

Around the time that there are fifteen or so workers supporting the colony, it first comes to the attention of the owner of the garage. He is getting out a stepladder stored in the garage, and its top comes dangerously close to the nest. Immediately, there are five wasps making warning flights around the ladder and his head, while the rest of the workers have assumed red alert posture. He carries the ladder down the driveway considerably faster than his usual pace. Later, at dinner, the wasp nest is a topic of conversation. His wife reminds him of a visitation of grandchildren the following month. He wonders whether the old can of spray under the sink is still any good. The following week, however, before he can get his act together, a red-bellied woodpecker makes an early raid on the nest, dislodging it from its conspicuous refuge, and gobbling down the larvae, in spite of the wasps buzzing around and attempting to sting.

Despite the uneasy relationship between homeowners and paper wasps, most of Florida's nine species of paper wasps have probably benefitted from human activities. The species that make nests in cavities in trees, a type of home site always in short supply, have an endless choice of buildings, other structures, and abandoned equipment in which to make their nests. The species that make nests in thickets and on the undersides of large palmetto leaves do not have their nests threatened by as many fires as in the days before human meddling with fire cycles in Florida.

Paper wasps are not particularly aggressive, and many biologists enjoy having the nests nearby where they can easily be observed. These wasps, however, vigorously defend the nest if it is threatened. Simply approaching the nest is not necessarily viewed as an attack. One can often get to within a few inches of the nest without any wasps leaving the nest, although they become increasingly alert and watch the intruder closely. Nests often go unobserved for months in places where there is plenty of human action, such as the underside of stadium bleachers, or the underside of a mailbox.

RFS

The paper wasp sting is painful, but these wasps are truly dangerous only to people who are strongly allergic to wasp venom. Since the nests are often high up, they may be encountered unexpectedly when one is at the top of a ladder.

Paper wasps have an annual cycle, even in Florida, with its warm winters. The nest is usually started by a single female, but sometimes several females cooperate. Worker daughters, which do not mate or produce offspring, are produced during the spring and summer. In fall, the queen lays the eggs that will develop into new queens and males. Mating is in late fall for most species, around Thanksgiving in southern Florida. The new queens then settle down in some sheltered place until the next year.

Mating groups often occur around tall, dead pines. Dozens of males, sometimes representing several species, wait for females to pass by. Paper wasps sometimes choose fire towers or other tall structures for their get-togethers. The gantry at the Kennedy Space Center, rising out of thousands of acres of flat countryside, is a magnet for male paper wasps. Maintenance workers and engineers may be a bit unnerved by the hundreds of wasps flying about. However, all these wasps are males. Since only female wasps can sting, the danger is not as great as it seems.

BK

BK

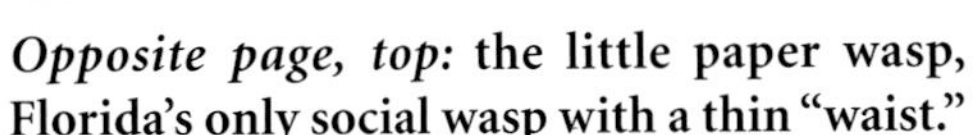

JHR

Opposite page, top: **the little paper wasp, Florida's only social wasp with a thin "waist."**

Opposite page, bottom: **the Carolina paper wasp, also known as the red paper wasp.**

Top, left: **a worker paper wasp on her nest in the "warning" position: wings half spread, slightly elevated, legs spread widely, head tilted toward the threat, in this case, a camera.**

Top, right: **a communal nest of the paper wasp. Notice the tiny, pearl-like eggs in some cells. Other cells contain larvae still in their cocoons.**

Right and far right: **paper wasps pulping insect prey as food for their young.**

BK

LL

LL

The species of paper wasps in Florida are generally difficult to tell apart since they are quite similar and also, there is much variation within each species. The little paper wasp is about half the size of any of the others. It has a long, narrow "wasp waist," and is the most easily recognized species. The many Florida paper wasp species are not identical in behavior and ecology. There is, for example, one species that is more aggressive than the others, and there is another species that almost always builds its nest on branches overhanging lakes or streams.

Left: **a paper wasp drinking at the nectar cup of a castor bean. This species (identified by the yellowish tips on the antennae) often nests in low shrubs, and is quite aggressive when the nest is approached.**

Right: **a queen paper wasp on a new nest that she has built. She is raising daughters that will take over most of the building and hunting duties that she now does by herself. The nest is suspended on a slender paper stem that the queen covers with ant repellent to keep ants away from her larvae.**

LL

JHR

Yellowjackets and Hornets

JLC

Top: the southern yellowjacket, Florida's most common species.

Above: two stripes on the thorax identify the southern yellowjacket.

Family Vespidae

The yellowjackets and hornets are wasps most famous for their fervent group defense of the nest. The paper nests of yellowjackets and hornets are strongly built, and there is even a large enough labor force to cover the combs of cells with a sturdy outside envelope. Thus these wasps can build their nests in the open, or in damp soil, greatly reducing their dependence on shelters such as hollow trees, which are often scarce. The individuals of a colony keep an eye on each other's activities, and quickly congregate for group projects, such as removing the remaining bits of meat on an abandoned chicken drumstick under a picnic table. It is not clear whether these "helpers" are cooperating, or merely taking advantage of the situation.

The names "yellowjacket" and "hornet" are not used very consistently, but most people call the yellow-and-black species yellowjackets, and the white-and-black species hornets. Some species build a nest in an underground cavity, others build nests above ground, either in trees and shrubs, or in buildings.

Yellowjackets and hornets feed their larvae minced insects. The insects are usually caught with a quick pounce, and chopped up with the mandibles. The sting of a yellowjacket or hornet is primarily defensive, and is not used to paralyze prey. Individual workers often become specialized. One may return over and over to a dried fish head to catch flies, another may come to a porch light every morning to catch insects attracted the previous night. The hunting behavior of yellowjackets clearly requires the ability to learn schedules, to develop several kinds of search images, and to become skilled in several different methods of prey capture. The learning ability of yellowjackets is probably at least as great as that of the honey bee, but is less well known, because yellowjackets are difficult to study.

Yellowjackets tend to be solitary hunters going after small game. Back in our own hunter-gatherer stage, there would have been no need to mobilize the whole village to hunt three squirrels and a rabbit. On the other hand, yellowjackets and hornets often join others working on large-scale efforts, such as dismembering a big dragonfly, or cutting chunks of bologna out of the edge of a sandwich.

While most yellowjacket and hornet colonies normally last for one year, southern yellowjacket colonies in Florida can persist two years, or even longer. In the old days, southern yellowjacket colonies may have been controlled by bears, which dig up colonies and eat the grubs, without showing much effect from the multiple stings.

JLC

Top, and below: yellowjacket nests are usually underground, or at the base of a tree. In a single year, a colony can grow to 4,000 workers.

Left: yellowjacket larvae in comb cells.

JLG

JLC

BBB

Above: in addition to the southern yellowjacket and another, smaller yellow-and-black species, Florida also has the white-faced hornet, sometimes called the bald-faced hornet whose large nests are usually up in trees. In southern Florida, this species is uncommon and usually found around water.

THE SHOPPING MALL WASP

The southern yellowjacket quickly learns that recently killed insects may be found on car grills, and regularly inspects the parking lots of supermarkets and malls. At least some individuals learn that a car that has just pulled into the lot is most likely to have freshly killed insects, and may appear at the front of the car before the driver has opened the door.

JHR

Honey Bees

Family Apidae, Apis mellifera

Honey bees, the smallest European domestic livestock, were brought to Florida in colonial times. They now occur both as wild colonies and domestic hives. More recently, many Florida honey bees have become migratory, wintering in Florida, and returning north in summer, usually in small flatbed trucks.

There is something romantic and magical about honey bees. Maybe it is the idea of having thousands of tiny furry servants who go out to collect droplets of nectar from innumerable flowers, and refine the liquor into a fragrant confection awaiting our sensuous tongues. Beekeepers are also slightly magical, with their ability to control the buzzing masses as surely as if they spoke the language of the bees. The amazing scientific discoveries about the life of the honey bee are themselves a magic window into the intricacies of insect behavior.

Whole books have been written about the behavior of honey bees. Like other social insects, the honey bee has a family-based colony. It consists of a queen, her daughters, and males (drones). The workers have the startling ability to dictate a symbolic map that directs other workers to a patch of flowers. Explanations of this now appear in standard biology texts, but when it was first described it seemed behavior well beyond insect capability. Another well-researched area is the change in adult worker bee behavior as it gets older. The bee starts by working in the hive, cleaning out cells, tending larvae and the queen, ventilating the nest by beating its wings near the entrance, and so forth. After ten days or so, the worker starts storing away nectar and pollen brought into the hive, and after this apprenticeship, begins to forage out among the flowers. Outside the hive, the bee memorizes the landmarks around the hive, but more impressively, she always knows where she is in relation to the hive, and can make a bee-line back no matter how many twists and turns she has made working her way through the flowers.

New colonies are formed by splitting a colony in two, a method of colony reproduction also found in a few species of Florida ants. The queen departs with a large entourage to find a new home, forming the well-known swarm that sometimes appears unexpectedly in a Florida yard, usually in early summer. The workers that remain behind raise a new queen, who mates in flight outside the nest with several drones from her own or nearby nests. The colonies of honey bees can persist for many years, with periodic replaçement of queens.

BK

Top: **a honey bee approaching a passion flower already occupied by a scarab wasp. Honey bees often displace native pollinators.** ***Above:*** **a honey bee swarm that has just left its home to establish a new hive. Such swarms are often seen in Florida in early summer.**

Honey bee workers are suicidal in their defense of the nest. The sting is barbed, and easily becomes embedded in the skin of an attacking animal, so the whole sting apparatus is torn from the bee. The value of this grim arrangement is that the venom gland can continue pumping venom into the attacker after the bee has been brushed off. Honey bees have an alarm odor that mobilizes the defense of the hive. All this defensive behavior is needed because the honey stores and larvae of the bee colony are sufficient incentive to induce a determined attack by an animal, such as the African honey badger in the native land of the honey bee, or a black bear in Florida.

JHR

Top: a honey bee visiting a flower. The yellow blob on the hind leg is pollen packed into the "pollen basket," a broad, concave section of the leg surrounded by long hairs. Pollen is the main food for the larvae of honey bees and also non-social bees. Honey bees rake pollen from flowers with their feet and comb it from the feathery hairs that cover their bodies.

Right: sometimes honey bees are unable to find a hollow tree or other shelter to build a nest and establish a nest in the open, here in an oak tree.

Far right: the cells of a commercial bee hive. Many cells are half-filled with honey. The honey cells are left open to evaporate water. As the nectar becomes more concentrated, it takes up less space and is less likely to spoil.

Bottom: a queen bee surrounded by her royal court. There is only one queen in the nest, and she lays all the eggs. Evolution has solved the problem of royal succession in a most ingenious way. Female eggs are not predestined to become workers or queens. They have the potential to become either. The workers control the situation. If the queen dies, or she is about to leave with part of the colony to found a new colony, the workers sense this through chemical signals, and begin to raise several larvae in larger cells and on a special diet. This triggers the development of these larvae into queens. Although there is normally no dispute, or even contact, between the old queen and the new queen, the succession is not totally harmonious. The workers raise several new queens at once, and the first queen to emerge kills all the others. If two emerge at once, they fight to the death.

CB

BK

BK

BK

Leaf Cutter Bees

Family Megachilidae

Leaf cutter bees are solitary (non-social) bees that get their name from the habit of some species of cutting circles and ovals of leaves to line their burrows. The pieces of leaves are cut quickly, the mandibles acting as scissors, so many people who notice the holes cut in the leaves never actually see the bee at work. A bee that is cutting leaves often returns to the same plant over a period of days, so the plant begins to look as if it had been attacked by peculiarly methodical caterpillars. Leaf cutter bees show preferences in the types of leaves they use for wallpapering their burrows. In Florida, favorite plants include grape, rose, and certain wild plants in the bean family. Leaves that are thin and flexible are easiest to cut, transport, and mold inside the burrow, but the bees may also be picking leaves with certain chemicals.

There are about 65 species of leaf cutter bees in Florida, and they are common throughout the state. Most of the species seen on flowers are medium-sized black bees, a little smaller than a honey bee, but some species are black with dark red markings. On the underside of the abdomen, female leaf cutter bees have dense rows of long, stiff, feathery hairs. The bee rakes pollen from flowers and stuffs it among these hairs, until the entire underside of

PC

the abdomen is packed with pollen. The mass of pale pollen on the belly of a dark bee is a distinctive field mark that allows naturalists to distinguish leaf cutter bees from the other solitary bees in Florida.

Solitary bees such as the leaf cutters need time for collecting nectar, pollen, and other supplies for the nest, and the nest is left unguarded during their absence. During this time the nest is vulnerable to insects such as velvet ants and certain flies, which can attack the larvae in the nest. It is also vulnerable to species of parasitic bees, which do not gather nectar or pollen, but sneak down the burrow of another bee and lay eggs on the pollen and nectar already stored. The newly hatched larva of most parasitic bees has sharp jaws with which it kills the host larva before settling

BBB

Top: **this particular species of leaf cutter bee makes molded resin nests attached to leaves or bark rather than the usual burrow nest.**

Left: **this bee has collected a load of pollen which is held underneath the abdomen by stiff hairs. This pollen held under the belly helps to identify a leaf cutter bee.**

Above: **holes left by a leaf cutter bee. As the bee finishes cutting, it begins to hover and grasps the piece of leaf with its legs so that it will not fall, all while buzzing loudly.**

down to feed on the nectar and pollen.

Surprisingly large numbers of parasitic bee species occur in Florida. Although it is easy to sympathize with the hard-working bees that gather the nectar and pollen, the parasitic bees are also interesting animals, and should not be condemned. Unlike human thieves, parasitic bees have no choice of profession. These bees are programmed to look for bee nests instead of nectar and pollen, and probably work as hard as any bee in a more traditional trade.

PATTERNS OF POLLINATION IN FLORIDA WILDFLOWERS

Already steaming gently, a Florida flatwoods strewn with flowers lies in the morning sunlight. From a nearby sandknoll, two identical solitary metallic green bees emerge from their separate burrows and fly out into the flatwoods. One bee is visiting flowers of blue-eyed grass, and flies from one widely separated clump to another. The other bee is visiting flat-top goldenrod, and flies right by the little patches of blue-eyed grass. These two bees are showing "flower constancy."

Many species of insects can get the nourishment they need from any one particular species of flowers. When they first start looking for nectar or pollen, these insects may visit several kinds of flowers, but soon begin to consistently visit a single kind of flower. This is because these insects, like ourselves, find it is much easier to find things for which they have a specific search image. If one is looking for a sandal lost at the beach, one needs to know what a sandal looks like, and one's chance of finding the missing sandal goes way up if one is shown the mate of the lost sandal. The ability to use search images proficiently often develops slowly in small children (this may frustrate and puzzle their parents), but most wild animals, birds, and many insects quickly develop search images.

Insect reliance on search images explains why Florida wildflowers occur in such glorious variety. Each species of flower needs to present a distinctive appearance if insects are to be trained to a search image that will cause the foraging insect to go from flower to flower of the same species and bring about cross-pollination. This is rather like the use of a consistent, distinctive logo, restaurant design, and menu selection by a fast food chain, so that travelers are easily trained to go from one restaurant to the other in the same chain. The actual quality of the food may be less important than the sense of security provided by knowing the features of these identical eateries. Some children go through a phase in which there is a conditioned response, shown by premature cries of hunger, at the mere appearance of their favorite restaurant logo along the highway. While there can be some degree of variation in the flowers in a population of wildflowers, if a flower is too different, it may fall outside the range of an insect's search image. Search images, therefore, dictate both the obvious differences between the flowers of different species, and the consistency in flowers of a single species.

In addition to appearance, odor, and situation on the plant, all of which are used to form search images, different species of wildflowers also differ in the placement of nectar and pollen in the flower. Insects must also train themselves in the best way to collect the nectar and pollen, and this increases the incentive to specialize on one kind of flower. A few insects, such as some bumble bees, seem able to work efficiently with several kinds of flowers at once, perhaps using multiple search images and handling techniques, but most flower-visiting insects learn to specialize. The system of flower constancy becomes even more efficient when, as often happens, an insect evolves to become rigidly specialized to feed on one kind of flower. In this case the insect is born with a search image and flower handling technique already implanted in its instincts. In Florida, there is a bee that specializes on prickly pear cactus, two that specialize on pond lilies, one on gallberry, two on silkgrass, and so on.

Specialization between plants and their pollinating insects is beneficial to both plant and insect in the short run. The two species can have synchronized seasonal appearances. The insect may have special body features suited to the shape of the flower. The insect's digestive system may be specially tailored to the nectar and pollen. The plant, in turn, has an insect species whose loyalty is inborn. A flower of this plant species is never competing for pollinators with other plant species whose flowers may be more common or more showy.

All this is good in the short run, but in the longer run, the specialized pollination system is more vulnerable. If anything happens to one member of the pair of species the other is in trouble. If for example, a late frost kills the flower buds, the insect pollinator may have nothing to eat that year, and the following year there may be no pollinators, even if there are plenty of flowers. In Florida, the number of wildflowers and insects that are absolutely dependent on each other seems relatively low.

As one learns more about how flowers function, one can develop a slight sense of hurt disappointment. All that beauty was not designed for our eyes, but for the eyes of some bug or hummingbird. Slowly one comes to realize that, while nature did not design flowers as a gift for us, we were designed so that we have an appreciation for the beauty of flowers. This itself is a gift that is unique and mysterious.

KILLER BEES

The honey bees brought to Florida are of stock that had long been domesticated in Europe. These bees do not get worked up very easily, perhaps because they have been bred for docility, perhaps because their colonies have been protected by humans for so long that there has been natural selection against colonies whose workers tend to lose their lives in unnecessary attacks. Much more recently, an African strain of bee, unmodified by domestication, was accidentally released in Brazil. This strain, called the Africanized bee or killer bee, has now reached Texas, and is expected to move across the southern US into Florida. The sting of the killer bee is no worse than that of a normal bee, but the killer bee stings with less provocation, and tends to pursue an intruder. Wild bees in Africa have a number of natural enemies, including humans, who have been exploiting wild honey bees for many thousands of years. Every bee nest is in constant danger of attack, so the workers are ever vigilant and prepared to use their stings. The nests tend to split as quickly as practical, because very large nests are more conspicuous and more worth robbing. Splitting the nest puts the colonies' eggs in two baskets rather than one. When the killer bee invades a new area, the result is large numbers of nests, each guarding a large territory. With killer bees around, a person has a much greater chance of wandering into the defensive zone of a nest, and once aroused, these bees tend to chase an intruder for a long distance, half a mile or so.

Nobody seems to know what will happen if killer bees thrive in Florida. It will certainly be a blow to beekeepers, since killer bees often displace or interbreed with European bees. Few Florida crops require bee pollination (citrus does not need to be pollinated), but Florida honey bees transported north in the summer are very important in pollination of crops. It is likely that a new profession, the bee patrol, will spring up around suburban developments to eliminate wild honey bees as they move in. In natural areas, the problem could be too large and expensive to contain easily, and both managers and visitors will need education about what to do if attacked.

From an ecological point of view, neither domestic bees or Africanized bees are desirable. These are exotic insects that appear to compete with local pollinators and are likely to disrupt the pollination systems of native plants. The honey bee is larger than most native pollinators, and readily displaces them from flowers. They dominate the best patches of flowers. Honey bees are willing to fly long distances into natural areas in search of flowers. The honey bee, for all its fascinating and useful characteristics, is still an invading, exotic animal in Florida.

BK

PC

Halictid Bees (Green Metallic Bees)

Family Halictidae

The halictid bees are a large family of solitary bees with 55 species in Florida. Most Florida species are small, about a quarter inch long, but there are some very common species about twice that size. The most conspicuous of these are eight species that are bright metallic green. These green bees are common in disturbed areas, as well as natural habitats, and usually nest in deep burrows in the soil. They gather nectar and pollen from a great variety of plants.

In some books, halictid bees are called "sweat bees," because of their habit of landing on bare skin to drink sweat. This habit seems strangely rare among bees in Florida. Human sweat has a number of components, including salt, urea, amino acids, and of course water. If salt is the important ingredient for sweat bees, it may be that salt deficiency is less likely in Florida, where onshore winds may be picking up salt spray and carrying it inland.

Small, solitary bees such as the halictid bees may be especially important for plants that occur in small patches. Such bees can keep seed set high in a patch that has only a few individual plants, which might escape the attention of more wide-ranging pollinators.

Above, left: **a common green metallic bee collecting nectar, while carrying a load of pollen on her hind legs. The bee digests some of the nectar she drinks, but most of it is regurgitated, along with salivary secretions, and used to moisten the mass of pollen that she is preparing for her larva. She completely stocks one chamber at a time, rather than giving each larva a little at each visit; if she dies while foraging, she leaves no starving young.**

Above, right: **some male green bees have yellow-and-black stripes, unlike the solid green females.**

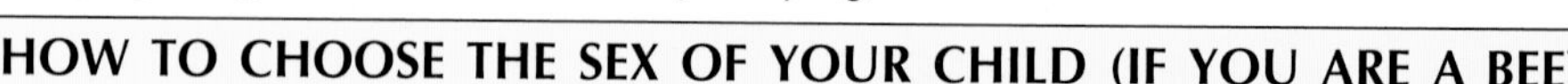

HOW TO CHOOSE THE SEX OF YOUR CHILD (IF YOU ARE A BEE)

As soon as biologists began to carefully study the colony cycles of ants, bees, and wasps, they realized that these insects must be able to control the sex of their offspring. Males are produced in relatively small numbers at specific times, and there were no observations of workers or queens killing-off half the eggs or larvae at times when males were not being raised. The mechanism for controlling sex was discovered about 150 years ago, and it turned out to be very simple, with all kinds of complicated implications. Male Hymenoptera, it was found, have only one set of chromosomes, and develop from unfertilized eggs. Females have two sets of chromosomes, and develop from fertilized eggs. The mated female stores the sperm in a small pouch, whose opening she is able to control. When she is to lay a female egg, she allows sperm to escape from the pouch as the egg passes by. For a male egg, the sperm pouch is kept closed.

This system is not restricted to the social Hymenoptera, but is also found in the solitary bees, wasps, and parasitic wasps. Here, too, it can be useful. In many instances, wasps are dealing with prey of different sizes or in different quantity. The amount of eggs a female can produce, and her ability to tackle prey is often correlated with size, and a small female has a great handicap. Males, on the other hand, need only to fly around and manufacture sperm, and are often at less of a disadvantage if they are small. Faced with large and small resources, the female can make good choices when she is laying eggs, since she is able to choose the sex of her young.

A great degree of maternal care is a feature of most Hymenoptera. In most species other than the sawflies, the mother provides her young with everything they will need for their entire growth to adult. The ability to determine the sex of the young is an important refinement on maternal care, allowing the female to not only make provision for an offspring that she will never see, but also make the provision appropriate to the sex of her offspring. In the social insects, this maternal control is used in an ingenious new way, to control the sexual cycle of an entire colony.

JLC

JLC

Carpenter Bees

Family Anthophoridae, Xylocopinae

There are only two species of carpenter bees in Florida, but they are large and common insects with interesting habits. Carpenter bees resemble bumble bees, but the head is more square and proportionally larger. The abdomen is more shiny black, not obscured by dense black fur. The square head accommodates the large jaw muscles, and large jaw muscles allow the bees to bore through solid wood. The tunnels made by carpenter bees are remarkably regular and smooth-sided, as if bored with a drill. Dead trees once provided home sites for carpenter bees, but these sites are now supplemented by timbers and thick boards used in construction. The actual amount of structural damage done by the bees is relatively minor, but when the burrows are in exposed boards, the nest chambers with larvae are near the surface of the wood where woodpeckers eventually find them and drill many large, messy holes in the board.

The burrows of carpenter bees are laborious to construct, and are not abandoned after a year, but are cleaned out and reused as long as the wood remains intact. They are probably passed down in successive generations of the same family. The males seem to do some nest guarding, an unusual role for male bees and wasps. There are often several families of carpenter bees in a single dead tree or timber, and this makes a busy sight, with females coming and going for loads of pollen and nectar, sawdust leaking steadily from a burrow under construction, and males zooming about looking for females and challenging each other and every other large insect that flies by.

All this activity can make people nervous, especially if they think the bees are bumble bees. Bumble bees can be quite aggressive around the nest, coming out to sting if one comes too close. Bumble bees, however, nest in the ground, not in wood. Carpenter bees are unlikely to sting, unless one is grabbed. Male carpenter bees, which are unable to sting, nevertheless can provoke the most anxiety. They often hover in the air near the nesting area, darting down to confront a passing human. Suspending themselves, buzzing loudly, only a few inches from the startled human eyes, these bees are rather impressive. Naturalists who know these bees recognize that they are being investigated by a harmless male, because the males have bright yellow faces, while the females' faces are black. A few nests of carpenter bees in the yard are an enjoyably and entertaining sight. Perhaps the various enterprises catering to backyard wildlife in Florida should turn their attention from butterfly houses, which no Florida butterfly would ever consider using, to carpenter bee timbers, suspended in a sleeve of chicken wire to keep out the woodpeckers.

BK

Top, left: a male carpenter bee emerging from a bee hole. Only the females do carpentry.

Top, right: a male carpenter bee. The yellow face of the male is the only obvious difference between the sexes.

Left: a Florida road sign illustrating how the habits of bees have become part of the English language. A bee flies directly home when returning to its hive. This has become synonymous with the straightest possible route.

ARISTOTLE AND THE GENDER OF HONEY BEES

The Greek encyclopedist Aristotle (384-322 BC) had a keen interest in honey bees, and understood a surprising amount about honey bee biology. He knew, for example, about flower constancy in honey bees, and about differences in defensiveness near and away from the hive. He was able to distinguish between queens, workers, and drones. He did not understand, however, that the drones were males, and queens and workers females. It is a good example of how cultural prejudices can lead to confusion. In this excerpt, what he calls "bees" are what we call workers.

"But, again, it is unreasonable to suppose that the bees (workers) are female and the drones are male, for nature does not give weapons for fighting to any female, and while the drones are stingless, all the bees have a sting. Nor is the opposite view reasonable, that the bees are male and the drones female, for no males are in the habit of working for their offspring, but the bees do this."

Even today, some of the confusion lingers on. For many of us, it requires a conscious effort to apply a female pronoun to a hefty bumble bee roughly agitating the anthers of a cactus flower.

BK

Bumble Bees

Family Apidae

Bumble bees are a northern group, and almost all of the seven species found in Florida seem equally at home in Maine. Bumble bees are not as prominent in Florida, where there are a couple of hundred other bee species, as they are in the arctic, where there are no other bees. Nevertheless, bumble bees are important pollinators of wild plants in Florida, and their complicated behavior is as interesting in Florida as anywhere else. Bumble bees in Florida retain their northern hardiness, and can be seen in central Florida visiting blooming citrus trees on chilly mornings when honey bees are still huddling in their hives.

Bumble bee nests have an annual cycle. The nest is founded by an overwintering queen, who usually starts her colony in a hole in the ground, such as an abandoned rodent burrow. The queens are the huge bumble bees that can be seen collecting nectar from azaleas in late winter. The queen raises several daughters at once, skimping on their food in order to produce more individuals. These daughters appear in early spring as miniature workers, and the big queens disappear from the flowers, spending their time underground taking care of the nest and laying eggs. If the supply of nectar and pollen is good, the colony grows during the spring and summer, and each set of workers may be a little larger than the last as the work force caring for them grows. In late fall, queens and males are raised by the last generations of workers, and after these queens and males have left the nest the social system of the colony collapses and the colony disappears. Social wasps, such as paper wasps and yellow jackets, usually have a similar annual cycle.

Away from the nest, bumble bees are not aggressive. Since bumble bees are cute and furry, children have discovered that with one little finger they can very gently pet the back of a bumble bee when it is intently working on a flower. These same children know that if they step on a bumble bee barefoot they will regret their carelessness. Very near the nest, bumble bees are strongly defensive, since they must be ever ready to repel predatory animals, such as skunks, which dig up the nest and eat the larvae whenever they can do so without getting severely stung. Unlike honey bees, bumble bees do not lose the stinger when they sting, so they can sting several times.

The behavior of bumble bees when they are visiting flowers is complicated. Like other bees, they are loyal to certain flowers. Individual bees learn the appearance, location, and floral structure of a species of flower, and are thus able to work that flower with great efficiency. Many flowers

RFS

Top: **the wings of bumble bees seem remarkably small relative to the size of the body. This is partly because the heavy coat of hair makes the bee look larger than it is. Also, we are used to seeing insects that have extra wing area which is helpful for acrobatic feats.**

Above: **the bumble bee has large eyes with many fine facets and appears to have excellent vision. The strong jaws are used for construction and gnawing. The long, nectar-sucking tongue is not visible here. It folds back against the underside of the head.**

have special puzzles that the bees must solve by trial and error to get nectar or pollen, and bumble bees solve these puzzles easily. Some wild flowers, such as those related to beans and peas, are closed, and the bee must learn to land in a particular place on the flower, force open the petals, and reach into a special pocket where the nectar is secreted. Some flowers, such as blueberries and cassias, have pollen contained in hollow anthers, and it only comes out when a bee lands on the flower and buzzes, vibrating the anthers so that the pollen pours out onto the bee. Bumble bees quickly learn this trick. If bumble bees are working in an area with relatively few flowers blooming at once, they may work on two or three species at once. In early spring in Florida, bumble bees can be seen flying directly from a cactus blooming on a scrub knoll to a Saint John's wort at the edge of a seasonal pond. Bumble bees that are unable to reach nectar that is at the end of a long flower tube, may learn to rob the nectar by chewing a hole through the tube.

A bumble bee working on a patch of flowers works through the patch methodically, like a person picking wild berries. It does not spend time revisiting plants where it just extracted the nectar. Recent studies show that bumble bees can detect whether a flower was recently visited by another bumble bee, even one of a different species. They can smell chemical traces left by the previous visitor on a flower, and they do not bother to search for nectar in that flower. Flowers do restock their nectar supply, which may take only a few minutes; or it may take as long as half an hour, depending on the species of flower. Bumble bees do not avoid for an indefinite time a flower that has had a previous visitor, and it may be that the chemical marker from the earlier bee fades after a short time. There is evidence that bees are quicker to revisit flowers of species that replenish their nectar more quickly. The simplest explanation for this is that bees learn to correlate the strength of the chemical marker with the presence of nectar in each plant species. Bumble bees are not the only bees to show complex behavior when visiting flowers. Carpenter bees and honey bees are equally sophisticated.

JHR

SOCIAL BEHAVIOR IN INSECTS

Some of Florida's most notable insects (including termites, ants, and some bees and wasps) have social systems. From the time of the ancient Greeks, writers have commented on the similarities between human and insect social systems, similarities that were even more striking when humans were divided into innumerable tribes and petty kingdoms.

The advantages of social systems for man and bug were obvious. Some of these are: banding together for common defense, pooling labor and resources for large-scale projects, coordination of activity under one leader, and specialized professionals, such as soldiers or artisans. The only one of these advantages that the ancients got wrong, was the coordination of activity under one leader, which is not a strong feature of social insects. A colony of social insects is strongly affected by the presence or absence of a queen, and her behavior and secretions may determine the actions of the workers, but she has almost none of the executive freedom that humans associate with high status.

Early observers of social insects failed to understand one of their key features. An insect colony is not a bunch of individuals that have come together for mutual advantage, like the citizens of a walled town in ancient Greece. An insect colony is a family, in the literal sense, not the "we're all one family" sense of politicians. As a family, it can have a feature not found in human societies: in the insect colony a great majority have no reproductive rights. The workers usually make up most of the colony, but do not raise any of their own children. They concentrate on raising and protecting their sisters and brothers. The workers cannot be called slaves, because they are working for their family, and raising their close relatives. There is no such thing as a human society composed of hundreds or thousands of siblings, and the implications of such a society are difficult to grasp.

The ecological importance of social insects is easily seen in Florida, where ants and termites are among the most abundant insects. Termites are the top decomposers, and ants are the top predators among the insects. These social insects increase their dominance even more in the tropics. In parts of Africa and South America it often seems that everything that is not devoured by ants is gobbled up by termites. Social bees and wasps are of less importance, but are still the most prominent pollinators and aerial predators, respectively, among the insects in many habitats.

For all their success, the social insects have not taken over completely, and the vast majority of insect species are not social. Only about one insect species in a hundred is social. There must, therefore, be disadvantages to the social way of life. The most obvious is that a colony of insects requires a lot of resources. The social insects have lost one of the special advantages of insects, the ability to use small resources in a very specialized and efficient way. A tiny, solitary, parasitic wasp, homing in on the odors coming from a decaying mushroom, finds and parasitizes dozens of little pupae of flies that were attracted to the fresh odor of the mushroom a few days earlier. Ants, living in the same forest, might carry away bits of the mushroom, and fly pupae, if they can find them, but they can never be as efficient either at finding or digesting these resources as the specialists. Up in the top of a maple, part of a poison ivy vine has died. Immediately it is invaded by tiny bark beetles and longhorn beetles that feed on dead poison ivy. Even if the termites on the ground below are able to deal with the chemicals found in poison ivy, making a covered trail up to the top of the tree would probably not be cost effective, considering the small amount of dead wood involved.

There are other less important disadvantages to insect social life. The gathering of insects into a dense colony allows group defense, but it also makes the colony easy to find and worth hunting for. Social insects themselves have their own specialized enemies. Big colonies are not easily relocated. Even nomadic colonies, such as those of army ants, lack the mobility in the face of a disaster, such as a big flood. The number of big colonies that can be supported by a small patch of habitat is small. The ground-nesting carpenter ant that lives in sandhill habitat is much less likely to persist in a small patch of overgrown sandhill than some scarab beetle that can have a big population underground in a few square meters.

Sometimes it seems possible to sum up all of ecology in a single, profound but unhelpful phrase: everything has its advantages and disadvantages.

Top: carpenter ants tend their cocoons inside a piece of rotted wood. Most carpenter ants in Florida take over cavities left in wood by termites, or nest in the ground.

Ants

Family Formicidae

Floridians could boast about their large numbers of ant species, the most diverse of any state in the eastern or midwestern US. There are 207 species of ants in Florida, compared with, for example Michigan, with a pathetic 113. Not only are there many kinds of ants in Florida, but ants are particularly abundant in the state, a fact that is somehow overlooked by the Florida Tourist Bureau when it is preparing promotional brochures. The reason for this rich ant population is that ants as a group are most dominant in warm areas, and Florida is the warmest state east of Texas.

Some residents and visitors are unfavorably impressed by Florida ants. This is because of crimes committed by a tiny minority of species. Only five or six species are major pests, led by the imported fire ant. If not for these pests, all of which were accidentally imported from other areas by humans, ants would be no more a problem in Florida than in the northern states. Florida native ants, for all their diversity and abundance, tend to be retiring creatures, and spend their lives in the soil, leaf litter, hollow twigs, or grass tussocks. These native ants have great ecological importance, especially as predators of other insects. Ants are also important food for many birds, especially woodpeckers, and for frogs, toads, and lizards.

Florida ants do all kinds of weird, wonderful things. Some species live on fungi that they grow in little chambers filled with compost. Some species live in hollow twigs and spend all their time gleaning leaves for food; these ants protect plants from caterpillars. Some species have long, snap-trap jaws and stalk minute organisms in leaf litter. Some species gather seeds, which they grind into pablum for their larvae. Some species make foraging tunnels through sand and never come to the surface. The natural history of many species is unknown and remarkable new discoveries await.

All ants are social insects. Like bee and wasp colonies, ant colonies are family units, consisting of queens, workers, and males, the latter appearing only at the appropriate time. Most Florida ant species have colonies that are started by a single queen, who settles down after her mating flight and begins to raise workers. The queens of some species go out looking for food for their young, the same as paper wasps and bumble bees.

Many other species of ants have queens that begin the colony in a more peculiar way. The young queen finds a place to live, perhaps a hollow twig, or a burrow deep in the ground. Here she seals herself in, and begins to lay eggs. She feeds a small number of young larvae on her salivary secretions and on extra eggs that she produces. The nutrients for this closed system of family support are derived from fat stored in her abdomen, and from the breakdown of the flight muscles, which will not be needed again. She raises several workers all the way to adulthood, although these workers are much smaller than normal. These workers break out of the sealed chamber, and look for the food to bring back to the nest. The advantage of this system is that the queen is not exposed to the many predators that she would encounter if she were out looking for food.

Males are not produced until the colony is large enough to support them. They are usually produced at the same time as young winged queens, but in most species of ants, siblings do not mate with each other in the nest. Many ant colonies of a single species send out their males and females at exactly the same time, the timing perhaps coordinated by local weather conditions as well as season. This greatly increases the chances of cross breeding. Queens and males usually mate in flight, with the male dying soon after mating. A queen may mate with several males in rapid succession, storing up enough sperm to last for the rest of her life, which may be several years.

FLORIDA'S NATIVE ANTS

Carpenter Ants. Among the native Florida ants, the species most likely to be noticed are the carpenter ants. These are large, fast-moving ants, usually nocturnal, and often contrastingly colored with a reddish head and thorax and a black abdomen, a color pattern found in many unrelated species of ants. This color pattern usually seems to mean: "Beware! I can spray formic acid!" The carpenter ants do not sting, but they can nip with the mandibles, and spray formic acid from the tip of the abdomen for a very short distance. For a small insect-eating bird, such as a wood warbler, the amount of formic acid that a carpenter ant could spray on its tongue should be a significant deterrent. There are birds in Florida, especially some of the woodpeckers, that seem to specialize in eating ants, and these must have some way to deal with formic acid. Carpenter ant workers occur in several sizes, and there are some differences in the behavior or the large and small members of the colony.

Carpenter ants in Florida are not likely to gnaw at the wood of buildings and cause structural damage of the kind that is caused by some northern species. A couple of species tend to move into wall voids from outside the house. When these species produce males and queens, they eventually open up new exits to allow the males and queens to leave for their mating flights. Sometimes these exits are opened into the house rather than to the outside, and suddenly large numbers of ants appear in the house, including winged forms that are often mistaken for giant termites. Florida carpenter ants also show a tendency to move into electrical appliances, such as the motors of refrigerators indoors, or pump boxes outdoors. This can cause the machine to short out or clog up. On the whole, however, Florida carpenter ants are interesting and harmless insects.

JHR

JLC

JHR

Top: **the powerful jaws of the carpenter ant. This species is sometimes called a bull ant.**
Left: **a young carpenter ant queen who has just left the nest and still has the wings she will use in her mating flight.**
Above: **a carpenter ant worker. The workers come in both large and small sizes within the same colony.**

MORE NATIVE ANTS

Fungus-growing Ant. Some of the ground-nesting species of ants in Florida are easily identified by the characteristic mounds of their nests. The fungus-growing ant, common in upland areas of Florida, makes a crescent-shaped mound composed of distinct little clumps of sand, ant-loads of moist sand brought up from far below. These ants gather bits of fallen flowers and caterpillar droppings, which are used to grow the fungus that the larvae eat as their only food. The fungus gardens are usually in chambers quite deep underground, where the temperature and humidity are relatively constant. These ants are related to the famous leaf-cutter ants of the tropics, and are occasionally known to cut little bits out of young leaves when there is nothing else to collect, for example, in the first few weeks after a fire in the scrub.

Cone Ants. Among the commonest ants of open areas of Florida are the cone-ants, which make volcano-shaped nest mounds. Although these ants are unable to sting, they appear to be able to compete with fire ants on the drier sites. After a flight of queen fire ants, the cone-ants can be seen attacking the fire ant queens that are trying to dig into the sand.

Harvester Ants. Florida harvester ants have large but low nest mounds, usually with several entrances, which are closed at night. The distinctive thing about harvester ant mounds is that they bring in fragments of twigs, or small bits of charcoal, that they arrange around the edge of the nest mound. Nobody is sure why they do this. Harvester ants feed their larvae on insects and ground-up seeds. The seeds may be harvested by the hundreds if there is a good source available, and in late summer there may be caravans of ants racing back and forth along a highway of scent markers between the nest and the nearest clump of rosemary or patch of yellow buttons. Some of the workers have greatly enlarged heads and work as specialized seed grinders. The sting of the harvester ant is the most powerful of all Florida ants, but few people are aware of this because the harvester ant is reluctant to use its sting. If one was digging up the nest with bare hands, it would be possible to get severely stung, but nobody does this.

Many ant species can live together in one area. At the Archbold Biological Station, in south-central Florida, 114 species of ants have been found on the property, the largest number of ant species at any site in the US. Listing the number of species, however, is only the beginning. The biology of most of these species is almost unknown. There is much to be discovered about ants (and other insects) in Florida.

Top, left: **a harvester ant, sometimes called a "bull ant," the same as the carpenter ant. The enlarged head accommodates the muscles for seed grinding. It nests in dry, sandy areas.**
Top, right: **harvester ants in their nest tending their brood. The paleness of these ants shows that they recently transformed from the pupal stage.**
Above: **a distinctive clearing with a ring of charcoal or plant bits surrounds the nest of the Florida harvester ant.**
Below: **the nest of a fungus-growing ant.**

JHR

HONEYDEW AND ANTS

The ant above is collecting a drop of honeydew from an aphid. Certain ants and aphids have a mutually beneficial relationship in which ants guard the aphids from predators and in turn receive honeydew, a sugary secretion that the aphids manufacture from plant sap. The aphids only release the honeydew when stroked by the ant.

JHR

THE ANT REPRODUCTIVE CYCLE

The photo above shows a young queen that has just emerged from her nest and is ready for her mating flight. At right, a group of male ants climb onto a grass tussock near their nest, preparing to fly. At certain times of year, ant colonies produce winged males and queens. They emerge from all the colonies in an area at the same time, synchronized by some environmental cue. Ants of some species mate high in the air, while members of other species mate in small swarms near the ground.

JHR

BIBLICAL ANTS

Respect for ants goes back thousands of years. Consider this verse:

"Go to the ant, thou sluggard; consider her ways, and be wise. Having no guide, overseer, or ruler, she provideth her meat in the summer and gathers her food for the harvest."

OGDEN NASH'S ANT

The ant has made himself illustrious
Through constant industry industrous.
So what?
Would you remain calm and placid
If you were full of formic acid?

Ogden Nash

THE HOLLYWOOD ANT

The recent animated movie, Antz, is based only loosely on the real world of ants. For this movie, the decision was made to portray many of the workers, including the soldiers and the most muscular laborer, as males. In reality, the females do every bit of the work, while the males sit around for their entire adult lives awaiting a single, brief, terminal moment of sex.

THE WANDERING ANT

Nobody is as lost as a lost ant. Deprived of the interaction with nestmates, and the chemical signals in the nest that help assign tasks and organize its life, the worker ant is a creature utterly adrift. As ants move about on the ground, or climb among plant stems, they are soon out of sight of the nest. Ants often forage distances of many meters, and it would seem likely that in this complicated, three dimensional landscape of huge objects, a tiny ant could easily go astray.

There are various ways by which ants avoid this terrible fate. Main routes that lead from the nest to an important temporary resource, such as a dead grasshopper or a small pine with many aphids, are marked out with scent trails, so large numbers of ants can move quickly back and forth without paying much attention to their surroundings. Most ants that forage by day have a good visual memory, and can use landmarks, such as clumps of grass or fallen pine cones. Ants that make long excursions orient by the sun, and as they move erratically through tangles of short vegetation or across featureless patches of sand, they keep track of their position with respect to the nest by constant recalculations, using the sun as a fixed point. If they are away from the nest for a long time, they adjust the calculations to allow for the movement of the sun. Some ants orient by the angle of polarization of sky light, which can be seen (by an ant) even when the sun is out of sight. These orienteering skills not only keep ants from getting lost, but they also allow an ant that has found a bit of food to go directly home, rather than retracing its complicated route as it moved from the nest searching for food.

Many other insects that have a fixed nest or burrow, such as sand wasps and solitary bees, also have the ability to navigate. Many humans, on the other hand, once out beyond familiar landmarks, would find it very difficult to use the sun to calculate the most direct route home. A person who is particularly good with directions, who never gets lost in the thousands of acres of piney woods of Apalachicola National Forest, or the tangle of streets of a Tampa suburb, is likely to attribute his ability to superior intelligence. He displays a facility, in fact, that is almost equal to that of an ant.

IDENTIFYING FLORIDA'S ANTS BY THEIR MOUNDS

The naturalist-detective can often identify the burrow entrances of various ants by the size of the entrance and adjacent mound of sand, its situation, and the way the sand is deposited. Such distinctions can be seen in the photographs in this chapter of the mounds of fungus-growing ants, harvester ants and fire ants.

In an open, sandy lot in Florida one might see several kinds of burrows, as in the little scene at right. Burrows are best observed early or late in the day when the low angle of the sun accentuates shadows. It also helps to find a place where a darker subsoil is being brought up so the pattern of deposition is clearer.

1. Yellow big-headed ant, whose burrow is usually near a clump of grass. 2. Not an ant, but a burrowing wolf spider. 3. The volcano-shaped mound of a cone ant. 4. Scattered small mounds of a nocturnal, native crazy ant. 5. A line of small mounds along an underground fire ant gallery.

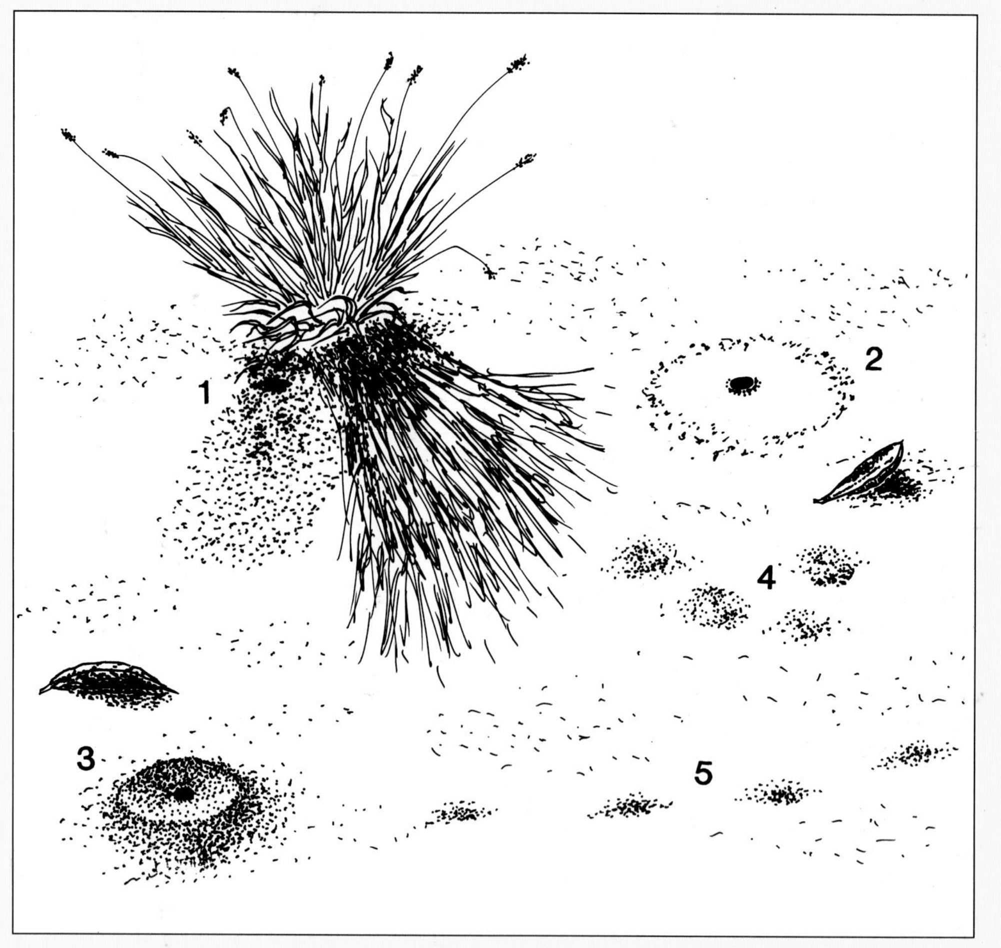

EXOTIC ANTS IN FLORIDA

Most species of ants that make themselves noticed in Florida are species that were accidentally imported. There are 53 exotic species of ants in Florida, the largest number for any state. This large number is partly due to the warm climate of Florida.

Pharaoh's Ant. *Among the annoying exotic species is pharaoh's ant, a small, yellowish-brown, elongate species. It makes very neat processions winding from the spot of jelly on the counter, up the wall, and behind the cupboards. This species is often found in multiple colonies that are closely related and completely compatible. The colonies may be scattered around the house, and thus difficult to control. Baits containing boric acid work well.*

Crazy and White-footed Ants. *The crazy ant and the white-footed ant are small, blackish species that move very fast and often run along wide scent trails, zigzagging from one side to the other. These species usually have their nests outside the house, and come in through open doors or windows to look for food. Neither of these ants bite or sting.*

Little Fire Ant. *There are a couple of imported stinging ants besides the fire ant. One of these is the little fire ant, which is a golden color, and about an eighth of an inch long. Its sting is out of all proportion to the size of the ant, and the pain can linger for 15 minutes or so. The sensation of being stung builds slowly and may not be noticed before the ant is gone. These ants are often up in trees or shrubs, and can fall down in numbers on a gardener who is pruning or staking. The little fire ant is most likely to sting when trapped under clothing, but also stings when caught in droplets of sweat on the bare skin. In Florida, this species is confined to the south and central areas, where it has been present for several decades at least. Its origin is probably South America.*

JLC

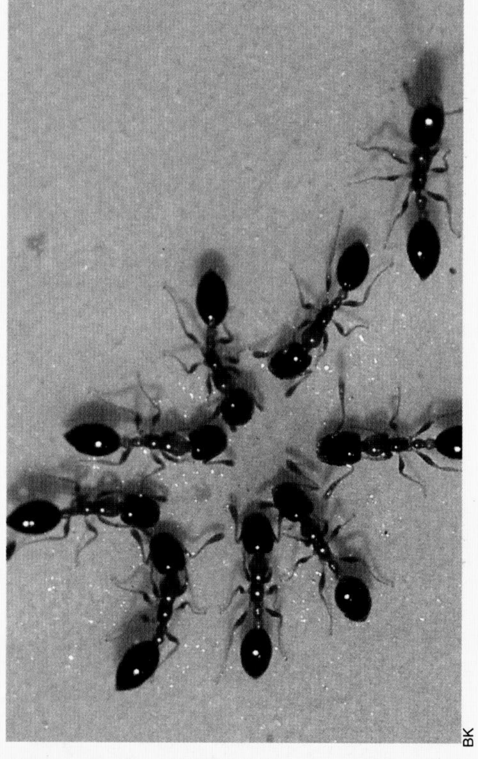
BK

Top, left: **a twig ant.**

Above: **bicolor trailing ants.**

Twig Ant. *Another stinging exotic ant is one of the elongate twig ants, a Mexican species that is about half-an-inch long, and attractively colored orange and black. The nests of these ants are in hollow twigs in trees and shrubs. When the nest is disturbed or broken open, the ants flee, and are not likely to sting. When a worker falls out of a tree, she climbs up the nearest tall object, which may be a person. When she crosses the collar and begins to climb up the neck, she is likely to get swatted, and immediately retaliates. This species is known locally as the "neck-biter ant." This species appeared in Florida in the 1960s, and quickly spread through the southern two-thirds of the peninsula.*

THE FIRE ANT STORY

For many Floridians, the ant in question is almost always the fire ant.

Above: note the hairs on this fire ant and the extended stinger.

Up to about 1945 one could most easily meet the fire ant by traveling to the open grasslands of Brazil, where seasonal flooding is a frequent problem for ants. The fire ant adapts to saturated soil by building a mound of dirt above the surface, and if the water creeps higher, the whole colony can cling to floating debris.

Above: fire ants making nest on weeds floating on water.

Since the beginning of this century, humans have been working unwittingly, but enthusiastically, to make the state of Florida more suitable for fire ants. Floridians cut trees to open the landscape, drained marshes to make a perfect habitat for fire ants, one that becomes saturated, but does not usually flood. Pastures have been improved by removing the rough tussocks of native grasses that harbor native ants, which are competitors of fire ants. In front of each house has been placed a welcome mat of short, well-watered grass, like a little bit of Brazil. Fire ants were accidentally introduced into the southeast in the 1940s. They soon found in Florida great expanses of ideal habitat. Since then, everything that has been done to natural habitats to accommodate the expanding human population has benefited fire ants.

The fire ant was imported into the US shortly after the invention of the first highly effective, inexpensive agricultural insecticides, such as DDT. In this period of happy confidence in the chemical age, it seemed possible that fire ants could be eradicated with specifically designed chemicals. Such a chemical was quickly developed, and deployed in aerial bombardments of a scale befitting the victors of World War II. Fire ants, however, are too stupid to understand the concept of surrender. Instead, the remnant populations moved back into the areas from which ants had been eradicated. Since native ants had been poisoned along with the fire ants, the fire ants were able to spread rapidly into places where they had formerly faced tough competition from native species. The resulting increase in fire ants was naturally met by an expansion of the eradication program.

Eventually, a University of Florida researcher studying the ecology of fire ants realized that the control program was fighting fire with gasoline, and produced experimental evidence to back his claim. At the same time, he discovered that the scientific name used for the fire ant was also incorrect, as it was first used for a different species of fire ant. He gave it a new name, invicta, *the "unconquered" ant. The imported fire ant is here to stay.*

Above: a typical fire ant mound.

The world will beat a path to the door to the person who invents a good way to control fire ants on a large scale. For small scale control of these wretched pests, there is a readily available, specialized insecticide that can be applied to the nest mound, though impatient lawn-owners become frustrated when it takes a colony a couple of weeks to disappear. Then there are all the folklore remedies. Some people suggest sprinkling the nest with grits, which the fire ants will eat, then swell up and explode. Since adult ants eat no solids, this is completely ineffective. Some prefer to drop a shovel-full from one colony into another to start an ant war. This is rather satisfying, but unlikely to eradicate colonies. Some suggest pouring boiling water on the nest, a remedy that sometimes actually works, especially if the entire colony is in a mound at the surface, as in early spring in North Florida. There are several ineffective methods too hazardous or bizarre to mention. It is also possible to change the habitat in a yard so it is less suitable for fire ants. Fire ants are not well adapted to shaded sites, especially if the soil is periodically dry.

On a large scale, however, there is as yet no practical control for fire ants, since large scale use of insecticides against fire ants is prohibitively expensive, often counter-productive, and destructive to the harmless native species. Researchers are now investigating natural enemiesin South America, in the hope that they could reduce the competitive advantage of fire ants to the extent that native ants could hold their own against the invaders. There are some examples of insects, including ants, that seem to have had a population explosion after invading a new area, followed by a population collapse, presumably due to natural enemies discovering this huge resource of hosts. The hope is to speed up this process by importing natural enemies. Meanwhile, the best way to exclude fire ants from a large area, such as a state forest or a cattle ranch, is to maintain habitats in as natural a condition as possible.

There is a legendary sign that once hung on the cages of fierce animals in some European zoo: "Warning! This animal is vicious. It will defend itself." This caution applies to the fire ant.

In its native Brazil, the fire ant lives in low, flat areas where the water table is often high and the soil saturated. When the soil is wet, fire ants build up a mound of soil, and the whole colony, including the queen and the larvae, is moved up into this mound. Many animals, including other ants, birds, reptiles, and mammals, would be more than happy to open the loose mound of soil and gobble up batches of fire ant larvae. For this reason, fire ants have evolved to be much more defensive than those species whose nest is more safely situated. At the least disturbance, workers pour out of the nest, ready to attack an intruder before it can dig into the nurseries filled with baby ants. Understanding the reason for fire ant ferocity does not make their stings easier to forgive, but it does assure us that a fire ant attack is not the kind of attack that we most fear: the random act of violence.

Above: fire ants swarm to attack.

Above: the pustule formed by a fire ant sting.

Visitors to Florida often ask about the place of fire ants in nature. Exotic species, those species that we humans have brought in and encouraged, do not have ancient linkages in natural systems. They are not part of the natural environment. Biologists see no redeeming features of fire ants in Florida habitats, although these ants are probably valuable members of natural ecosystems in South America where they evolved. In Florida, fire ants reduce the populations of many native insects, and attack helpless vertebrates, such as ground-nesting birds just hatching from the egg. In lawns, gardens, and fields, fire ants are a nuisance because of their aggressiveness. Native species that eat large amounts of fire ants may benefit, although this is not sufficient cause for celebration.

TABLE OF CONTENTS

COMMON NAMES INDEX